HAMMOND

ODYSSEY WORLD ATLAS

Contents

LIBRARY OF CONGRESS
CATALOGING-IN-PUBLICATION DATA

Hammond World Atlas Corporation.
    Hammond odyssey world atlas
        p. cm.
    Rev. ed. of Hammond odyssey atlas of the world/
Hammond Incorporated
    Includes indexes.
    ISBN 0–8437–1188–4 (pbk.)
    1. Atlases. I. Hammond Incorporated.
Hammond odyssey atlas of the world.
II Title. III.Title: Odyssey world atlas
    Odyssey atlas of the world.
G1021.H27447   1999   <G&M>
912—dc21   99–34155
                                 CIP
                                MAPS

Map Projections

Simply stated, the map-maker's challenge is to project the earth's curved surface onto a flat plane. To achieve this elusive goal, cartographers have developed map projections — equations which govern this conversion of geographic data.

This section explores some of the most widely used projections. It also introduces a new projection, the Hammond Optimal Conformal.

GENERAL PRINCIPLES AND TERMS

The earth rotates around its axis once a day. Its end points are the North and South poles; the line circling the earth midway between the poles is the equator. The arc from the equator to either pole is divided into 90 degrees of latitude. The equator represents 0° latitude. Circles of equal latitude, called parallels, are traditionally shown at every fifth or tenth degree.

The equator is divided into 360 degrees. Lines circling the globe from pole to pole through the degree points on the equator are called meridians, or great circles. All meridians are equal in length, but by international agreement the meridian passing through the Greenwich Observatory near London has been chosen as the prime meridian or 0° longitude. The distance in degrees from the prime meridian to any point east or west is its longitude.

While meridians are all equal in length, parallels become shorter as they approach the poles. Whereas one degree of latitude represents approximately 69 miles (112 km.) anywhere on the globe, a degree of longitude varies from 69 miles (112 km.) at the equator to zero at the poles. Each degree of latitude and longitude is divided into 60 minutes. One minute of latitude equals one nautical mile (1.15 land miles or 1.85 km.).

HOW TO FLATTEN A SPHERE: THE ART OF CONTROLLING DISTORTION

There is only one way to represent a sphere with absolute precision: on a globe. All attempts to project our planet's surface onto a plane unevenly stretch or tear the sphere as it flattens, inevitably distorting shapes, distances, area (sizes appear larger or smaller than actual size), angles or direction.

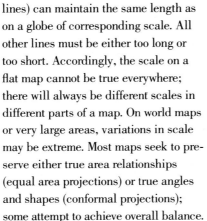

FIGURE 1 **Mercator Projection**

FIGURE 2 **Robinson Projection**

Since representing a sphere on a flat plane always creates distortion, only the parallels or the meridians (or some other set of lines) can maintain the same length as on a globe of corresponding scale. All other lines must be either too long or too short. Accordingly, the scale on a flat map cannot be true everywhere; there will always be different scales in different parts of a map. On world maps or very large areas, variations in scale may be extreme. Most maps seek to preserve either true area relationships (equal area projections) or true angles and shapes (conformal projections); some attempt to achieve overall balance.

PROJECTIONS: SELECTED EXAMPLES

Mercator (Fig. 1): This projection is especially useful because all compass directions appear as straight lines, making it a valuable navigational tool. Moreover, every small region conforms to its shape on a globe — hence the name conformal. But because its meridians are evenly-spaced vertical lines which never converge (unlike the globe), the horizontal parallels must be drawn farther and farther apart at higher latitudes to maintain a correct relationship.

Only the equator is true to scale, and the size of areas in the higher latitudes is dramatically distorted.

Robinson (Fig. 2): To create the thematic maps in Global Relationships and the two-page world map in the Maps of the World section, the Robinson projection was used. It combines elements of both conformal and equal area projections to show the whole earth with relatively true shapes and reasonably equal areas.

Conic (Fig. 3): This projection has been used frequently for air navigation charts and to create most of the national and regional maps in this atlas. (See text in margin at left).

HAMMOND'S OPTIMAL CONFORMAL

As its name implies, this new conformal projection (Fig. 4) presents the optimal view of an area by reducing shifts in scale over an entire region to the minimum degree possible. While conformal maps generally preserve all small shapes, large shapes can become very distorted because of varying scales, causing considerable inaccuracy in distance measurements. The concept underlying the Optimal Conformal is that for any region on the globe, there is an ideal projection for which scale variation can be made as small as possible. Consequently, unlike other projections, the Optimal Conformal does not use one standard formula to construct a map. Each map is a unique projection — the optimal projection for that particular area.

After a cartographer defines the subject area, a sophisticated computer program evaluates the size and shape of the region, projecting the most distortion-free map possible. All of the continent maps in this atlas, except Antarctica, have been drawn using the Optimal projection.

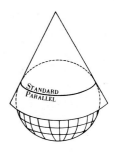

FIGURE 3
Conic Projection
The original idea of a conic projection is to cap the globe with a cone, and then project onto the cone from the planet's center the lines of latitude and longitude (the parallels and meridians). To produce a working map, the cone is simply cut open and laid flat. The conic projection used here is a modification of this idea. A cone can be made tangent to any standard parallel you choose. One popular version of a conic projection, the Lambert Conformal Conic, uses two standard parallels near the top and bottom of the map to further reduce errors of scale.

FIGURE 4
Hammond's Optimal Conformal Projection
Like all conformal maps, the Optimal projection preserves angles exactly and minimizes distortion in shapes. This projection is more successful than any previous projection at spreading curvature across the entire map, producing the most distortion-free map possible.

Using This Atlas

How to Locate
Information Quickly
This atlas is organized by
continent. If you're looking
for a major region of the
world, consult the Contents
on page two.

Australia
Page/Location: 7
Area: 2,966,136 s
7,682,300
Population: 17,
Capital: Canb
Largest C

World Reference Guide
This concise guide lists the
countries of the world
alphabetically. If you're
looking for the largest scale
map of any country, you'll
find a page and alpha-
numeric reference at a
glance, as well as
information about each
country, including its flag.

Master Index
When you're looking for a
specific place or physical
feature, your quickest route
is the Master Index. This
7,000-entry alphabetical
index lists both the page
number and alpha-numeric
reference for major places
and features in the world.

This new atlas is created from a unique digital database, and its computer-generated maps represent a new phase in map-making technology.

HOW COMPUTER-GENERATED MAPS ARE MADE

To build a digital database capable of generating this world atlas, the latitude and longitude of every significant town, river, coastline, boundary, trans-portation network and peak elevation was researched and digitized. Hundreds of millions of data points describing every important geographic feature are organized into thousands of different map feature codes.

There are no maps in this unique system. Rather, it consists entirely of coded points, lines and polygons. To create a map, cartographers simply determine what specific information they wish to show, based upon considerations of scale, size, density and importance of different features.

New technology developed by Hammond describes and re-configures coastlines, borders and other linework to fit a variety of map scales and projections. A computerized type placement program allows thousands of map labels to be placed accurately in minutes.

This atlas has been designed to be both easy and enjoyable to use. Familiarizing yourself with its organization will help you to benefit fully from its use.

WORLD FLAGS AND REFERENCE GUIDE

This colorful section portrays each nation of the world, its flag, important geographical data, such as size, population and capital, and its location in the atlas.

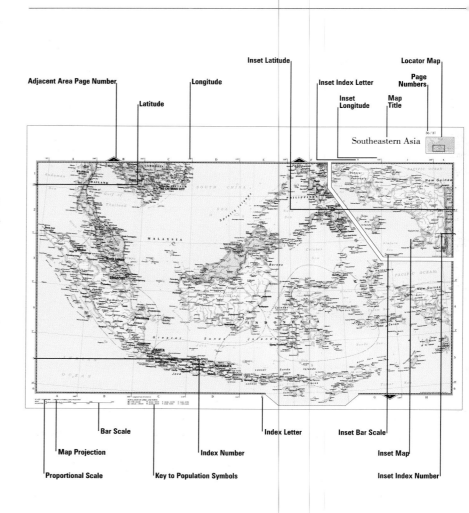

Adjacent Area Page Number · Latitude · Longitude · Inset Latitude · Inset Index Letter · Inset Longitude · Map Title · Locator Map · Page Numbers

Southeastern Asia

Bar Scale · Map Projection · Proportional Scale · Key to Population Symbols · Index Number · Index Letter · Inset Bar Scale · Inset Map · Inset Index Number

SYMBOLS USED ON MAPS OF THE WORLD

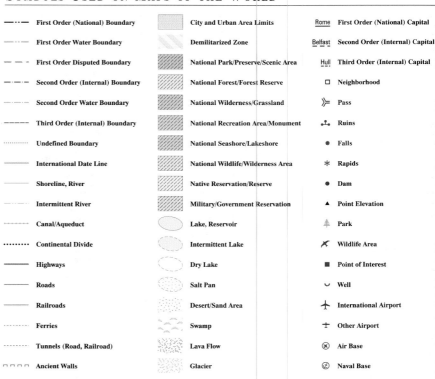

First Order (National) Boundary	City and Urban Area Limits	Rome First Order (National) Capital
First Order Water Boundary	Demilitarized Zone	Belfast Second Order (Internal) Capital
First Order Disputed Boundary	National Park/Preserve/Scenic Area	Hull Third Order (Internal) Capital
Second Order (Internal) Boundary	National Forest/Forest Reserve	Neighborhood
Second Order Water Boundary	National Wilderness/Grassland	Pass
Third Order (Internal) Boundary	National Recreation Area/Monument	Ruins
Undefined Boundary	National Seashore/Lakeshore	Falls
International Date Line	National Wildlife/Wilderness Area	Rapids
Shoreline, River	Native Reservation/Reserve	Dam
Intermittent River	Military/Government Reservation	Point Elevation
Canal/Aqueduct	Lake, Reservoir	Park
Continental Divide	Intermittent Lake	Wildlife Area
Highways	Dry Lake	Point of Interest
Roads	Salt Pan	Well
Railroads	Desert/Sand Area	International Airport
Ferries	Swamp	Other Airport
Tunnels (Road, Railroad)	Lava Flow	Air Base
Ancient Walls	Glacier	Naval Base

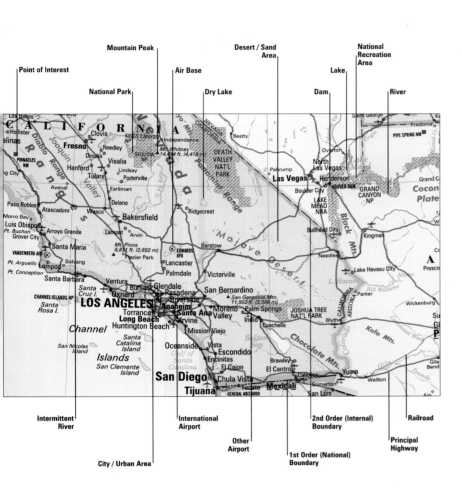

Point of Interest

Mountain Peak

National Park

Air Base

Dry Lake

Desert / Sand Area

Lake

Dam

National Recreation Area

River

Intermittent River

International Airport

Other Airport

City / Urban Area

1st Order (National) Boundary

2nd Order (Internal) Boundary

Railroad

Principal Highway

PHYSICAL MAPS

The topography (relief) as well as the linework, colors and type for the continents and ocean floors is computer-generated and presents the relationships of land and sea forms with startling realism.

MAPS OF THE WORLD

These detailed regional maps are arranged by continent and introduced by physical and political maps of that continent which utilize Hammond's new Optimal Conformal projection.

On the regional maps, individual colors for each country highlight political divisions. A country's color remains the same on all regional maps. These maps also provide considerable information by locating numerous political and physical geographic features.

MASTER INDEX

This is an A-Z listing of names found on the political maps. It also has its own abbreviation list which, along with other Index keys, appears on page 65.

MAP SCALES

A map's scale is the relationship of any length on the map to an identical length on the earth's surface. A scale of 1:3,000,000 means that one inch on the map represents 3,000,000 inches (47 miles, 76 km.) on the earth's surface. A 1:1,000,000 scale (1/1) is larger than a 1:3,000,000 scale (1/3).

In this atlas, regional maps in Europe and North America are shown at scales of 1:7,000,000 and 1:10,500,000; Asia 1:10,500,000; South America 1:15,000,000; Africa 1:17,500,000; Australia 1:19,400,000.

In addition to these fractional scales, each map is accompanied by a linear scale for measuring distances (in miles and kilometers) on the map.

Boundary Policies

This atlas observes the boundary policies of the U.S. Department of State. Boundary disputes are customarily handled with a special symbol treatment, but de facto boundaries are favored if they seem to have any degree of permanence, in the belief that boundaries should reflect current geographic and political realities. The portrayal of independent nations in the atlas follows their recognition by the United Nations and/or the United States government.

Hammond also uses accepted conventional names for certain major foreign places. Usually, space permits the inclusion of the local form in parentheses. To make the maps more readily understandable to English-speaking readers, many foreign physical features are translated into more recognizable English forms.

A Word About Names

Our source for all foreign names and physical names in the United States is the decision lists of the U.S. Board of Geographic Names, which contain hundreds of thousands of place names. If a place is not listed, the Atlas follows the name form appearing on official foreign maps or in official gazetteers of the country concerned. For rendering domestic city, town and village names, this atlas follows the forms and spelling of the U.S. Postal Service.

PRINCIPAL MAP ABBREVIATIONS

ABOR. RSV.	ABORIGINAL RESERVE	IND. RES.	INDIAN RESERVATION	NWR	NATIONAL WILDLIFE RESERVE
ADMIN.	ADMINISTRATION	INT'L	INTERNATIONAL		
AFB	AIR FORCE BASE	IR	INDIAN RESERVATION	OBL.	OBLAST
AMM. DEP.	AMMUNITION DEPOT	ISTH.	ISTHMUS	OCC.	OCCUPIED
ARCH.	ARCHIPELAGO	JCT.	JUNCTION	OKR.	OKRUG
ARPT.	AIRPORT	L.	LAKE	PAR.	PARISH
AUT.	AUTONOMOUS	LAG.	LAGOON	PASSG.	PASSAGE
B.	BAY	LAKESH.	LAKESHORE	PEN.	PENINSULA
BFLD.	BATTLEFIELD	MEM.	MEMORIAL	PK.	PEAK
BK.	BROOK	MIL.	MILITARY	PLAT.	PLATEAU
BOR.	BOROUGH	MISS.	MISSILE	PN	PARK NATIONAL
BR.	BRANCH	MON.	MONUMENT	PREF.	PREFECTURE
C.	CAPE	MT.	MOUNT	PROM.	PROMONTORY
CAN.	CANAL	MTN.	MOUNTAIN	PROV.	PROVINCE
CAP.	CAPITAL	MTS.	MOUNTAINS	PRSV.	PRESERVE
C.G.	COAST GUARD	NAT.	NATURAL	PT.	POINT
CHAN.	CHANNEL	NAT'L	NATIONAL	R.	RIVER
CO.	COUNTY	NAV.	NAVAL	RA	RECREATION AREA
CR.	CREEK	NB	NATIONAL BATTLEFIELD	RA.	RANGE
CTR.	CENTER			REC.	RECREATION(AL)
DEP.	DEPOT	NBP	NATIONAL BATTLEFIELD PARK	REF.	REFUGE
DEPR.	DEPRESSION			REG.	REGION
DEPT.	DEPARTMENT	NBS	NATIONAL BATTLEFIELD SITE	REP.	REPUBLIC
DES.	DESERT			RES.	RESERVOIR, RESERVATION
DIST.	DISTRICT	NHP	NATIONAL HISTORICAL PARK		
DMZ	DEMILITARIZED ZONE			RVWY.	RIVERWAY
DPCY.	DEPENDENCY	NHPP	NATIONAL HISTORICAL PARK AND PRESERVE	SA.	SIERRA
ENG.	ENGINEERING			SD.	SOUND
EST.	ESTUARY	NHS	NATIONAL HISTORIC SITE	SEASH.	SEASHORE
FD.	FIORD, FJORD			SO.	SOUTHERN
FED.	FEDERAL	NL	NATIONAL LAKESHORE	SP	STATE PARK
FK.	FORK	NM	NATIONAL MONUMENT	SPR., SPRS.	SPRING, SPRINGS
FLD.	FIELD	NMEMP	NATIONAL MEMORIAL PARK	ST.	STATE
FOR.	FOREST			STA.	STATION
FT.	FORT	NMILP	NATIONAL MILITARY PARK	STM.	STREAM
G.	GULF			STR.	STRAIT
GOV.	GOVERNOR	NO.	NORTHERN	TERR.	TERRITORY
GOVT.	GOVERNMENT	NP	NATIONAL PARK	TUN.	TUNNEL
GD.	GRAND	NPP	NATIONAL PARK AND PRESERVE	TWP.	TOWNSHIP
GT.	GREAT			VAL.	VALLEY
HAR.	HARBOR	NPRSV	NATIONAL PRESERVE	VILL.	VILLAGE
HD.	HEAD	NRA	NATIONAL RECREATION AREA	VOL.	VOLCANO
HIST.	HISTORIC(AL)			WILD.	WILDLIFE,
HTS.	HEIGHTS	NRSV	NATIONAL RESERVE		WILDERNESS
I., IS.	ISLAND(S)	NS	NATIONAL SEASHORE	WTR.	WATER

World Flags and Reference Guide

Afghanistan
Page/Location: 33/H2
Area: 250,775 sq. mi.
649,507 sq. km.
Population: 23,738,085
Capital: Kabul
Largest City: Kabul
Highest Point: Noshaq
Monetary Unit: afghani

Albania
Page/Location: 21/H3
Area: 11,100 sq. mi.
28,749 sq. km.
Population: 3,293,252
Capital: Tiranë
Largest City: Tiranë
Highest Point: Korab
Monetary Unit: lek

Algeria
Page/Location: 40/F2
Area: 919,591 sq. mi.
2,381,740 sq. km.
Population: 29,830,370
Capital: Algiers
Largest City: Algiers
Highest Point: Tahat
Monetary Unit: Algerian dinar

Andorra
Page/Location: 20/D3
Area: 174 sq. mi.
450 sq. km.
Population: 74,839
Capital: Andorra la Vella
Largest City: Andorra la Vella
Highest Point: Coma Pedrosa
Monetary Unit: Fr. franc, Sp. peseta

Angola
Page/Location: 42/C3
Area: 481,351 sq. mi.
1,246,700 sq. km.
Population: 10,623,994
Capital: Luanda
Largest City: Luanda
Highest Point: Morro de Môco
Monetary Unit: new kwanza

Antigua and Barbuda
Page/Location: 59/J4
Area: 171 sq. mi.
443 sq. km.
Population: 66,175
Capital: St. John's
Largest City: St. John's
Highest Point: Boggy Peak
Monetary Unit: East Caribbean dollar

Argentina
Page/Location: 64/C4
Area: 1,068,296 sq. mi.
2,766,890 sq. km.
Population: 35,797,536
Capital: Buenos Aires
Largest City: Buenos Aires
Highest Point: Cerro Aconcagua
Monetary Unit: nuevo peso argentino

Armenia
Page/Location: 23/F5
Area: 11,506 sq. mi.
29,800 sq. km.
Population: 3,465,611
Capital: Yerevan
Largest City: Yerevan
Highest Point: Alagez
Monetary Unit: dram

Australia
Page/Location: 45
Area: 2,966,136 sq. mi.
7,682,300 sq. km.
Population: 18,438,824
Capital: Canberra
Largest City: Sydney
Highest Point: Mt. Kosciusko
Monetary Unit: Australian dollar

Austria
Page/Location: 21/G2
Area: 32,375 sq. mi.
83,851 sq. km.
Population: 8,054,078
Capital: Vienna
Largest City: Vienna
Highest Point: Grossglockner
Monetary Unit: schilling

Azerbaijan
Page/Location: 23/G5
Area: 33,436 sq. mi.
86,600 sq. km.
Population: 7,735,918
Capital: Baku
Largest City: Baku
Highest Point: Bazardyuzyu
Monetary Unit: manat

Bahamas
Page/Location: 59/F2
Area: 5,382 sq. mi.
13,939 sq. km.
Population: 262,034
Capital: Nassau
Largest City: Nassau
Highest Point: 207 ft. (63 m)
Monetary Unit: Bahamian dollar

Bahrain
Page/Location: 32/F3
Area: 240 sq. mi.
622 sq. km.
Population: 603,318
Capital: Manama
Largest City: Manama
Highest Point: Jabal Dukhān
Monetary Unit: Bahraini dinar

Bangladesh
Page/Location: 34/E3
Area: 55,598 sq. mi.
144,000 sq. km.
Population: 125,340,261
Capital: Dhākā
Largest City: Dhākā
Highest Point: Keokradong
Monetary Unit: taka

Barbados
Page/Location: 59/J5
Area: 166 sq. mi.
430 sq. km.
Population: 257,731
Capital: Bridgetown
Largest City: Bridgetown
Highest Point: Mt. Hillaby
Monetary Unit: Barbadian dollar

Belarus
Page/Location: 19/L3
Area: 80,154 sq. mi.
207,600 sq. km.
Population: 10,439,916
Capital: Minsk
Largest City: Minsk
Highest Point: Dzerzhinskaya
Monetary Unit: Belarusian ruble

Belgium
Page/Location: 18/E4
Area: 11,781 sq. mi.
30,513 sq. km.
Population: 10,203,683
Capital: Brussels
Largest City: Brussels
Highest Point: Botrange
Monetary Unit: Belgian franc

Belize
Page/Location: 58/D4
Area: 8,867 sq. mi.
22,966 sq. km.
Population: 224,663
Capital: Belmopan
Largest City: Belize City
Highest Point: Victoria Peak
Monetary Unit: Belize dollar

Benin
Page/Location: 40/F5
Area: 43,483 sq. mi.
112,620 sq. km.
Population: 5,342,000
Capital: Porto-Novo
Largest City: Cotonou
Highest Point: Nassoukou
Monetary Unit: CFA franc

Bhutan
Page/Location: 34/E2
Area: 18,147 sq. mi.
47,000 sq. km.
Population: 1,865,191
Capital: Thimphu
Largest City: Thimphu
Highest Point: Kula Kangri
Monetary Unit: ngultrum

Bolivia
Page/Location: 62/F7
Area: 424,163 sq. mi.
1,098,582 sq. km.
Population: 7,669,868
Capital: La Paz; Sucre
Largest City: La Paz
Highest Point: Nevado Ancohuma
Monetary Unit: boliviano

Bosnia and Herzegovina
Page/Location: 21/H2
Area: 19,940 sq. mi.
51,645 sq. km.
Population: 2,607,734
Capital: Sarajevo
Largest City: Sarajevo
Highest Point: Maglič
Monetary Unit: dinar

Botswana
Page/Location: 42/D5
Area: 231,803 sq. mi.
600,370 sq. km.
Population: 1,500,765
Capital: Gaborone
Largest City: Gaborone
Highest Point: Tsodilo Hills
Monetary Unit: pula

Brazil
Page/Location: 61/D3
Area: 3,286,470 sq. mi.
8,511,965 sq. km.
Population: 164,511,366
Capital: Brasília
Largest City: São Paulo
Highest Point: Pico da Neblina
Monetary Unit: real

Brunei
Page/Location: 36/D2
Area: 2,226 sq. mi.
5,765 sq. km.
Population: 307,616
Capital: Bandar Seri Begawan
Largest City: Bandar Seri Begawan
Highest Point: Bukit Pagon
Monetary Unit: Brunei dollar

Bulgaria
Page/Location: 21/K3
Area: 42,823 sq. mi.
110,912 sq. km.
Population: 8,652,745
Capital: Sofia
Largest City: Sofia
Highest Point: Musala
Monetary Unit: lev

Burkina Faso
Page/Location: 40/E5
Area: 105,869 sq. mi.
274,200 sq. km.
Population: 10,891,159
Capital: Ouagadougou
Largest City: Ouagadougou
Highest Point: 2,405 ft. (733 m)
Monetary Unit: CFA franc

Burundi
Page/Location: 42/E1
Area: 10,747 sq. mi.
27,835 sq. km.
Population: 6,052,614
Capital: Bujumbura
Largest City: Bujumbura
Highest Point: 8,760 ft. (2,670 m)
Monetary Unit: Burundi franc

Cambodia
Page/Location: 35/H5
Area: 69,898 sq. mi.
181,036 sq. km.
Population: 11,163,861
Capital: Phnom Penh
Largest City: Phnom Penh
Highest Point: Phnum Aoral
Monetary Unit: new riel

Cameroon
Page/Location: 40/H7
Area: 183,568 sq. mi.
475,441 sq. km.
Population: 14,677,510
Capital: Yaoundé
Largest City: Douala
Highest Point: Mt. Cameroon
Monetary Unit: CFA franc

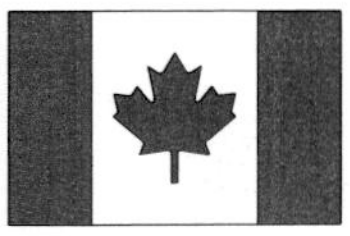

Canada
Page/Location: 49/G4
Area: 3,851,787 sq. mi.
9,976,139 sq. km.
Population: 29,123,194
Capital: Ottawa
Largest City: Toronto
Highest Point: Mt. Logan
Monetary Unit: Canadian dollar

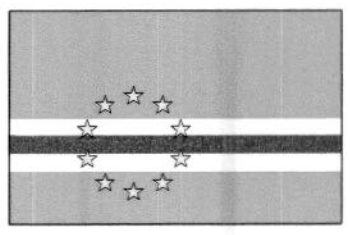

Cape Verde
Page/Location: 14/H5
Area: 1,557 sq. mi.
4,033 sq. km.
Population: 393,843
Capital: Praia
Largest City: Praia
Highest Point: 9,282 ft. (2,829 m)
Monetary Unit: Cape Verde escudo

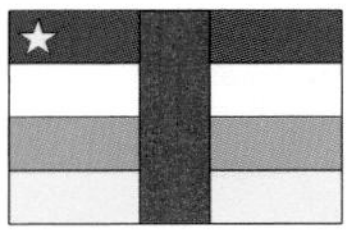

Central African Republic
Page/Location: 41/J6
Area: 240,533 sq. mi.
622,980 sq. km.
Population: 3,342,051
Capital: Bangui
Largest City: Bangui
Highest Point: Mt. Kayagangiri
Monetary Unit: CFA franc

Chad
Page/Location: 41/J4
Area: 495,752 sq. mi.
1,283,998 sq. km.
Population: 7,166,023
Capital: N'Djamena
Largest City: N'Djamena
Highest Point: Emi Koussi
Monetary Unit: CFA franc

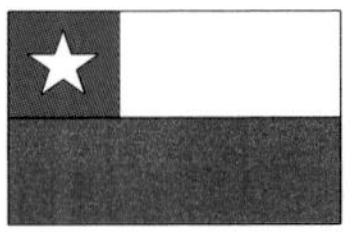

Chile
Page/Location: 64/B3
Area: 292,257 sq. mi.
756,946 sq. km.
Population: 14,508,168
Capital: Santiago
Largest City: Santiago
Highest Point: Nevado Ojos del Salado
Monetary Unit: Chilean peso

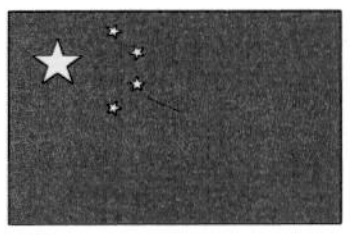

China
Page/Location: 27/J6
Area: 3,705,386 sq. mi.
9,596,960 sq. km.
Population: 1,221,591,778
Capital: Beijing
Largest City: Shanghai
Highest Point: Mt. Everest
Monetary Unit: yuan

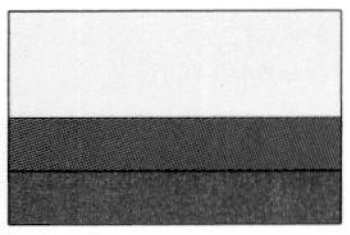

Colombia
Page/Location: 62/D3
Area: 439,513 sq. mi.
1,138,339 sq. km.
Population: 37,418,290
Capital: Bogotá
Largest City: Bogotá
Highest Point: Pico Cristóbal Colón
Monetary Unit: Colombian peso

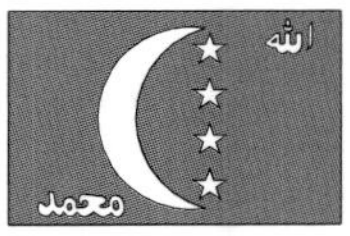

Comoros
Page/Location: 39/G6
Area: 838 sq. mi.
2,170 sq. km.
Population: 589,797
Capital: Moroni
Largest City: Moroni
Highest Point: Karthala
Monetary Unit: Comorian franc

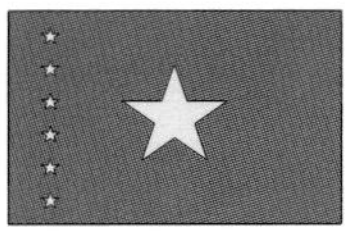

Congo, Dem. Rep. of the
Page/Location: 39/E5
Area: 905,563 sq. mi.
2,345,410 sq. km.
Population: 47,440,362
Capital: Kinshasa
Largest City: Kinshasa
Highest Point: Margherita Peak
Monetary Unit: zaire

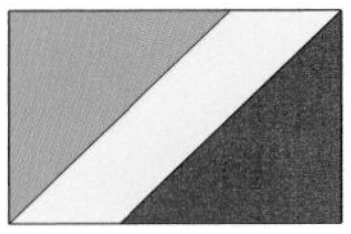

Congo, Rep. of the
Page/Location: 39/D4
Area: 132,046 sq. mi.
342,000 sq. km.
Population: 2,583,198
Capital: Brazzaville
Largest City: Brazzaville
Highest Point: Lékéti Mts.
Monetary Unit: CFA franc

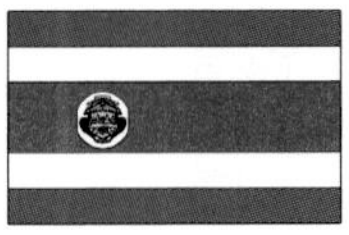

Costa Rica
Page/Location: 58/E5
Area: 19,730 sq. mi.
51,100 sq. km.
Population: 3,534,174
Capital: San José
Largest City: San José
Highest Point: Cerro Chirripó Grande
Monetary Unit: Costa Rican colón

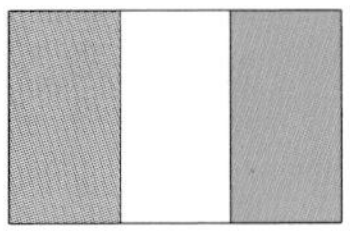

Côte d'Ivoire
Page/Location: 40/D6
Area: 124,504 sq. mi.
322,465 sq. km.
Population: 14,986,218
Capital: Yamoussoukro
Largest City: Abidjan
Highest Point: Mt. Nimba
Monetary Unit: CFA franc

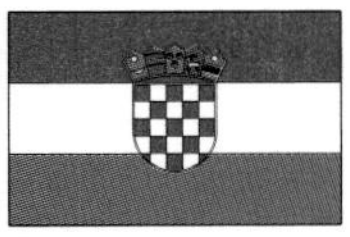

Croatia
Page/Location: 21/G2
Area: 22,050 sq. mi.
57,110 sq. km.
Population: 5,026,995
Capital: Zagreb
Largest City: Zagreb
Highest Point: Veliki Troglav
Monetary Unit: Croatian kuna

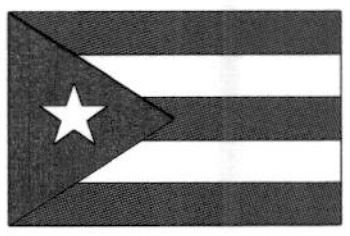

Cuba
Page/Location: 59/F3
Area: 42,803 sq. mi.
110,860 sq. km.
Population: 10,999,041
Capital: Havana
Largest City: Havana
Highest Point: Pico Turquino
Monetary Unit: Cuban peso

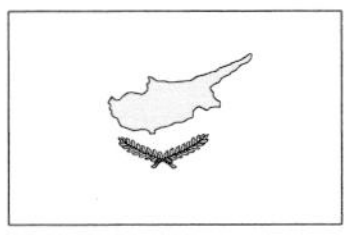

Cyprus
Page/Location: 32/B1
Area: 3,571 sq. mi.
9,250 sq. km.
Population: 752,808
Capital: Nicosia
Largest City: Nicosia
Highest Point: Olympus
Monetary Unit: Cypriot pound

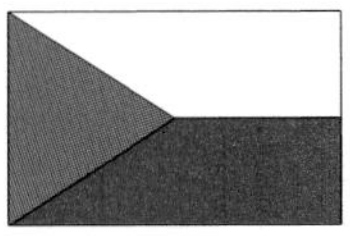

Czech Republic
Page/Location: 19/H4
Area: 30,387 sq. mi.
78,703 sq. km.
Population: 10,318,958
Capital: Prague
Largest City: Prague
Highest Point: Sněžka
Monetary Unit: Czech koruna

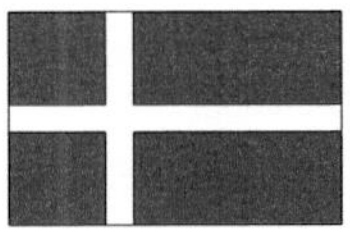

Denmark
Page/Location: 18/G3
Area: 16,629 sq. mi.
43,069 sq. km.
Population: 5,268,775
Capital: Copenhagen
Largest City: Copenhagen
Highest Point: Yding Skovhøj
Monetary Unit: Danish krone

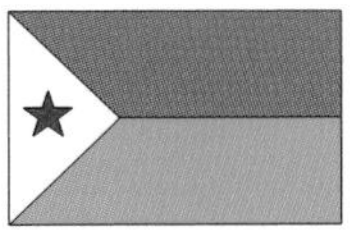

Djibouti
Page/Location: 41/P5
Area: 8,494 sq. mi.
22,000 sq. km.
Population: 434,116
Capital: Djibouti
Largest City: Djibouti
Highest Point: Moussa Ali
Monetary Unit: Djibouti franc

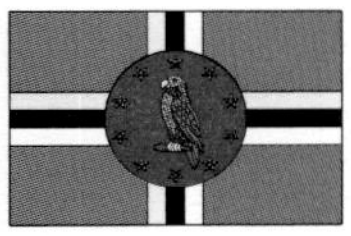

Dominica
Page/Location: 59/J4
Area: 290 sq. mi.
751 sq. km.
Population: 83,226
Capital: Roseau
Largest City: Roseau
Highest Point: Morne Diablotin
Monetary Unit: EC dollar

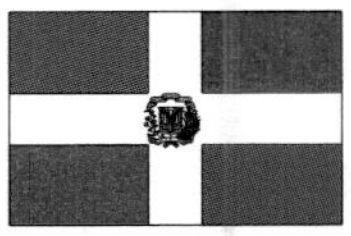

Dominican Republic
Page/Location: 59/H4
Area: 18,815 sq. mi.
48,730 sq. km.
Population: 8,228,151
Capital: Santo Domingo
Largest City: Santo Domingo
Highest Point: Pico Duarte
Monetary Unit: Dominican peso

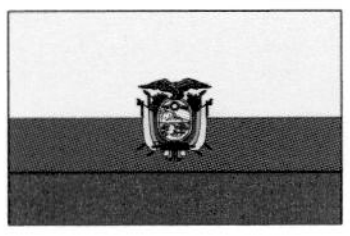

Ecuador
Page/Location: 62/C4
Area: 109,483 sq. mi.
283,561 sq. km.
Population: 11,690,535
Capital: Quito
Largest City: Guayaquil
Highest Point: Chimborazo
Monetary Unit: sucre

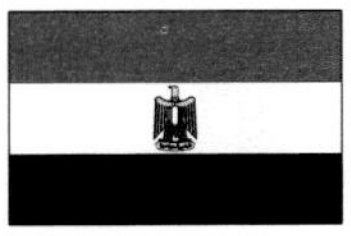

Egypt
Page/Location: 41/L2
Area: 386,659 sq. mi.
1,001,447 sq. km.
Population: 64,791,891
Capital: Cairo
Largest City: Cairo
Highest Point: Mt. Catherine
Monetary Unit: Egyptian pound

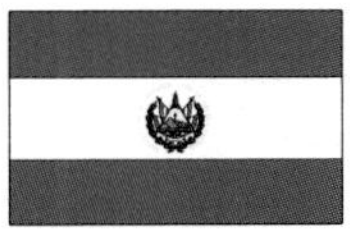

El Salvador
Page/Location: 58/C5
Area: 8,124 sq. mi.
21,040 sq. km.
Population: 5,661,827
Capital: San Salvador
Largest City: San Salvador
Highest Point: Santa Ana
Monetary Unit: Salvadoran colón

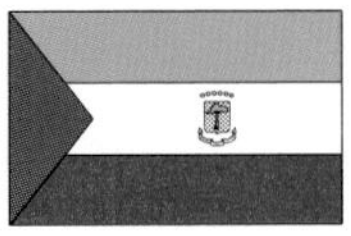

Equatorial Guinea
Page/Location: 40/G7
Area: 10,831 sq. mi.
28,052 sq. km.
Population: 442,516
Capital: Malabo
Largest City: Malabo
Highest Point: Pico de Santa Isabel
Monetary Unit: CFA franc

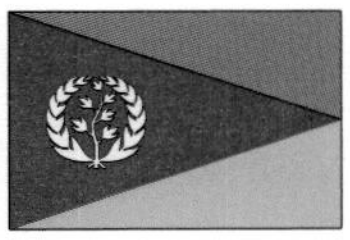

Eritrea
Page/Location: 41/N5
Area: 46,842 sq. mi.
121,320 sq. km.
Population: 3,589,687
Capital: Asmara
Largest City: Asmara
Highest Point: Soira
Monetary Unit: nafka

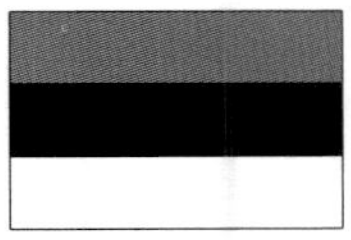

Estonia
Page/Location: 19/L2
Area: 17,413 sq. mi.
45,100 sq. km.
Population: 1,444,721
Capital: Tallinn
Largest City: Tallinn
Highest Point: Munamägi
Monetary Unit: kroon

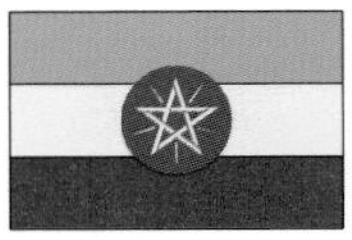

Ethiopia
Page/Location: 41/N5
Area: 435,184 sq. mi.
1,127,127 sq. km.
Population: 58,732,577
Capital: Addis Ababa
Largest City: Addis Ababa
Highest Point: Ras Dashen Terara
Monetary Unit: birr

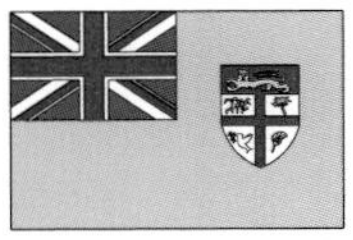

Fiji
Page/Location: 46/G6
Area: 7,055 sq. mi.
18,272 sq. km.
Population: 792,441
Capital: Suva
Largest City: Suva
Highest Point: Tomaniivi
Monetary Unit: Fijian dollar

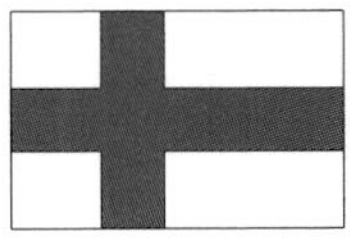

Finland
Page/Location: 22/H2
Area: 130,128 sq. mi.
337,032 sq. km.
Population: 5,109,148
Capital: Helsinki
Largest City: Helsinki
Highest Point: Kahperusvaara
Monetary Unit: markka

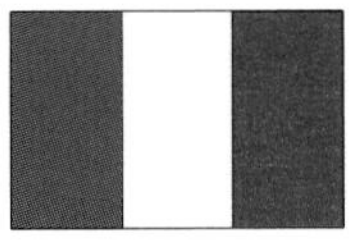

France
Page/Location: 20/D2
Area: 211,208 sq. mi.
547,030 sq. km.
Population: 58,470,421
Capital: Paris
Largest City: Paris
Highest Point: Mont Blanc
Monetary Unit: French franc

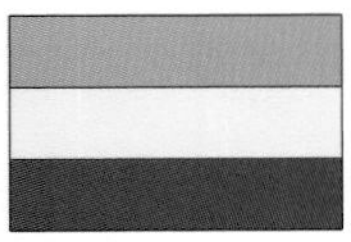

Gabon
Page/Location: 40/H7
Area: 103,346 sq. mi.
267,666 sq. km.
Population: 1,190,159
Capital: Libreville
Largest City: Libreville
Highest Point: Mt. Iboundji
Monetary Unit: CFA franc

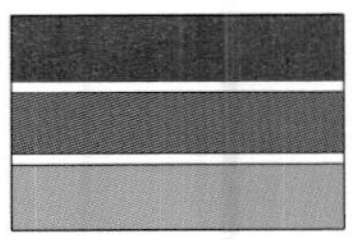

Gambia, The
Page/Location: 40/B5
Area: 4,363 sq. mi.
11,300 sq. km.
Population: 1,248,085
Capital: Banjul
Largest City: Banjul
Highest Point: 98 ft. (30 m)
Monetary Unit: dalasi

Georgia
Page/Location: 23/F5
Area: 26,911 sq. mi.
69,700 sq. km.
Population: 5,174,642
Capital: T'bilisi
Largest City: T'bilisi
Highest Point: Kazbek
Monetary Unit: lari

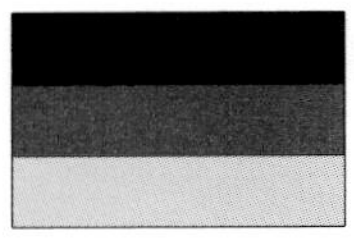

Germany
Page/Location: 18/G4
Area: 137,803 sq. mi.
356,910 sq. km.
Population: 84,068,216
Capital: Berlin
Largest City: Berlin
Highest Point: Zugspitze
Monetary Unit: Deutsche mark

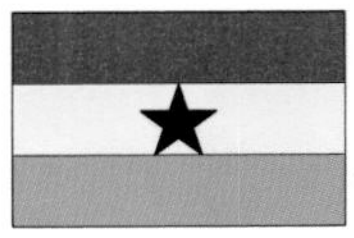

Ghana
Page/Location: 40/E6
Area: 92,099 sq. mi.
238,536 sq. km.
Population: 18,100,703
Capital: Accra
Largest City: Accra
Highest Point: Afadjoto
Monetary Unit: new cedi

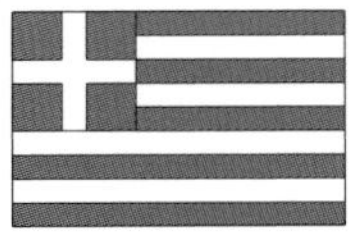

Greece
Page/Location: 21/J4
Area: 50,944 sq. mi.
131,945 sq. km.
Population: 10,583,126
Capital: Athens
Largest City: Athens
Highest Point: Mt. Olympus
Monetary Unit: drachma

World Flags and Reference Guide

Grenada
Page/Location: 59/J5
Area: 133 sq. mi.
344 sq. km.
Population: 95,537
Capital: St. George's
Largest City: St. George's
Highest Point: Mt. St. Catherine
Monetary Unit: East Caribbean dollar

Guatemala
Page/Location: 58/C4
Area: 42,042 sq. mi.
108,889 sq. km.
Population: 11,558,407
Capital: Guatemala
Largest City: Guatemala
Highest Point: Tajumulco
Monetary Unit: quetzal

Guinea
Page/Location: 40/C5
Area: 94,925 sq. mi.
245,856 sq. km.
Population: 7,405,375
Capital: Conakry
Largest City: Conakry
Highest Point: Mt. Nimba
Monetary Unit: Guinea franc

Guinea-Bissau
Page/Location: 40/B5
Area: 13,948 sq. mi.
36,125 sq. km.
Population: 1,178,584
Capital: Bissau
Largest City: Bissau
Highest Point: 689 ft. (210 m)
Monetary Unit: Guinea-Bissau peso

Guyana
Page/Location: 62/G3
Area: 83,000 sq. mi.
214,970 sq. km.
Population: 706,116
Capital: Georgetown
Largest City: Georgetown
Highest Point: Mt. Roraima
Monetary Unit: Guyana dollar

Haiti
Page/Location: 59/G4
Area: 10,694 sq. mi.
27,697 sq. km.
Population: 6,611,407
Capital: Port-au-Prince
Largest City: Port-au-Prince
Highest Point: Pic la Selle
Monetary Unit: gourde

Honduras
Page/Location: 58/D4
Area: 43,277 sq. mi.
112,087 sq. km.
Population: 5,751,384
Capital: Tegucigalpa
Largest City: Tegucigalpa
Highest Point: Cerro de las Minas
Monetary Unit: lempira

Hungary
Page/Location: 21/H2
Area: 35,919 sq. mi.
93,030 sq. km.
Population: 9,935,774
Capital: Budapest
Largest City: Budapest
Highest Point: Kékes
Monetary Unit: forint

Iceland
Page/Location: 22/N7
Area: 39,768 sq. mi.
103,000 sq. km.
Population: 272,550
Capital: Reykjavík
Largest City: Reykjavík
Highest Point: Hvannadalshnúkur
Monetary Unit: króna

India
Page/Location: 34/C3
Area: 1,269,339 sq. mi.
3,287,588 sq. km.
Population: 967,612,804
Capital: New Delhi
Largest City: Calcutta
Highest Point: Nanda Devi
Monetary Unit: Indian rupee

Indonesia
Page/Location: 37/E4
Area: 741,096 sq. mi.
1,919,440 sq. km.
Population: 209,774,138
Capital: Jakarta
Largest City: Jakarta
Highest Point: Puncak Jaya
Monetary Unit: rupiah

Iran
Page/Location: 32/F2
Area: 636,293 sq. mi.
1,648,000 sq. km.
Population: 67,540,002
Capital: Tehrān
Largest City: Tehrān
Highest Point: Qolleh-ye Damāvand
Monetary Unit: Iranian rial

Iraq
Page/Location: 32/D2
Area: 168,753 sq. mi.
437,072 sq. km.
Population: 22,219,289
Capital: Baghdad
Largest City: Baghdad
Highest Point: Haji Ibrahim
Monetary Unit: Iraqi dinar

Ireland
Page/Location: 18/B3
Area: 27,136 sq. mi.
70,282 sq. km.
Population: 3,555,500
Capital: Dublin
Largest City: Dublin
Highest Point: Carrantuohill
Monetary Unit: Irish pound

Israel
Page/Location: 32/B2
Area: 8,019 sq. mi.
20,770 sq. km.
Population: 5,534,672
Capital: Jerusalem
Largest City: Tel Aviv-Yafo
Highest Point: Har Meron
Monetary Unit: new Israeli shekel

Italy
Page/Location: 21/F3
Area: 116,303 sq. mi.
301,225 sq. km.
Population: 57,534,088
Capital: Rome
Largest City: Rome
Highest Point: Monte Rosa
Monetary Unit: Italian lira

Jamaica
Page/Location: 59/F4
Area: 4,243 sq. mi.
10,990 sq. km.
Population: 2,615,582
Capital: Kingston
Largest City: Kingston
Highest Point: Blue Mountain Pk.
Monetary Unit: Jamaican dollar

Japan
Page/Location: 29/M4
Area: 145,882 sq. mi.
377,835 sq. km.
Population: 125,716,637
Capital: Tokyo
Largest City: Tokyo
Highest Point: Fujiyama
Monetary Unit: yen

Jordan
Page/Location: 32/C2
Area: 34,445 sq. mi.
89,213 sq. km.
Population: 4,324,638
Capital: Ammān
Largest City: Ammān
Highest Point: Jabal Ramm
Monetary Unit: Jordanian dinar

Kazakhstan
Page/Location: 24/G5
Area: 1,049,150 sq. mi.
2,717,300 sq. km.
Population: 16,898,572
Capital: Astana
Largest City: Almaty
Highest Point: Khan-Tengri
Monetary Unit: Kazakstani tenge

Kenya
Page/Location: 41/N7
Area: 224,960 sq. mi.
582,646 sq. km.
Population: 28,803,085
Capital: Nairobi
Largest City: Nairobi
Highest Point: Mt. Kenya
Monetary Unit: Kenya shilling

Kiribati
Page/Location: 46/H5
Area: 277 sq. mi.
717 sq. km.
Population: 82,449
Capital: Tarawa
Largest City: —
Highest Point: Banaba Island
Monetary Unit: Australian dollar

Korea, North
Page/Location: 29/K3
Area: 46,540 sq. mi.
120,539 sq. km.
Population: 24,317,004
Capital: P'yŏngyang
Largest City: P'yŏngyang
Highest Point: Paektu-san
Monetary Unit: North Korean won

Korea, South
Page/Location: 29/K4
Area: 38,023 sq. mi.
98,480 sq. km.
Population: 45,948,811
Capital: Seoul
Largest City: Seoul
Highest Point: Halla-san
Monetary Unit: South Korean won

Kuwait
Page/Location: 32/E3
Area: 6,880 sq. mi.
17,820 sq. km.
Population: 2,076,805
Capital: Kuwait
Largest City: Kuwait
Highest Point: 951 ft. (290 m)
Monetary Unit: Kuwaiti dinar

Kyrgyzstan
Page/Location: 31/B3
Area: 76,641 sq. mi.
198,500 sq. km.
Population: 4,540,185
Capital: Bishkek
Largest City: Bishkek
Highest Point: Pik Pobedy
Monetary Unit: som

Laos
Page/Location: 35/H3
Area: 91,428 sq. mi.
236,800 sq. km.
Population: 5,116,959
Capital: Vientiane
Largest City: Vientiane
Highest Point: Phou Bia
Monetary Unit: new kip

Latvia
Page/Location: 19/L2
Area: 24,749 sq. mi.
64,100 sq. km.
Population: 2,437,649
Capital: Riga
Largest City: Riga
Highest Point: Gaizina Kalns
Monetary Unit: Latvian let

Lebanon
Page/Location: 32/C2
Area: 4,015 sq. mi.
10,399 sq. km.
Population: 3,858,736
Capital: Beirut
Largest City: Beirut
Highest Point: Qurnat as Sawdā'
Monetary Unit: Lebanese pound

Lesotho
Page/Location: 42/E6
Area: 11,720 sq. mi.
30,355 sq. km.
Population: 2,007,814
Capital: Maseru
Largest City: Maseru
Highest Point: Thabana-Ntlenyana
Monetary Unit: loti

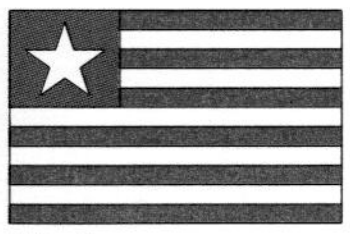

Liberia
Page/Location: 40/D6
Area: 43,000 sq. mi.
111,370 sq. km.
Population: 2,602,068
Capital: Monrovia
Largest City: Monrovia
Highest Point: Mt. Wuteve
Monetary Unit: Liberian dollar

Libya
Page/Location: 41/J2
Area: 679,358 sq. mi.
1,759,537 sq. km.
Population: 5,648,359
Capital: Tripoli
Largest City: Tripoli
Highest Point: Picco Bette
Monetary Unit: Libyan dinar

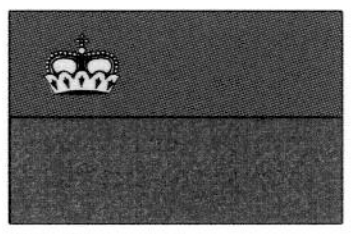

Liechtenstein
Page/Location: 18/G5
Area: 61 sq. mi.
158 sq. km.
Population: 31,461
Capital: Vaduz
Largest City: Vaduz
Highest Point: Grauspitz
Monetary Unit: Swiss franc

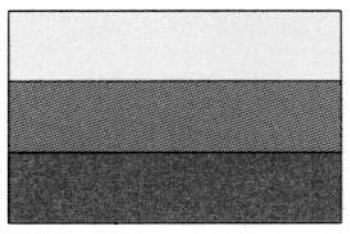

Lithuania
Page/Location: 19/K3
Area: 25,174 sq. mi.
65,200 sq. km.
Population: 3,635,932
Capital: Vilnius
Largest City: Vilnius
Highest Point: Nevaišių
Monetary Unit: litas

Luxembourg
Page/Location: 18/F4
Area: 999 sq. mi.
2,587 sq. km.
Population: 422,474
Capital: Luxembourg
Largest City: Luxembourg
Highest Point: Ardennes Plateau
Monetary Unit: Luxembourg franc

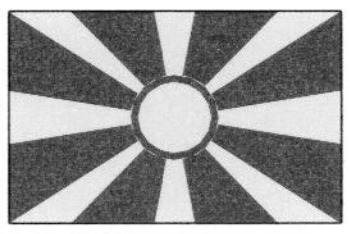

Macedonia (F.Y.R.O.M.)
Page/Location: 21/J3
Area: 9,781 sq. mi.
25,333 sq. km.
Population: 2,113,866
Capital: Skopje
Largest City: Skopje
Highest Point: Korab
Monetary Unit: denar

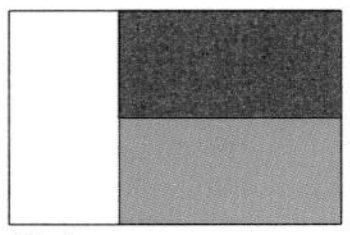

Madagascar
Page/Location: 42/K10
Area: 226,657 sq. mi.
587,041 sq. km.
Population: 14,061,627
Capital: Antananarivo
Largest City: Antananarivo
Highest Point: Maromokotro
Monetary Unit: Malagasy franc

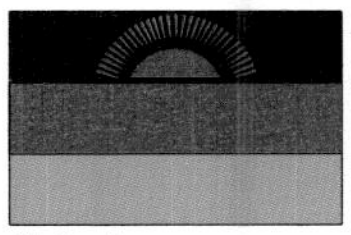

Malawi
Page/Location: 42/F3
Area: 45,747 sq. mi.
118, 485 sq. km.
Population: 9,609,081
Capital: Lilongwe
Largest City: Blantyre
Highest Point: Mulanje Mts.
Monetary Unit: Malawi kwacha

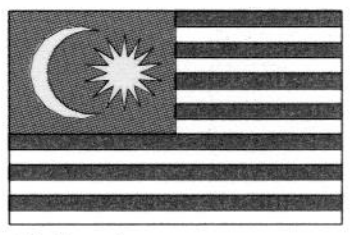

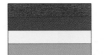

Malaysia
Page/Location: 36/C2
Area: 127,316 sq. mi.
329,750 sq. km.
Population: 20,376,235
Capital: Kuala Lumpur
Largest City: Kuala Lumpur
Highest Point: Gunung Kinabalu
Monetary Unit: ringgit

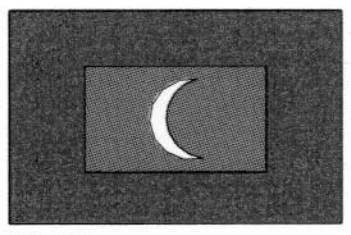

Maldives
Page/Location: 27/G9
Area: 115 sq. mi.
298 sq. km.
Population: 280,391
Capital: Male
Largest City: Male
Highest Point: 20 ft. (6 m)
Monetary Unit: rufiyaa

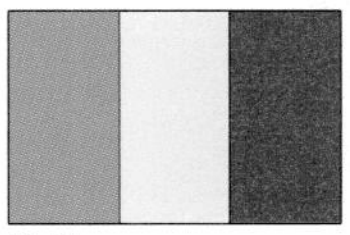

Mali
Page/Location: 40/E4
Area: 478,764 sq. mi.
1,240,000 sq. km.
Population: 9,945,383
Capital: Bamako
Largest City: Bamako
Highest Point: Hombori Tondo
Monetary Unit: CFA franc

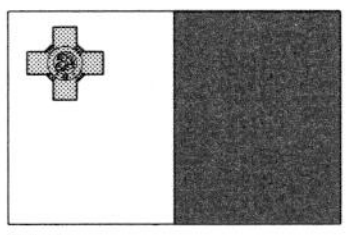

Malta
Page/Location: 21/G5
Area: 122 sq. mi.
316 sq. km.
Population: 379,365
Capital: Valletta
Largest City: Sliema
Highest Point: 830 ft. (253 m)
Monetary Unit: Maltese lira

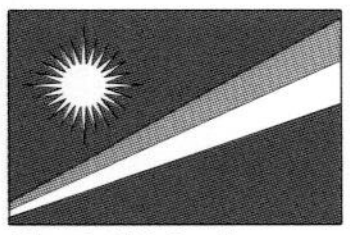

Marshall Islands
Page/Location: 46/G3
Area: 70 sq. mi.
181 sq. km.
Population: 60,652
Capital: Majuro
Largest City: —
Highest Point: 20 ft. (6 m)
Monetary Unit: U.S. dollar

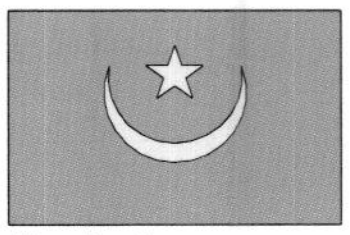

Mauritania
Page/Location: 40/C4
Area: 397,953 sq. mi.
1,030,700 sq. km.
Population: 2,411,317
Capital: Nouakchott
Largest City: Nouakchott
Highest Point: Kediet Ijill
Monetary Unit: ouguiya

Mauritius
Page/Location: 15/M7
Area: 718 sq. mi.
1,860 sq. km.
Population: 1,154,272
Capital: Port Louis
Largest City: Port Louis
Highest Point: 2,713 ft. (827 m)
Monetary Unit: Mauritian rupee

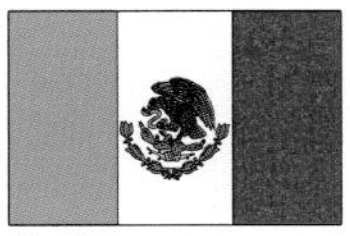

Mexico
Page/Location: 58/A3
Area: 761,601 sq. mi.
1,972,546 sq. km.
Population: 97,563,374
Capital: Mexico
Largest City: Mexico
Highest Point: Citlaltépetl
Monetary Unit: new Mexican peso

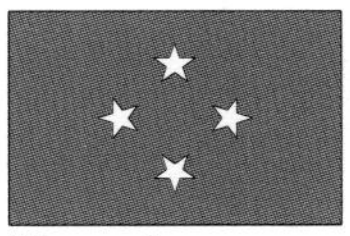

Micronesia
Page/Location: 46/D4
Area: 271 sq. mi.
702 sq. km.
Population: 122,950
Capital: Palikir
Largest City: —
Highest Point: —
Monetary Unit: U.S. dollar

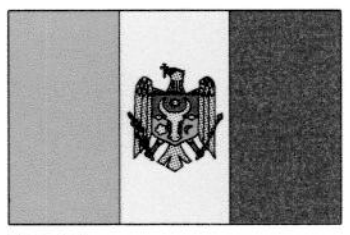

Moldova
Page/Location: 19/L5
Area: 13,012 sq. mi.
33,700 sq. km.
Population: 4,475,232
Capital: Chişinău
Largest City: Chişinău
Highest Point: 1,408 ft. (429 m)
Monetary Unit: leu

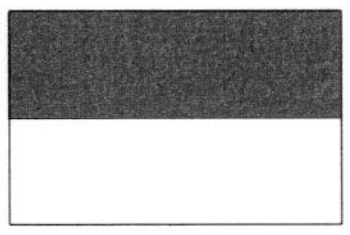

Monaco
Page/Location: 20/E3
Area: 0.7 sq. mi.
1.9 sq. km.
Population: 31,892
Capital: Monaco
Largest City: —
Highest Point: —
Monetary Unit: French franc

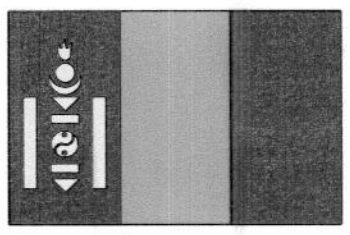

Mongolia
Page/Location: 28/D2
Area: 606,163 sq. mi.
1,569, 962 sq. km.
Population: 2,538,211
Capital: Ulaanbaatar
Largest City: Ulaanbaatar
Highest Point: Tavan Bogd Uul
Monetary Unit: tughrik

Morocco
Page/Location: 40/C1
Area: 172,414 sq. mi.
446,550 sq. km.
Population: 30,391,423
Capital: Rabat
Largest City: Casablanca
Highest Point: Jebel Toubkal
Monetary Unit: Moroccan dirham

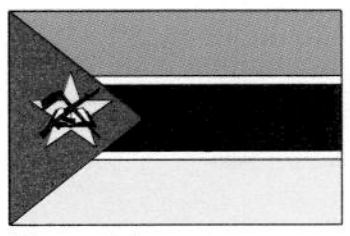

Mozambique
Page/Location: 42/G4
Area: 309,494 sq. mi.
801,590 sq. km.
Population: 18,165,476
Capital: Maputo
Largest City: Maputo
Highest Point: Monte Binga
Monetary Unit: metical

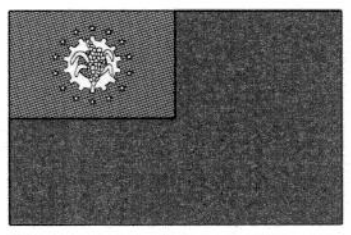

Myanmar (Burma)
Page/Location: 35/G3
Area: 261,969 sq. mi.
678,500 sq. km.
Population: 46,821,943
Capital: Rangoon
Largest City: Rangoon
Highest Point: Hkakabo Razi
Monetary Unit: kyat

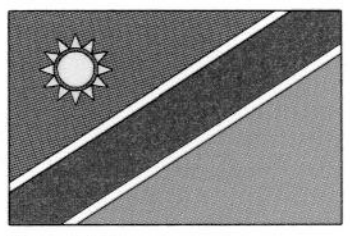

Namibia
Page/Location: 42/C5
Area: 318,694 sq. mi.
825,418 sq. km.
Population: 1,727,183
Capital: Windhoek
Largest City: Windhoek
Highest Point: Brandberg
Monetary Unit: Namibian dollar

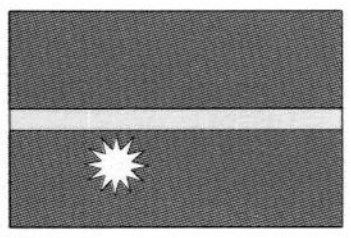

Nauru
Page/Location: 46/F5
Area: 7.7 sq. mi.
20 sq. km.
Population: 10,390
Capital: Yaren (district)
Largest City: —
Highest Point: 230 ft. (70 m)
Monetary Unit: Australian dollar

Nepal
Page/Location: 34/D2
Area: 54,663 sq. mi.
141,577 sq. km.
Population: 22,641,061
Capital: Kāthmāndu
Largest City: Kāthmāndu
Highest Point: Mt. Everest
Monetary Unit: Nepalese rupee

Netherlands
Page/Location: 18/F3
Area: 14,413 sq. mi.
37,330 sq. km.
Population: 15,653,091
Capital: The Hague; Amsterdam
Largest City: Amsterdam
Highest Point: Vaalserberg
Monetary Unit: Netherlands guilder

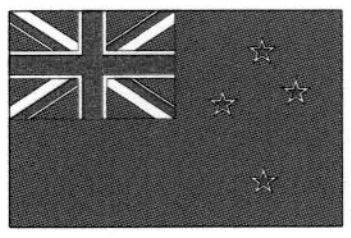

New Zealand
Page/Location: 45/H6
Area: 103,736 sq. mi.
268,676 sq. km.
Population: 3,587,275
Capital: Wellington
Largest City: Auckland
Highest Point: Mt. Cook
Monetary Unit: New Zealand dollar

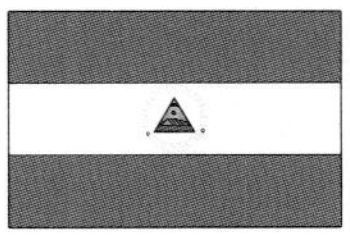

Nicaragua
Page/Location: 58/D5
Area: 49,998 sq. mi.
129,494 sq. km.
Population: 4,386,399
Capital: Managua
Largest City: Managua
Highest Point: Pico Mogotón
Monetary Unit: gold cordoba

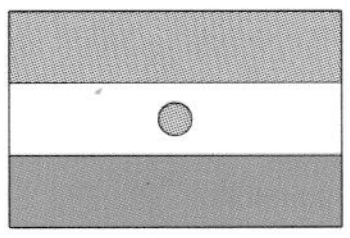

Niger
Page/Location: 40/G4
Area: 489,189 sq. mi.
1,267,000 sq. km.
Population: 9,388,859
Capital: Niamey
Largest City: Niamey
Highest Point: Bagzane
Monetary Unit: CFA franc

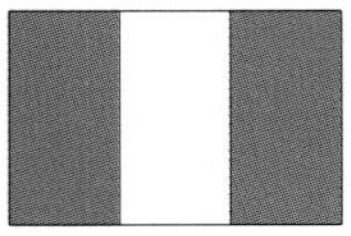

Nigeria
Page/Location: 40/G6
Area: 356,668 sq. mi.
923,770 sq. km.
Population: 107,129,469
Capital: Abuja
Largest City: Lagos
Highest Point: Dimlang
Monetary Unit: naira

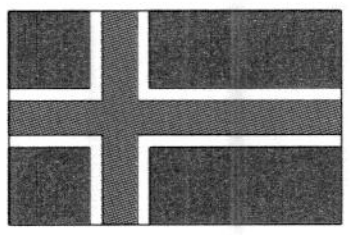

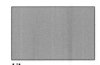

Norway
Page/Location: 22/C3
Area: 125,053 sq. mi.
323,887 sq. km.
Population: 4,404,456
Capital: Oslo
Largest City: Oslo
Highest Point: Glittertjnden
Monetary Unit: Norwegian krone

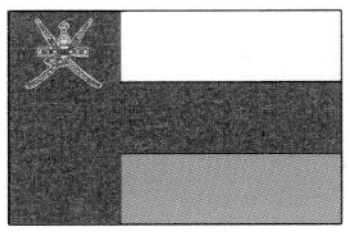

Oman
Page/Location: 33/G4
Area: 82,031 sq. mi.
212,460 sq. km.
Population: 2,264,590
Capital: Muscat
Largest City: Muscat
Highest Point: Jabal ash Shām
Monetary Unit: Omani rial

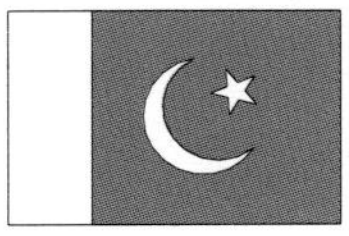

Pakistan
Page/Location: 33/H3
Area: 310,403 sq. mi.
803,944 sq. km.
Population: 132,185,299
Capital: Islāmābād
Largest City: Karāchi
Highest Point: K2 (Godwin Austen)
Monetary Unit: Pakistani rupee

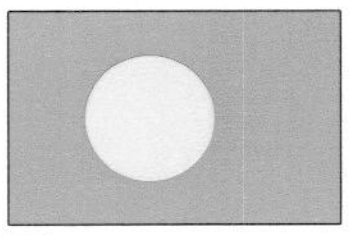

Palau
Page/Location: 46/C4
Area: 177 sq. mi.
458 sq. km.
Population: 17,240
Capital: Koror
Largest City: Koror
Highest Point: 699 ft. (213m)
Monetary Unit: U.S. dollar

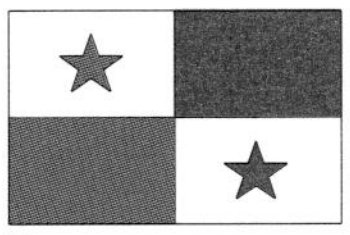

Panama
Page/Location: 58/E6
Area: 30,193 sq. mi.
78,200 sq. km.
Population: 2,693,417
Capital: Panamá
Largest City: Panamá
Highest Point: Barú
Monetary Unit: balboa

World Flags and Reference Guide

Papua New Guinea
Page/Location: 46/D5
Area: 178,259 sq. mi.
    461,690 sq. km.
Population: 4,496,221
Capital: Port Moresby
Largest City: Port Moresby
Highest Point: Mt. Wilhelm
Monetary Unit: kina

Paraguay
Page/Location: 61/D5
Area: 157,047 sq. mi.
    406,752 sq. km.
Population: 5,651,634;
Capital: Asunción
Largest City: Asunción
Highest Point: Sierra de Amambay
Monetary Unit: guaraní

Peru
Page/Location: 62/C5
Area: 496,222 sq. mi.
    1,285,215 sq. km.
Population: 24,949,512
Capital: Lima
Largest City: Lima
Highest Point: Nevado Huascarán
Monetary Unit: nuevo sol

Philippines
Page/Location: 30/D5
Area: 115,830 sq. mi.
    300,000 sq. km.
Population: 76,103,564
Capital: Manila
Largest City: Manila
Highest Point: Mt. Apo
Monetary Unit: Philippine peso

Poland
Page/Location: 19/J3
Area: 120,725 sq. mi.
    312,678 sq. km.
Population: 38,700,291
Capital: Warsaw
Largest City: Warsaw
Highest Point: Rysy
Monetary Unit: zloty

Portugal
Page/Location: 20/A4
Area: 35,549 sq. mi.
    92,072 sq. km.
Population: 9,867,654
Capital: Lisbon
Largest City: Lisbon
Highest Point: Serra da Estrela
Monetary Unit: Portuguese escudo

Qatar
Page/Location: 32/F3
Area: 4,247 sq. mi.
    11,000 sq. km.
Population: 665,485
Capital: Doha
Largest City: Doha
Highest Point: Dukhān Heights
Monetary Unit: Qatari riyal

Romania
Page/Location: 21/J2
Area: 91,699 sq. mi.
    237,500 sq. km.
Population: 21,399,114
Capital: Bucharest
Largest City: Bucharest
Highest Point: Moldoveanul
Monetary Unit: leu

Russia
Page/Location: 24/H3
Area: 6,592,812 sq. mi.
    17,075,400 sq. km.
Population: 147,987,101
Capital: Moscow
Largest City: Moscow
Highest Point: El'brus
Monetary Unit: Russian ruble

Rwanda
Page/Location: 42/E1
Area: 10,169 sq. mi.
    26,337 sq. km.
Population: 7,737,537
Capital: Kigali
Largest City: Kigali
Highest Point: Karisimbi
Monetary Unit: Rwanda franc

Saint Kitts and Nevis
Page/Location: 59/J4
Area: 104 sq. mi.
    269 sq. km.
Population: 41,803
Capital: Basseterre
Largest City: Basseterre
Highest Point: Mt. Misery
Monetary Unit: East Caribbean dollar

Saint Lucia
Page/Location: 59/J5
Area: 238 sq. mi.
    616 sq. km.
Population: 159,639
Capital: Castries
Largest City: Castries
Highest Point: Mt. Gimie
Monetary Unit: East Caribbean dollar

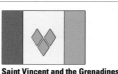

Saint Vincent and the Grenadines
Page/Location: 59/J5
Area: 131 sq. mi.
    340 sq. km.
Population: 119,092
Capital: Kingstown
Largest City: Kingstown
Highest Point: Soufrière
Monetary Unit: East Caribbean dollar

Samoa
Page/Location: 47/H6
Area: 1,104 sq. mi.
    2,860 sq. km.
Population: 219,509
Capital: Apia
Largest City: Apia
Highest Point: Mt. Silisili
Monetary Unit: tala

San Marino
Page/Location: 21/G3
Area: 23.4 sq. mi.
    60.6 sq. km.
Population: 24,714
Capital: San Marino
Largest City: San Marino
Highest Point: Monte Titano
Monetary Unit: Italian lira

São Tomé and Príncipe
Page/Location: 40/F7
Area: 371 sq. mi.
    960 sq. km.
Population: 147,865
Capital: São Tomé
Largest City: São Tomé
Highest Point: Pico de São Tomé
Monetary Unit: dobra

Saudi Arabia
Page/Location: 32/D4
Area: 756,981 sq. mi.
    1,960,582 sq. km.
Population: 20,087,965
Capital: Riyadh
Largest City: Riyadh
Highest Point: Jabal Sawdā'
Monetary Unit: Saudi riyal

Senegal
Page/Location: 40/B5
Area: 75,954 sq. mi.
    196,720 sq. km.
Population: 9,403,546
Capital: Dakar
Largest City: Dakar
Highest Point: Fouta Djallon
Monetary Unit: CFA franc

Seychelles
Page/Location: 15/M6
Area: 176 sq. mi.
    455 sq. km.
Population: 78,142
Capital: Victoria
Largest City: Victoria
Highest Point: Morne Seychellois
Monetary Unit: Seychelles rupee

Sierra Leone
Page/Location: 40/C6
Area: 27,699 sq. mi.
    71,740 sq. km.
Population: 4,891,546
Capital: Freetown
Largest City: Freetown
Highest Point: Loma Mansa
Monetary Unit: leone

Singapore
Page/Location: 36/B3
Area: 244 sq. mi.
    632.6 sq. km.
Population: 3,461,929
Capital: Singapore
Largest City: Singapore
Highest Point: Bukit Timah
Monetary Unit: Singapore dollar

Slovakia
Page/Location: 19/J4
Area: 18,924 sq. mi.
    49,013 sq. km.
Population: 5,393,016
Capital: Bratislava
Largest City: Bratislava
Highest Point: Gerlachovský Štít
Monetary Unit: Slovak koruna

Slovenia
Page/Location: 21/G2
Area: 7,898 sq. mi.
    20,456 sq. km.
Population: 1,945,998
Capital: Ljubljana
Largest City: Ljubljana
Highest Point: Triglav
Monetary Unit: tolar

Solomon Islands
Page/Location: 46/E6
Area: 11,500 sq. mi.
    29,785 sq. km.
Population: 462,855
Capital: Honiara
Largest City: Honiara
Highest Point: Mt. Makarakomburu
Monetary Unit: Solomon Islands dollar

Somalia
Page/Location: 41/Q6
Area: 246,200 sq. mi.
    637,658 sq. km.
Population: 9,940,232
Capital: Mogadishu
Largest City: Mogadishu
Highest Point: Shimber Berris
Monetary Unit: Somali shilling

South Africa
Page/Location: 42/D6
Area: 471,008 sq. mi.
    1,219,912 sq. km.
Population: 42,327,458
Capital: Cape Town; Pretoria
Largest City: Johannesburg
Highest Point: Injasuti
Monetary Unit: rand

Spain
Page/Location: 20/B3
Area: 194,881 sq. mi.
    504,742 sq. km.
Population: 39,244,195
Capital: Madrid
Largest City: Madrid
Highest Point: Pico de Teide
Monetary Unit: peseta

Sri Lanka
Page/Location: 34/D6
Area: 25,332 sq. mi.
    65,610 sq. km.
Population: 18,762,075
Capital: Colombo
Largest City: Colombo
Highest Point: Pidurutalagala
Monetary Unit: Sri Lanka rupee

Sudan
Page/Location: 41/L5
Area: 967,494 sq. mi.
    2,505,809 sq. km.
Population: 32,594,128
Capital: Khartoum
Largest City: Omdurman
Highest Point: Jabal Marrah
Monetary Unit: Sudanese pound

Suriname
Page/Location: 63/G3
Area: 63,039 sq. mi.
    163,270 sq. km.
Population: 443,446
Capital: Paramaribo
Largest City: Paramaribo
Highest Point: Juliana Top
Monetary Unit: Suriname guilder

Swaziland
Page/Location: 42/F6
Area: 6,705 sq. mi.
17,366 sq. km.
Population: 1,031,600
Capital: Mbabane; Lobamba
Largest City: Mbabane
Highest Point: Emlembe
Monetary Unit: lilangeni

Sweden
Page/Location: 22/E3
Area: 173,665 sq. mi.
449,792 sq. km.
Population: 8,946,193
Capital: Stockholm
Largest City: Stockholm
Highest Point: Kebnekaise
Monetary Unit: krona

Switzerland
Page/Location: 20/E2
Area: 15,943 sq. mi.
41,292 sq. km.
Population: 7,248,984
Capital: Bern
Largest City: Zürich
Highest Point: Dufourspitze
Monetary Unit: Swiss franc

Syria
Page/Location: 32/C1
Area: 71,498 sq. mi.
185,180 sq. km.
Population: 16,137,899
Capital: Damascus
Largest City: Damascus
Highest Point: Jabal ash Shaykh
Monetary Unit: Syrian pound

Taiwan
Page/Location: 30/D3
Area: 13,971 sq. mi.
36,185 sq. km.
Population: 21,655,515
Capital: T'aipei
Largest City: T'aipei
Highest Point: Yü Shan
Monetary Unit: new Taiwan dollar

Tajikistan
Page/Location: 24/H6
Area: 55,251 sq. mi.
143,100 sq. km.
Population: 6,013,855
Capital: Dushanbe
Largest City: Dushanbe
Highest Point: Communism Peak
Monetary Unit: Tajikistani ruble

Tanzania
Page/Location: 42/F2
Area: 364,699 sq. mi.
945,090 sq. km.
Population: 29,460,753
Capital: Dar es Salaam
Largest City: Dar es Salaam
Highest Point: Kilimanjaro
Monetary Unit: Tanzanian shilling

Thailand
Page/Location: 35/H4
Area: 198,455 sq. mi.
513,998 sq. km.
Population: 59,450,818
Capital: Bangkok
Largest City: Bangkok
Highest Point: Doi Inthanon
Monetary Unit: baht

Togo
Page/Location: 40/F6
Area: 21,927 sq. mi.
56,790 sq. km.
Population: 4,735,610
Capital: Lomé
Largest City: Lomé
Highest Point: Mt. Agou
Monetary Unit: CFA franc

Tonga
Page/Location: 47/H7
Area: 289 sq. mi.
748 sq. km.
Population: 107,335
Capital: Nuku'alofa
Largest City: Nuku'alofa
Highest Point: Kao Island
Monetary Unit: pa'anga

Trinidad and Tobago
Page/Location: 59/J5
Area: 1,980 sq. mi.
5,128 sq. km.
Population: 1,273,141
Capital: Port-of-Spain
Largest City: Port-of-Spain
Highest Point: El Cerro del Aripo
Monetary Unit: Trin. & Tobago dollar

Tunisia
Page/Location: 40/G1
Area: 63,170 sq. mi.
163,610 sq. km.
Population: 9,183,097
Capital: Tūnis
Largest City: Tūnis
Highest Point: Jabal ash Sha'nabī
Monetary Unit: Tunisian dinar

Turkey
Page/Location: 23/D6
Area: 301,382 sq. mi.
780,580 sq. km.
Population: 63,528,225
Capital: Ankara
Largest City: Istanbul
Highest Point: Mt. Ararat
Monetary Unit: Turkish lira

Turkmenistan
Page/Location: 24/F6
Area: 188,455 sq. mi.
488,100 sq. km.
Population: 4,225,351
Capital: Ashgabat
Largest City: Ashgabat
Highest Point: Rize
Monetary Unit: manat

Tuvalu
Page/Location: 46/G5
Area: 9.78 sq. mi.
25.33 sq. km.
Population: 10,297
Capital: Funafuti
Largest City: —
Highest Point: 16 ft. (5 m)
Monetary Unit: Australian dollar

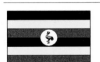

Uganda
Page/Location: 41/M7
Area: 91,076 sq. mi.
235,887 sq. km.
Population: 20,604,874
Capital: Kampala
Largest City: Kampala
Highest Point: Margherita Peak
Monetary Unit: Ugandan shilling

Ukraine
Page/Location: 23/C4
Area: 233,089 sq. mi.
603,700 sq. km.
Population: 50,684,635
Capital: Kiev
Largest City: Kiev
Highest Point: Goverla
Monetary Unit: hryvnia

United Arab Emirates
Page/Location: 32/F4
Area: 29,182 sq. mi.
75,581 sq. km.
Population: 2,262,309
Capital: Abu Dhabi
Largest City: Dubayy
Highest Point: Hajar Mts.
Monetary Unit: Emirian dirham

United Kingdom
Page/Location: 18/C3
Area: 94,399 sq. mi.
244,493 sq. km.
Population: 58,610,182
Capital: London
Largest City: London
Highest Point: Ben Nevis
Monetary Unit: pound sterling

United States
Page/Location: 49/G5
Area: 3,618,765 sq. mi.
9,372,610 sq. km.
Population: 267,954,767
Capital: Washington, D.C.
Largest City: New York
Highest Point: Mt. McKinley
Monetary Unit: U.S. dollar

Uruguay
Page/Location: 64/E3
Area: 68,039 sq. mi.
176,220 sq. km.
Population: 3,261,707
Capital: Montevideo
Largest City: Montevideo
Highest Point: Cerro Catedral
Monetary Unit: Uruguayan peso

Uzbekistan
Page/Location: 24/G5
Area: 172,741 sq. mi.
447,400 sq. km.
Population: 23,860,452
Capital: Tashkent
Largest City: Tashkent
Highest Point: Khodzha-Pir'yakh
Monetary Unit: som

Vanuatu
Page/Location: 46/F6
Area: 5,700 sq. mi.
14,763 sq. km.
Population: 181,358
Capital: Port-Vila
Largest City: Port-Vila
Highest Point: Tabwemasana
Monetary Unit: vatu

Vatican City
Page/Location: 21/F3
Area: 0.17 sq. mi.
0.44 sq. km.
Population: 830
Capital: —
Largest City: —
Highest Point: —
Monetary Unit: Vatican lira

Venezuela
Page/Location: 62/E2
Area: 352,143 sq. mi.
912,050 sq. km.
Population: 22,396,407
Capital: Caracas
Largest City: Caracas
Highest Point: Pico Bolívar
Monetary Unit: bolívar

Vietnam
Page/Location: 35/J5
Area: 127,243 sq. mi.
329,560 sq. km.
Population: 75,123,880
Capital: Hanoi
Largest City: Ho Chi Minh City
Highest Point: Fan Si Pan
Monetary Unit: new dong

Yemen
Page/Location: 32/E5
Area: 203,849 sq. mi.
527,970 sq. km.
Population: 13,972,477
Capital: Sanaa
Largest City: Aden
Highest Point: Nabī Shu'ayb
Monetary Unit: Yemeni rial

Yugoslavia
Page/Location: 21/J3
Area: 39,517 sq. mi.
102,350 sq. km.
Population: 10,655,317
Capital: Belgrade
Largest City: Belgrade
Highest Point: Đaravica
Monetary Unit: Yugoslav new dinar

Zambia
Page/Location: 42/E3
Area: 290,586 sq. mi.
752,618 sq. km.
Population: 9,349,975
Capital: Lusaka
Largest City: Lusaka
Highest Point: Sunzu
Monetary Unit: Zambian kwacha

Zimbabwe
Page/Location: 42/E4
Area: 150,803 sq. mi.
390,580 sq. km.
Population: 11,423,175
Capital: Harare
Largest City: Harare
Highest Point: Inyangani
Monetary Unit: Zimbabwe dollar

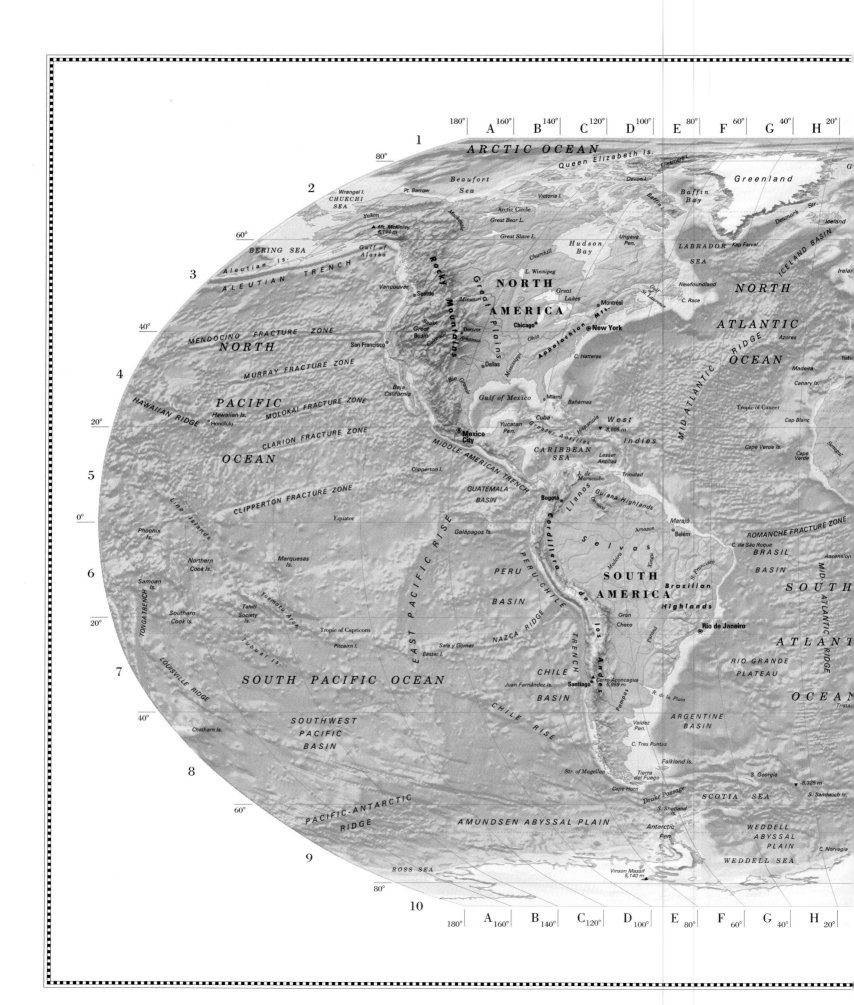

ARCTIC OCEAN

Queen Elizabeth Is.

Greenland

1

80°

2
Beaufort
Sea
Wrangel I.
CHUKCHI
SEA
Pt. Barrow
Victoria I.
Devon I.
Ellesmere I.
Baffin
Bay
Denmark
Iceland
G

60°
Yukon
Mackenzie
Arctic Circle
Great Bear L.
Baffin
LABRADOR
Kap Farvel
▲ Mt. McKinley
6,194 m
Great Slave L.
Hudson
Bay
Ungava
Pen.
SEA

3
BERING SEA
Aleutian Is.
Gulf of
Alaska
Churchill
L. Winnipeg
Newfoundland
NORTH
Ireland

ALEUTIAN TRENCH
Vancouver
Seattle
Great
Lakes
Montréal
St. Lawrence
C. Race
ATLANTIC

40°
Mendocino FRACTURE ZONE
NORTH
San Francisco
Missouri
Snake
Denver
Colorado
Arkansas
Chicago
Ohio
New York
Appalachian
C. Hatteras
OCEAN
MID-ATLANTIC RIDGE
Azores

4
MURRAY FRACTURE ZONE
PACIFIC
Baja
California
Rio Grande
Gulf of Mexico
Miami
Bahamas
Tropic of Cancer
Madeira
Canary Is.

20°
HAWAIIAN RIDGE
Hawaiian Is.
Honolulu
MOLOKAI FRACTURE ZONE
Mexico
City
Yucatan
Pen.
Cuba
Greater Antilles
Hispaniola
West
▲ 8,605 m
Indies
Cap Blanc
Cape Verde Is.
Cape
Verde

CLARION FRACTURE ZONE
OCEAN
Clipperton I.
CARIBBEAN
SEA
Lesser
Antilles
Trinidad
Senegal

5
0°
Line Islands
CLIPPERTON FRACTURE ZONE
Equator
GUATEMALA
BASIN
MIDDLE AMERICAN TRENCH
L. de
Maracaibo
Bogotá
Llanos
Orinoco
Guiana Highlands

Phoenix
Is.
Galápagos Is.
Cordillera
Selvas
Amazon
Marajó
Belém
ROMANCHE FRACTURE ZONE
Ascension
SOUTH

6
Northern
Cook Is.
Marquesas
Is.
EAST PACIFIC RISE
PERU-CHILE
PERU
BASIN
de
SOUTH
AMERICA
Xingu
Madeira
S. Francisco
BRASIL
BASIN
MID-ATLANTIC RIDGE
Brazilian
Highlands

Samoan
Is.
Tuamotu Arch.
Tahiti
Society
Is.
20°
Southern
Cook Is.
Tropic of Capricorn
Pitcairn I.
Sala y Gomez
Easter I.
NAZCA RIDGE
los
Gran
Chaco
Potosi
Rio de Janeiro
ATLANTIC

7
TONGA TRENCH
Tubuai Is.
CHILE
BASIN
Andes
Cerro Aconcagua
6,959 m
Juan Fernández Is.
Santiago
Pampas
R. de la Plata
RIO GRANDE
PLATEAU
OCEAN
Tristan

LOUISVILLE RIDGE
SOUTH PACIFIC OCEAN
CHILE RISE
40°
ARGENTINE
BASIN
Valdez
Pen.

8
Chatham Is.
SOUTHWEST
PACIFIC
BASIN
Str. of Magellan
Tierra
del Fuego
C. Tres Puntes
Falkland Is.
S. Georgia
▲ 8,325 m
S. Sandwich Is.

60°
PACIFIC-ANTARCTIC
RIDGE
Cape Horn
Drake Passage
S. Shetland
Is.
SCOTIA SEA
WEDDELL
ABYSSAL
PLAIN
C. Norvegia

9
AMUNDSEN ABYSSAL PLAIN
Antarctic
Pen.
WEDDELL SEA

80°
ROSS SEA
Vinson Massif
5,140 m

10

| 180° | A 160° | B 140° | C 120° | D 100° | E 80° | F 60° | G 40° | H 20° |

World - Physical

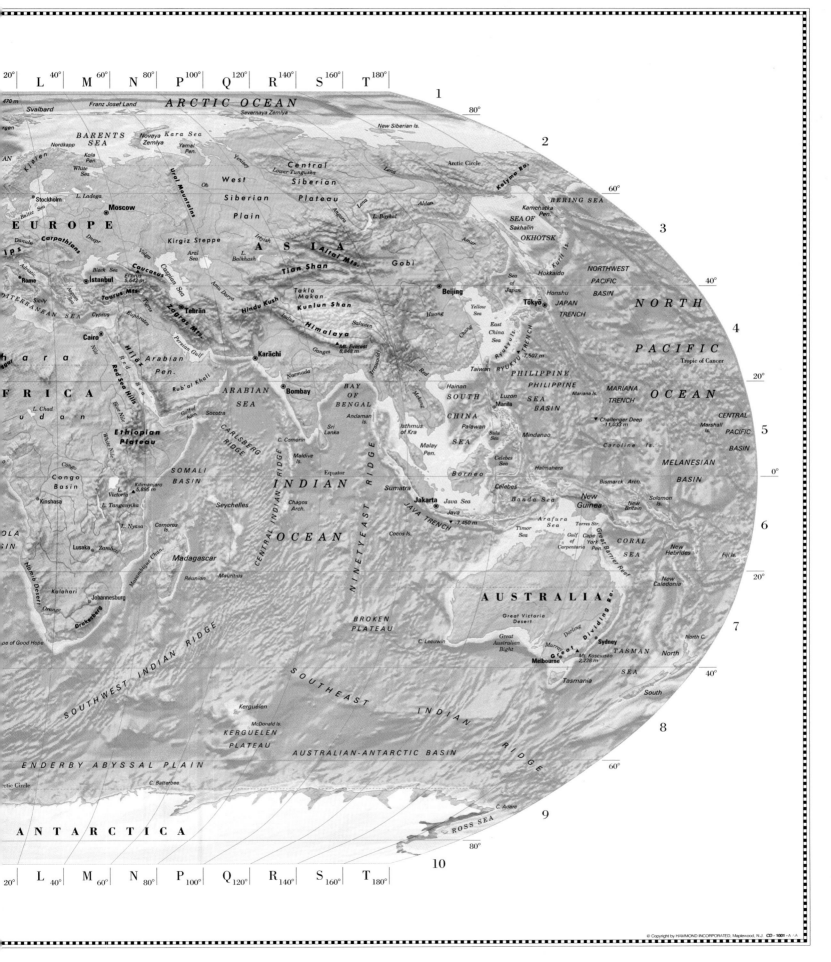

POPULATION OF CITIES AND TOWNS

⊛ OVER 5,000,000   ⊙ 500,000 - 1,999,999
⦿ 2,000,000 - 4,999,999   ○ UNDER 500,000

SCALE 1:81,700,000   ROBINSON PROJECTION   STANDARD PARALLELS 38°N AND 38°S

MILES   0 — 1000 — 2000 — 3000 — 4000
KILOMETERS   0 — 1000 — 2000 — 3000 — 4000

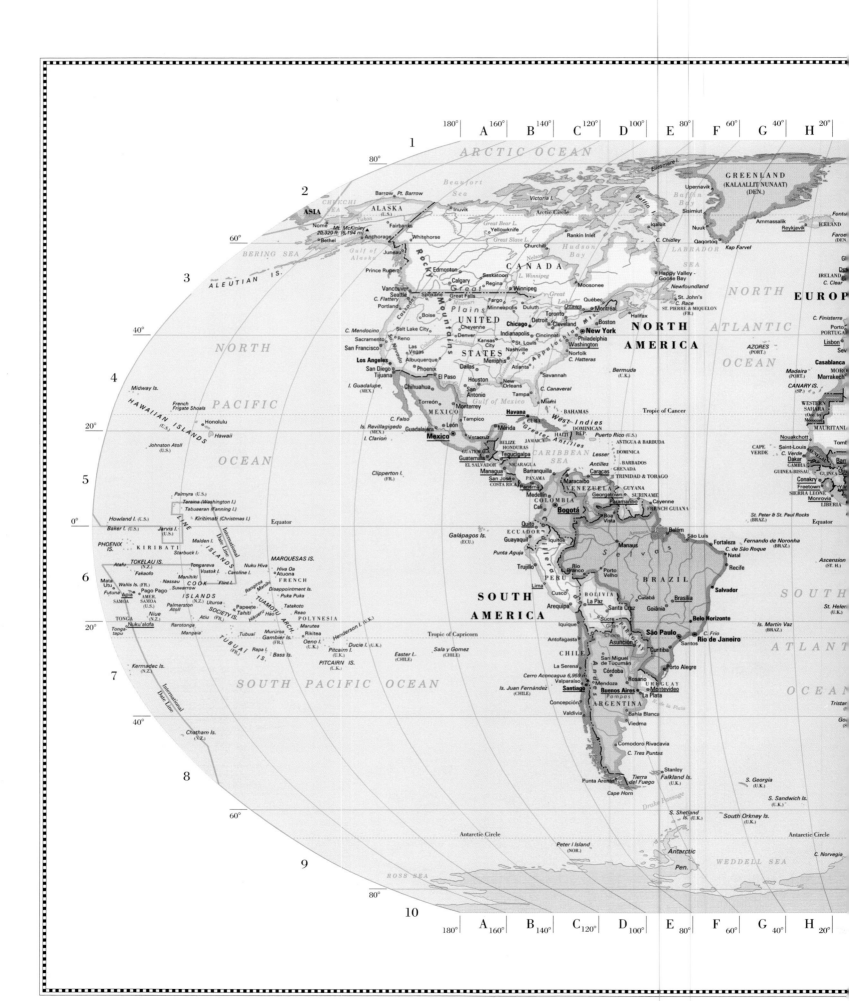

World - Political

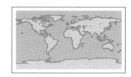

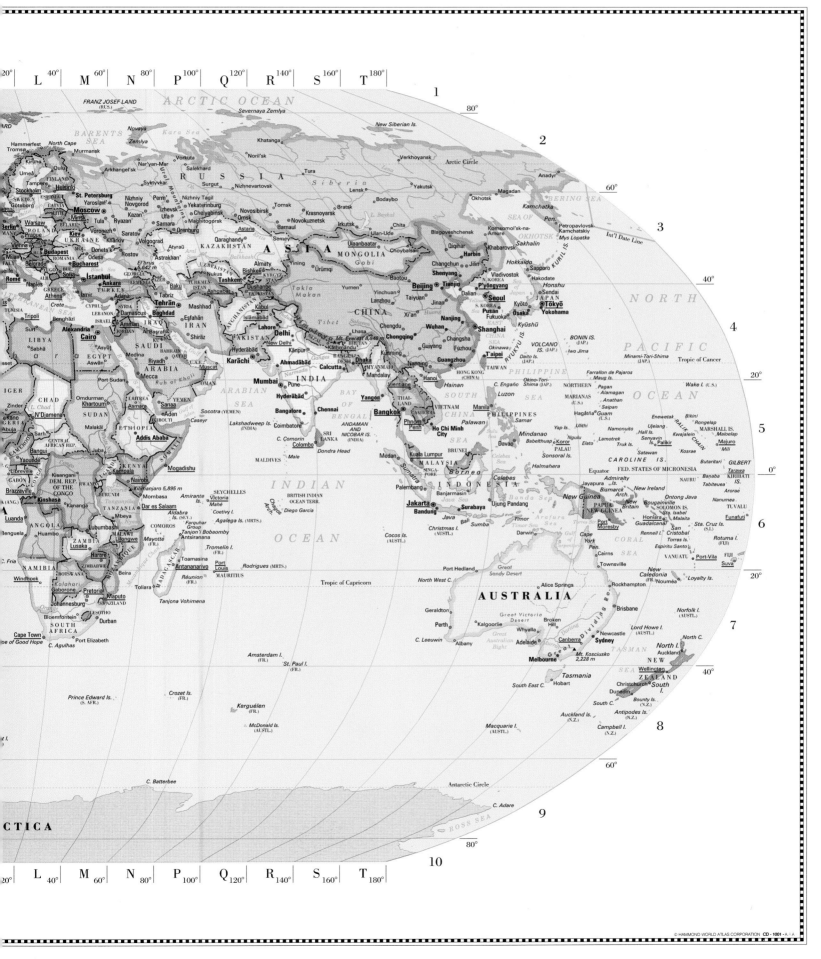

POPULATION OF CITIES AND TOWNS

◉ OVER 5,000,000   ○ 500,000 - 1,999,999
● 2,000,000 - 4,999,999   ○ UNDER 500,000

SCALE 1:81,700,000   ROBINSON PROJECTION STANDARD PARALLELS 38°N AND 38°S

MILES 0   1000   2000   3000   4000
KILOMETERS 0   1000   2000   3000   4000

Europe - Physical

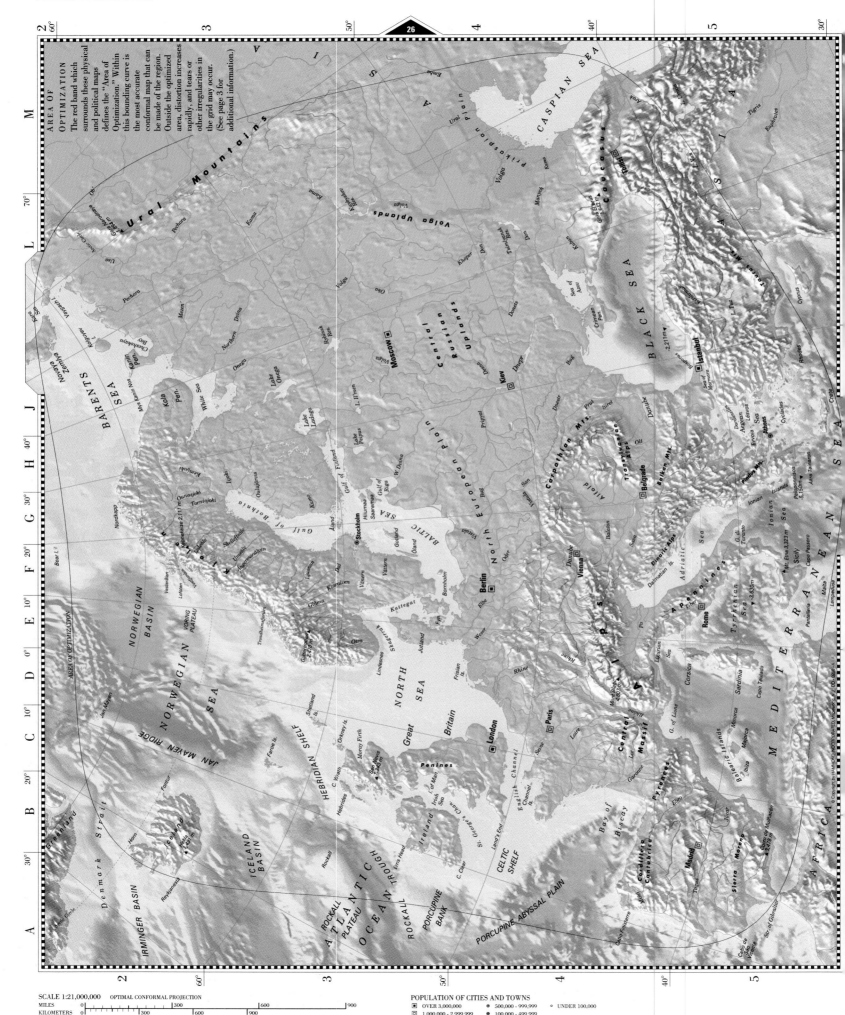

AREA OF OPTIMIZATION
The red band which surrounds these physical and political maps defines the "Area of Optimization." Within this bounding curve is the most accurate conformal map that can be made of the region. Outside the optimized area, distortion increases rapidly, and tears or other irregularities in the grid may occur. (See page 3 for additional information.)

SCALE 1:21,000,000   OPTIMAL CONFORMAL PROJECTION

MILES   0   300   600   900
KILOMETERS 0   300   600   900

POPULATION OF CITIES AND TOWNS

▣ OVER 3,000,000   ⊛ 500,000 - 999,999   ∘ UNDER 100,000
▢ 1,000,000 - 2,999,999   ● 100,000 - 499,999

Europe - Political

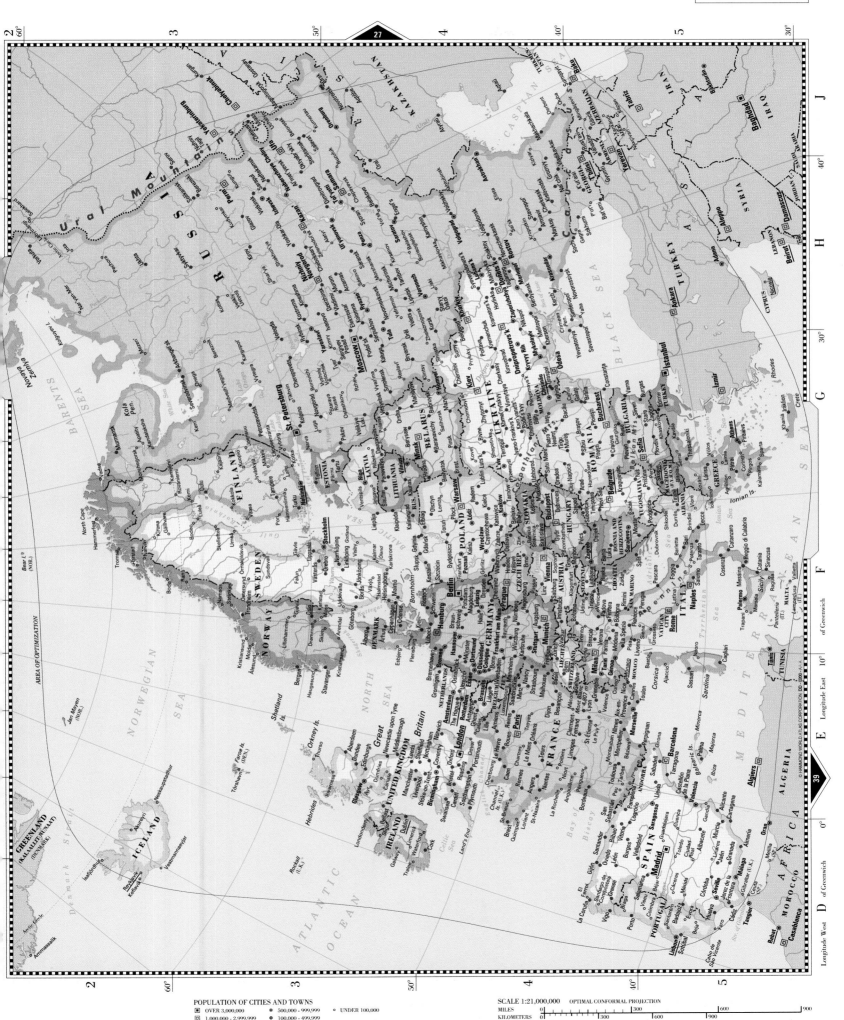

SCALE 1:21,000,000   OPTIMAL CONFORMAL PROJECTION

POPULATION OF CITIES AND TOWNS

■ OVER 3,000,000   ● 500,000 - 999,999   ○ UNDER 100,000
▣ 1,000,000 - 2,999,999   ● 100,000 - 499,999

Western and Central Europe

Southern Europe

POPULATION OF CITIES AND TOWNS

■ OVER 2,000,000	● 300,000 - 999,999	⊕ 100,000 - 249,999	⊙ 10,000 - 29,999
▣ 1,000,000 - 1,999,999	⊙ 250,000 - 499,999	⊕ 30,000 - 99,999	○ UNDER 10,000

SCALE 1:7,000,000   LAMBERT CONFORMAL CONIC PROJECTION

MILES   0   100   200   300

KILOMETERS 0   100   200   300

Scandinavia and Finland, Iceland

Eastern Europe and Turkey

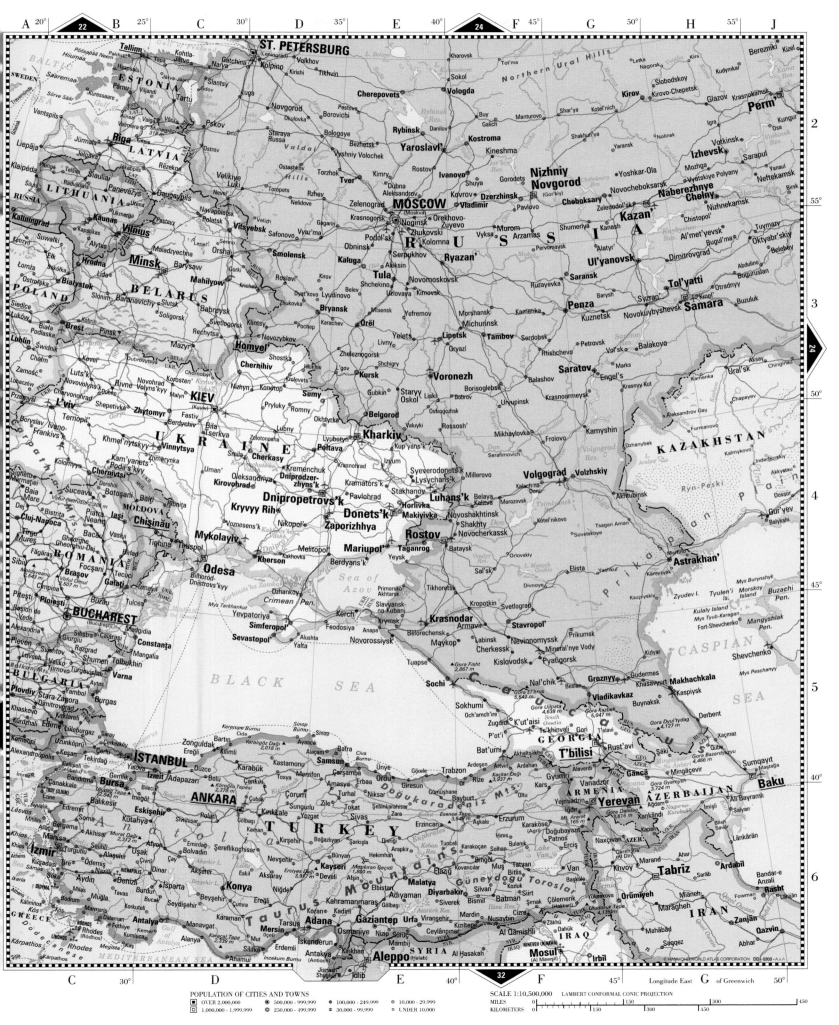

POPULATION OF CITIES AND TOWNS

■ OVER 2,000,000 ◻ 500,000 - 999,999 ● 100,000 - 249,999 ● 10,000 - 29,999
◻ 1,000,000 - 1,999,999 ◻ 250,000 - 499,999 ● 30,000 - 99,999 ● UNDER 10,000

SCALE 1:10,500,000   LAMBERT CONFORMAL CONIC PROJECTION
MILES 0   150   150   300   450
KILOMETERS 0   150   300   450

Longitude East of Greenwich

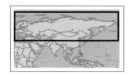

Asia - Physical

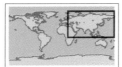

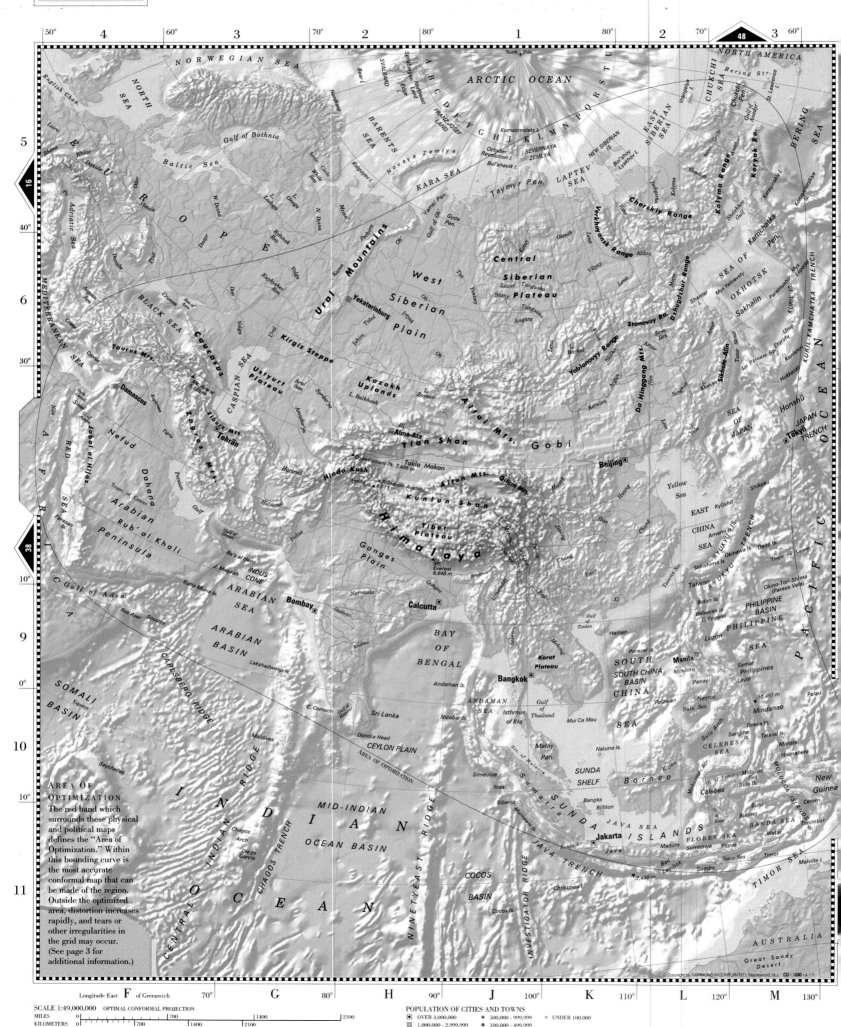

AREA OF OPTIMIZATION
The red band which surrounds these physical and political maps defines the "Area of Optimization." Within this bounding curve is the most accurate conformal map that can be made of the region. Outside the optimized area, distortion increases rapidly, and tears or other irregularities in the grid may occur. (See page 3 for additional information.)

SCALE 1:49,000,000   OPTIMAL CONFORMAL PROJECTION

Longitude East **F** of Greenwich   70°   **G**   80°   **H**   90°   **J**   100°   **K**   110°   **L**   120°   **M**   130°

MILES   0   700   1400   2100
KILOMETERS 0   700   1400   2100

POPULATION OF CITIES AND TOWNS
▣ OVER 3,000,000   ⊕ 500,000 - 999,999   ○ UNDER 100,000
▣ 1,000,000 - 2,999,999   ⊕ 100,000 - 499,999

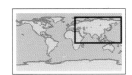

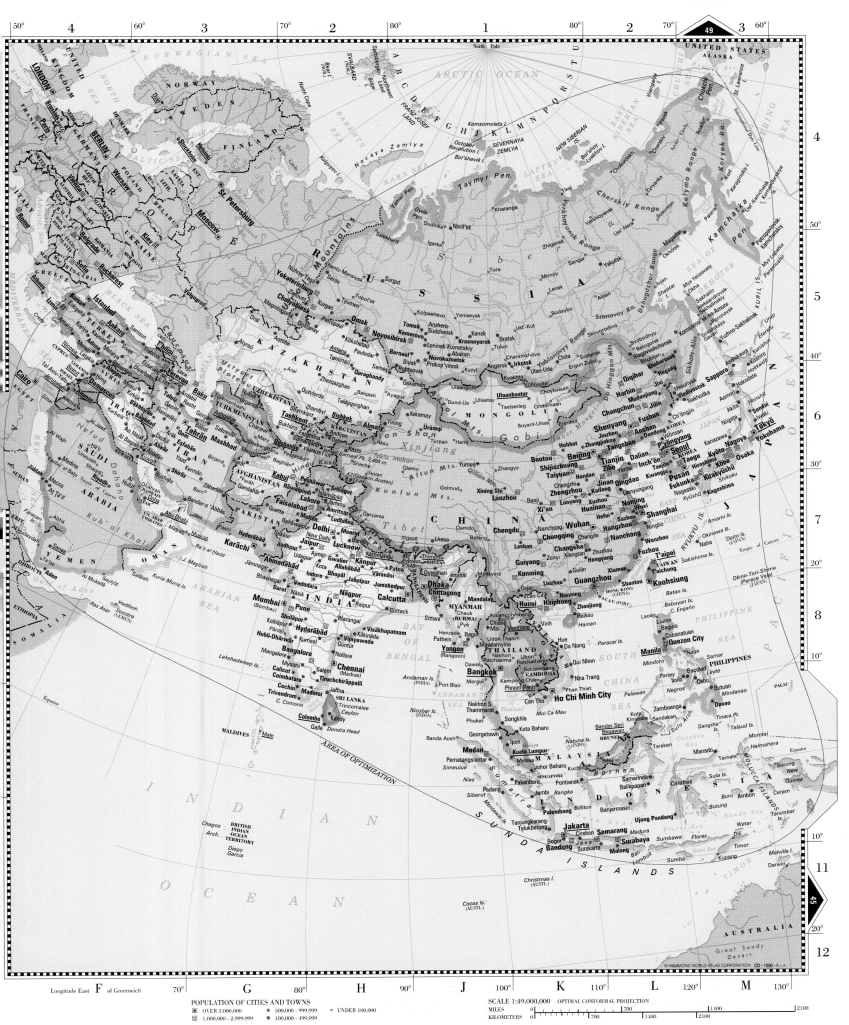

POPULATION OF CITIES AND TOWNS

■ OVER 3,000,000 ● 500,000 - 999,999 ○ UNDER 100,000
▣ 1,000,000 - 2,999,999 ● 100,000 - 499,999

SCALE 1:49,000,000   OPTIMAL CONFORMAL PROJECTION

MILES   0   700   1400   2100
KILOMETERS   0   700   1400   2100

Longitude East F of Greenwich   70°   G   80°   H   90°   J   100°   K   110°   L   120°   M   130°

© HAMMOND WORLD ATLAS CORPORATION   CD - 1030 - A - A

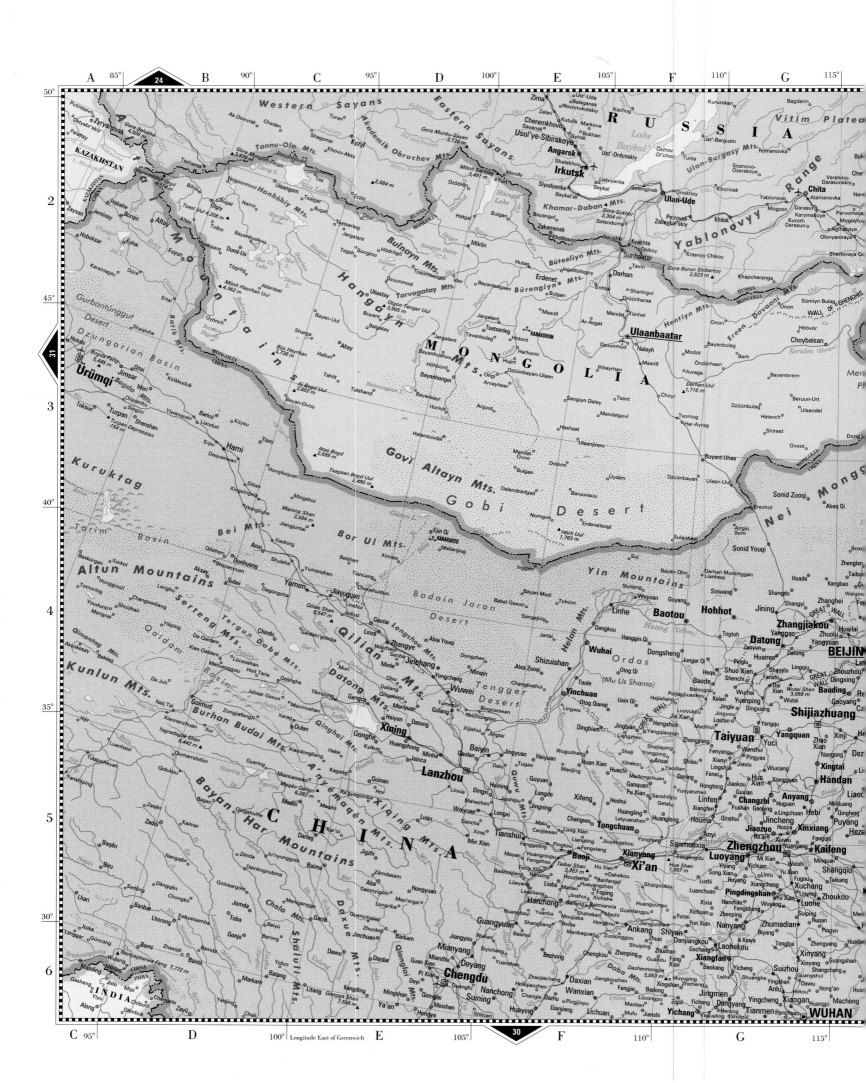

Eastern Asia

Southeastern China, Taiwan, Philippines

SCALE 1:10,500,000 LAMBERT CONFORMAL CONIC PROJECTION

MILES 0 150 150 300 450

KILOMETERS 0 150 300 450

Central Asia

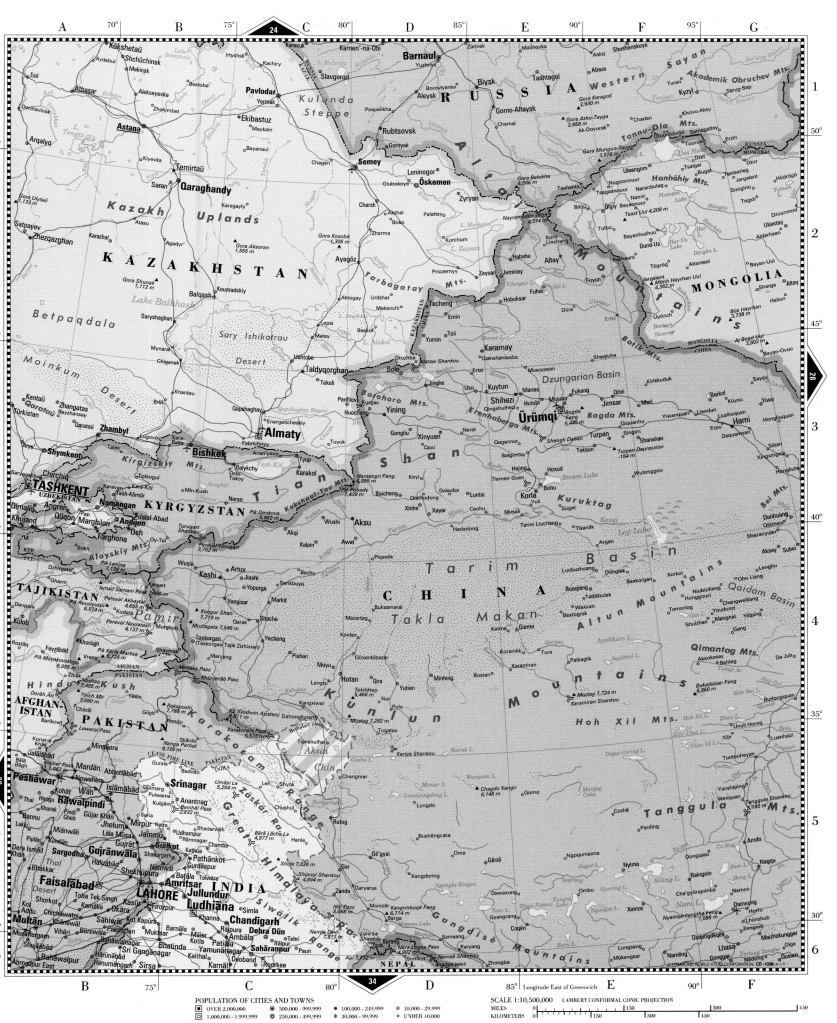

POPULATION OF CITIES AND TOWNS

■ OVER 2,000,000 ● 500,000 - 999,999 ● 100,000 - 249,999 ○ 10,000 - 29,999
◻ 1,000,000 - 1,999,999 ● 250,000 - 499,999 ○ 30,000 - 99,999 ○ UNDER 10,000

SCALE 1:10,500,000 LAMBERT CONFORMAL CONIC PROJECTION

MILES 0   150   300   450
KILOMETERS 0   150   300   450

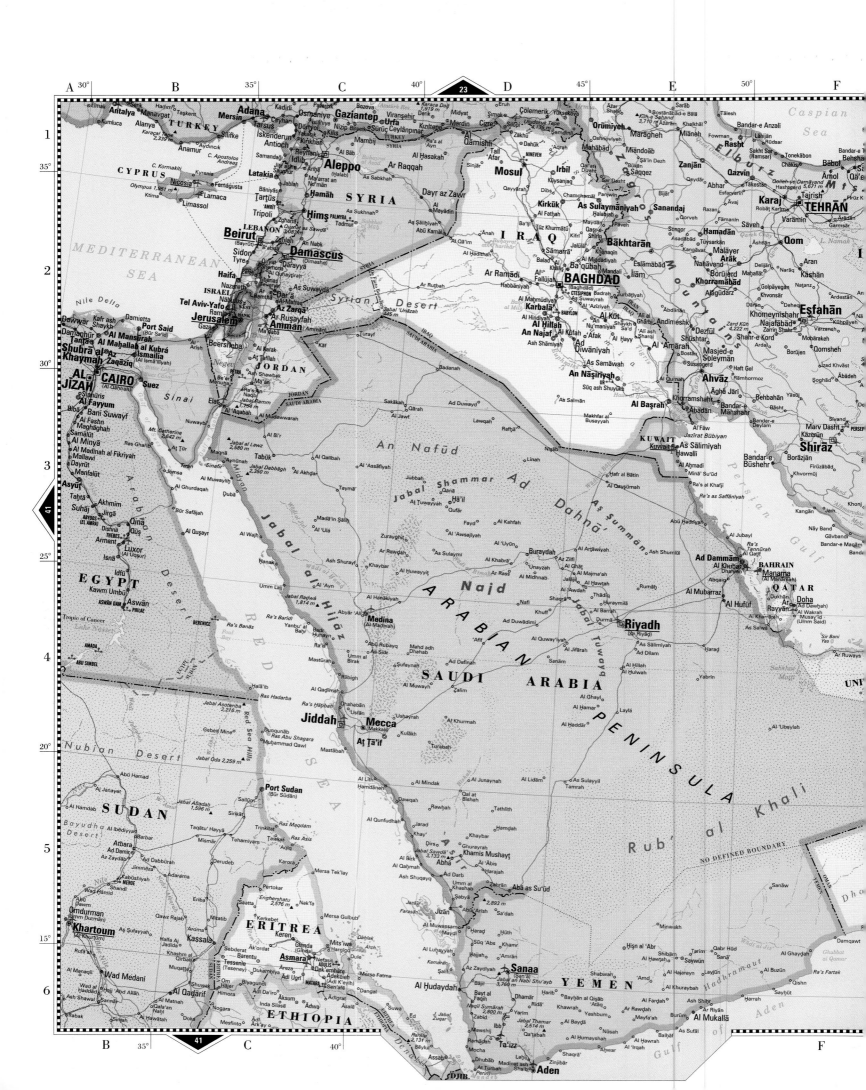

Southwestern Asia

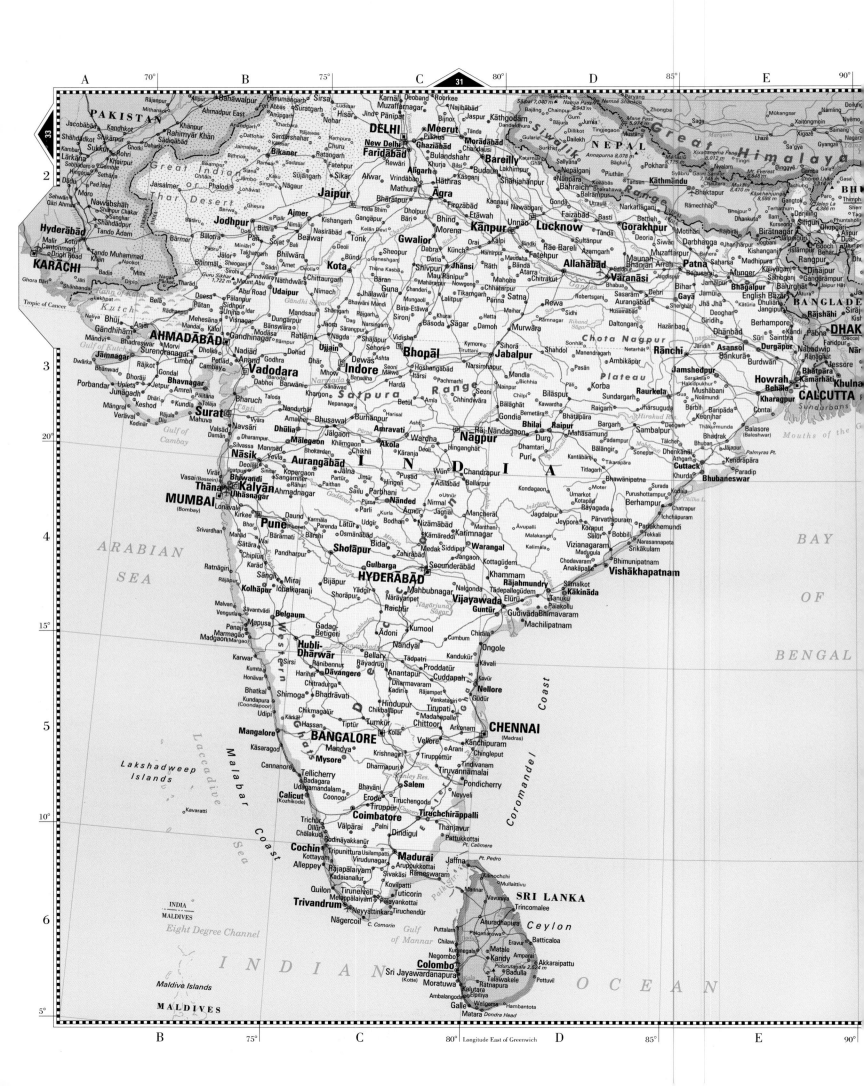

Southern Asia

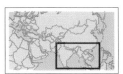

POPULATION OF CITIES AND TOWNS

■ OVER 2,000,000 ● 500,000 - 999,999 ● 100,000 - 249,999 ⊙ 10,000 - 29,999
□ 1,000,000 - 1,999,999 ● 250,000 - 499,999 ⊙ 30,000 - 99,999 ○ UNDER 10,000

SCALE 1:10,500,000   LAMBERT CONFORMAL CONIC PROJECTION

MILES 0 ___ 150 ___ 300 ___ 450
KILOMETERS 0 ___ 150 ___ 300 ___ 450

95° A 100° B 105° C 110° D 11

Andaman

Mergui
Archipelago
Mergui
(Myeik)
Letsôk-Aw I.
Lenya
Bokpyin
Zadetkyi I.

Cha-am
Hua Hin
Tha Mai
Chanthaburi
Rayong
Khlung
Trat
Kut I.

Batdambang
Beng Kesei
Phnum Tumbôt
1,563 m
Leach
Krakor
Phumi Prek
Pursat
Kampong
Thum
Kampong
Chhnang
Kampong
Spoe
Phumi Phsa
Phnum Aôral
1,771 m
Kompong Cham
Tbong
Prey Veng
Svay Rieng
Tay Ninh
Thu Dau
Mot

CAMBODIA

Ban Ay Rieng
BanDon
Trapeang Veng
Serimonorom
Ap Lac Thien
 Dien khanh
Bo-Duc
Lộc Ninh
Bi Doup
2,289 m
B'nôm M'hai
1,642 m
Di
Linh
Xa Binh Long
My An Phuoc

Cung Son
Buon Mrong
Buon Me Thuot
Ba Râ
Gia
Nghia

Tuy An
Tuy Hoa

Ninh Hoa
Nha Trang

Da Lat
Phan Rang
Phan Thiet

Cam Ranh
Thon Lac
Nghiep

**MYANMAR
(BURMA)**
Tenasserim
Prachuap Khiri
Khan
Maw-daung Pass
Khao Daen Noi
582 m
Kra Buri
Ranong

Khao Namno
755 m
Pathiu
Chumphon

Phangan I.
Samui I.

VIETNAM
Bien Hoa
HO CHI MINH CITY
(Saigon)
Long Xuyen
Rach Gia
Sa Dec
Chau Doc
Vinh Long
Can Tho
Tra Vinh
Soc Trang

Kampong Saom
Phu Quoc I.
Kien Thanh
Ap Loc
Go Cong
Thoi Binh
Bac Lieu
Ca Mau
Mui Cà Mau
Con Son

Gulf of

Thailand

THAILAND

Khao Lang Kha Tuk
1,395 m
Chaiya
Surat Thani
Ban Na San
Nakhon Si
Thammarat
Ban Pak
Phanang

Phangnga
Khao Luang
1,835 m
Krabi
Phuket I.
Phuket
Laem Mum Nauk
Lanta I.
Trang

Phatthalung
Songkhla

Hat Yai
Laem Pho
Sai Buri
Pattani
Yala
Narathiwat
Tumpat
Kota Baharu
Kampong Kuala
Besut

Terutao I.
Satun
Langkawi I.
Kangar
Tanjong Pinang
Bukit Bubat
1,145 m
Sungai
Kolok
Pulau We
Sabang
Banda Aceh
Sigli
Seulimeum
Padangtiji
Lhokkruet
Keudeteunom

Pusat Gayo Mts.
G. Geureudong
2,855 m
Isak
Lhoksukon
Langsa
Kualasimpang
Pangkalanberandan
Tanjungpura

Sungai Petani
George Town
Pinang I.
Butterworth
Taiping
Port Weld
Lumut
Ipoh
Batu Gajah
Kampar

Alor Setar
Baling
G. Bintang
1,862 m
G. Chamah
2,171 m
Tanah Merah
Jerteh
Kuala Krai
Kuala Terengganu

Marang

Kuala Dungun

Kemasik
Chukai
Kuantan

MALAYSIA

Natuna
Is.
Ranai
Bunguran I.

SOUTH CHI

SEA

Spratly

(Sovereign

BRUN
Bandar Seri Begawa
Kuala Belait
Tanjung Baram
Lutong
Miri

Ujung Raja
Gunung Lembu
3,014 m
Binjai
Medan
Tebingtinggi
Pematangsiantar

Tanjungbalai
Bakungan
Simeulue I.
L. Toba
Prapat

Pusat Gayo Mts.
G. Leuser
3,466 m

Kuala Lipis
G. Tahan
2,187 m
Raub
Bentong
Temerloh
Kuala Lumpur
Shah Alam
Kelang
Seremban
Kuala Pilah
Port Dickson
Gemas
Melaka
Segamat
Muar
Batu Pahat
Rengam
Kluang
Keluang

G. Batu Puteh
2,130 m
Gunung Tapis
1,512 m
Pekan

Kuala Lumpur
Malaya

Mersing
Tioman I.

Johor Baharu
SINGAPORE
SINGAPORE
Tanjungpinang

Anambas
Is.
Letong
Subi I.

Terempa
Serasan

Tambelan
Is.

Equator

Ujung Dewa

Sibolga
Nias I.
Tuhemberua
Lahewa
Gunungsitoli
Sirombu
Batatstoru

Tuangku
Barus

Tuka
Singkuang

Tabuyung
Muarasoma
Natal

Airbangis
Ujung Tuan

G. Sorikmerapi
2,145 m
Padangsidempuan

Bengkalis
Tanjung Punggai

Bengkalis I.

Rupat I.
Dumai

Rokan
Pakanbaru

Siak
Pekan Nanas

Riau Islands

Lingga

Singkawang
G. Niut
1,701 m
Bengkayang
Ngabang
Pontianak

Tanjong Sirik
Bruit I.
Tanjong Datu
Paloh
Sambas
Kuching
1,285 m

Benua Martinus
Selimbau
Nangamahap
Sanggau
Sintang
Bukit Batuensambang
1,770 m
Gunung Sarah
1,759 m
Semitau
Melawi
Putussibau
Kapuas Hulu Mts.
Jungkat

Sarawak

Sibu
Kanowit
Sarikei
Saratok
Kabong
Oya
Tatau
Bintulu
Labang
Bukit Batu
2,012 m
Clangbrap
2,240 m
Nahabuan
Bukit Lesung
1,730 m
Kuda

Serasan Strait

Bay
Rajang

Kalimanta

Indragiri
Cerenti
Rengat
Tembilahan
Taluk
Kuantan
Airmolek
Lubuksikaping
Payakumbuh
Bukittinggi
G. Marapi
2,891 m
Padangpanjang
Sawahlunto
Solok
Gunung Talang
2,597 m
Padang
Pasaman
G. Pasaman
2,912 m
Singkuang
Muarasipongi

Singkep I.
Tg. Buku
Tg. Datuk
Kualamandah
Pulaukijang
Tg. Jabung

Muarabungo
Bangko
Rantaupanjang
Sarolangun
Tapan
Muaratebo
Jambi
Muararupit
Babat
Surulangun

Gunung Kerinci
3,805 m
Sungaipenuh
Gunung Masurai
2,933 m

Sumatra

Muntok
Bangka I.
Tanjung Samak
Sungailiat
Pangkalpinang

Karimata I.
Sukadana
Bukit Sebayan
1,377 m

Jawi
Maya I.
Telukmelano
Bukit Tukung
1,175 m
Bukit Raya
2,278 m
Tumbangkaman
Schwaner Mts.
Tumbangsenamang

Sukaraja
Bawan
Kasongan
Hanjalipan
Kotabesi
Sampit
Palangka
Sukamara
Pangkalanbuun
Gelinggang
Buang
Malika
Banjarmasin
Martapura
Pagatan
Tg. Selatan
Batakan
Pelaihari

Muller Mts.

Kayuagung
Lubuklinggau
Curup
Gunung Dempo
3,159 m
Bengkulu
Lahat
Baturaja
Martapura
Kotabumi
Menggala
Gunung Patah
2,817 m
Manna
Bandingagung
Gunung Pesagi
2,232 m
Krui
Kotaagung
Pringsewu
Ngaras
Enggano I.
Kotajawa
Balimbing
Tanjung Rata

Perabumulih
Pagerdewa
Wiralaga
Tangkit Tebak 2,116 m
Ketapang
Tg. Pujut
Kalianda
Tg. Tua
Merak

Pagerdewa
Koba
Tg. Berikat
Tanjungpandan
Belitung I.
Membalong
Tanjung Puting
Tanjung Sambar

Pagatan

Greater Sunda

Kayuagung
Perabumulih
Palembang
Sekayu
Sungsang

Belitung I.

Gaspar Strait
Karimata Strait

**Tanjungkarang-
Telukbetung**
JAKARTA
Bekasi
Serang
Merak
Krakatoa
Panaitan I.
Tanjung Cangkuang
Sunda Strait
Depok
Karawang
Subang
Bogor
Cianjur
Sukabumi
Tanjung Genteng
Ujunggenteng
Sindangbarang

Karimunjawa
Is.
Bawean I.

Java Sea

Tanjung Indramayu
Cirebon
Klangenan
Kuningan
BANDUNG
Garut
Ciamis
Tasikmalaya
Cijulang
Cilacap
Yogyakarta
Kebumen
Pacitan

Pekalongan
Kudus
Tegal
Purwokerto
Magelang
Gunung Mura
1,602 m
Pati
Blora
Semarang
Taman
Madiun
G. Lawu
3,265 m
Surakarta
Kediri
Pare

Rembang
Tuban
Jombang

Ujung Bugel

Madura

Sumenep
SURABAYA
Pasuruan
Tg. Pacinan
Probolinggo
G. Semeru
3,676 m
Malang
Bondowoso
Jember
Genteng
Tg. Selatan

Java

INDIAN

OCEAN

95° A 100° B 105° Longitude East of Greenwich C 110° D

POPULATION OF CITIES AND TOWNS

| ■ OVER 2,000,000 | ● 500,000 - 999,999 | ● 100,000 - 249,999 | ● 10,000 - 29,999 |
| ▣ 1,000,000 - 1,999,999 | ◉ 250,000 - 499,999 | ● 30,000 - 99,999 | ○ UNDER 10,000 |

Southeastern Asia

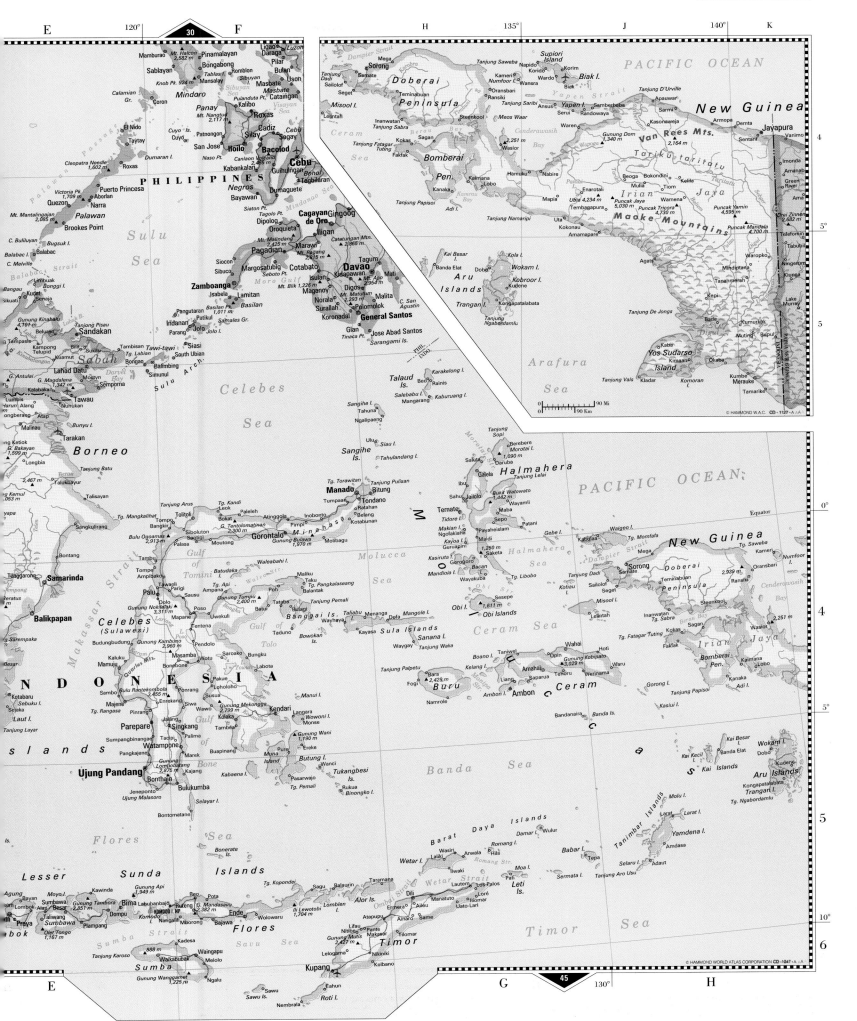

Africa - Physical

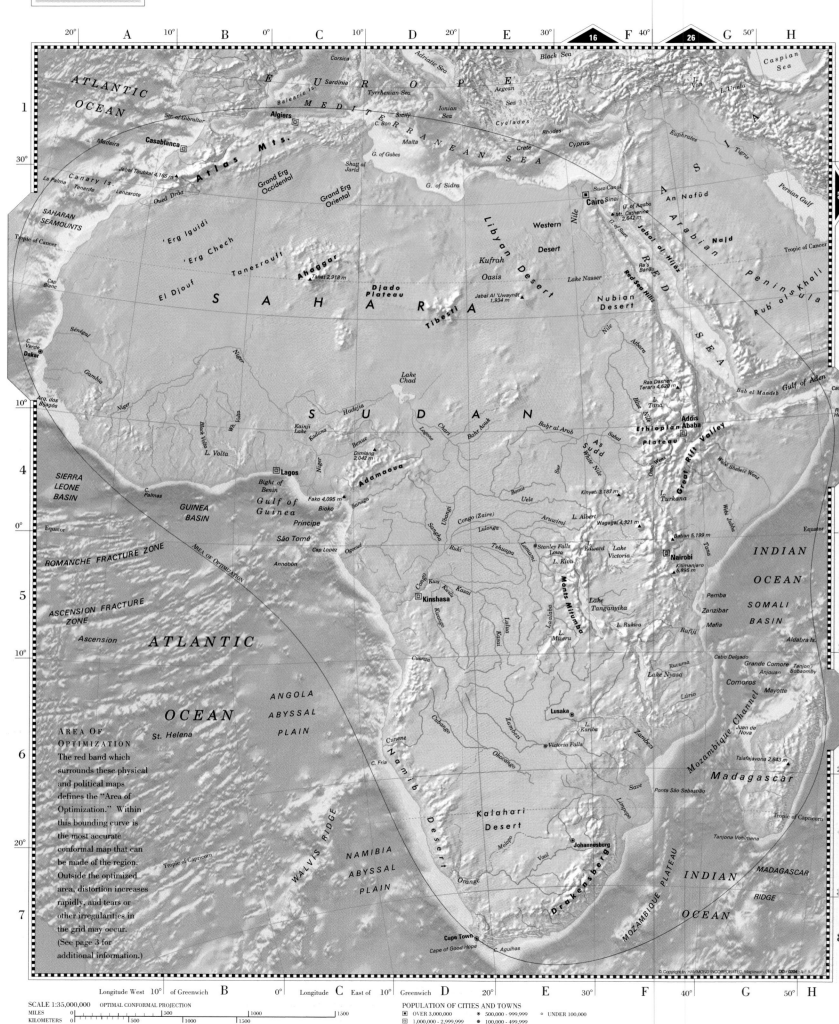

AREA OF
OPTIMIZATION
The red band which
surrounds these physical
and political maps
defines the "Area of
Optimization." Within
this bounding curve is
the most accurate
conformal map that can
be made of the region.
Outside the optimized
area, distortion increases
rapidly, and tears or
other irregularities in
the grid may occur.
(See page 3 for
additional information.)

SCALE 1:35,000,000   OPTIMAL CONFORMAL PROJECTION

MILES

KILOMETERS

POPULATION OF CITIES AND TOWNS
☐ OVER 3,000,000   ⊡ 500,000 - 999,999   ○ UNDER 100,000
☐ 1,000,000 - 2,999,999   ⊙ 100,000 - 499,999

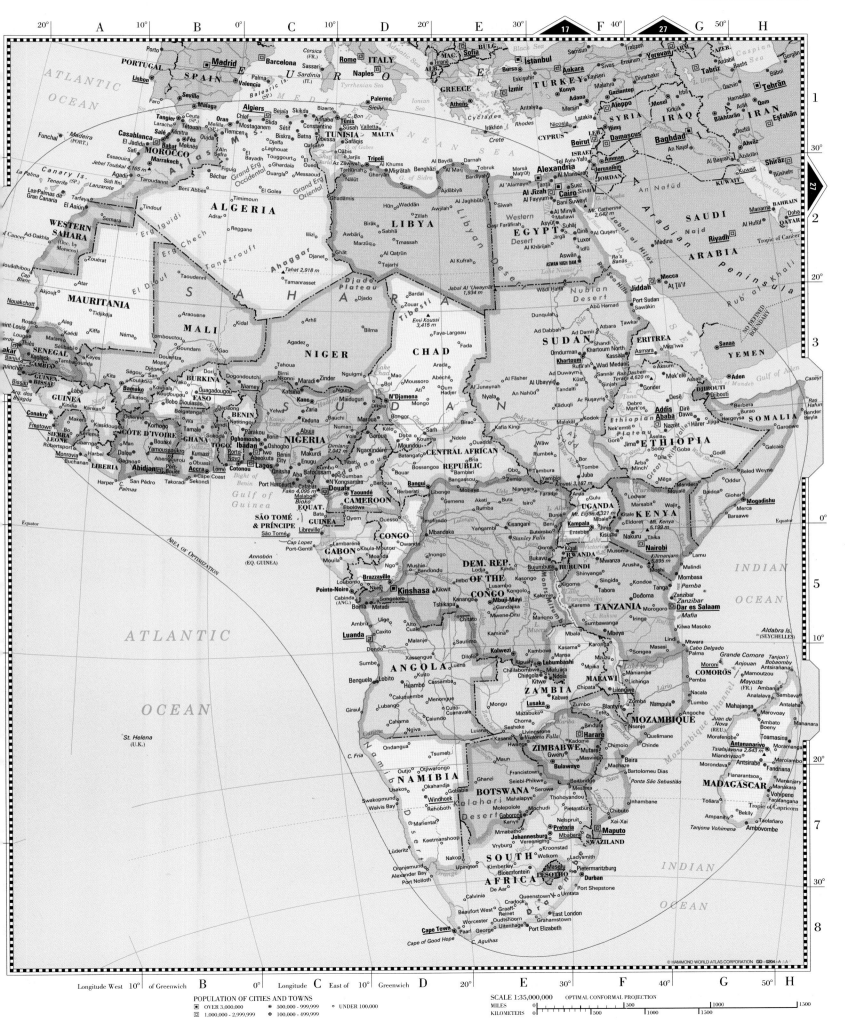

POPULATION OF CITIES AND TOWNS

■ OVER 3,000,000   ● 500,000 - 999,999   ○ UNDER 100,000
▣ 1,000,000 - 2,999,999   ◉ 100,000 - 499,999

SCALE 1:35,000,000   OPTIMAL CONFORMAL PROJECTION

MILES   0   500   1000   1500
KILOMETERS   0   500   1000   1500

© HAMMOND WORLD ATLAS CORPORATION   DD-0204-A

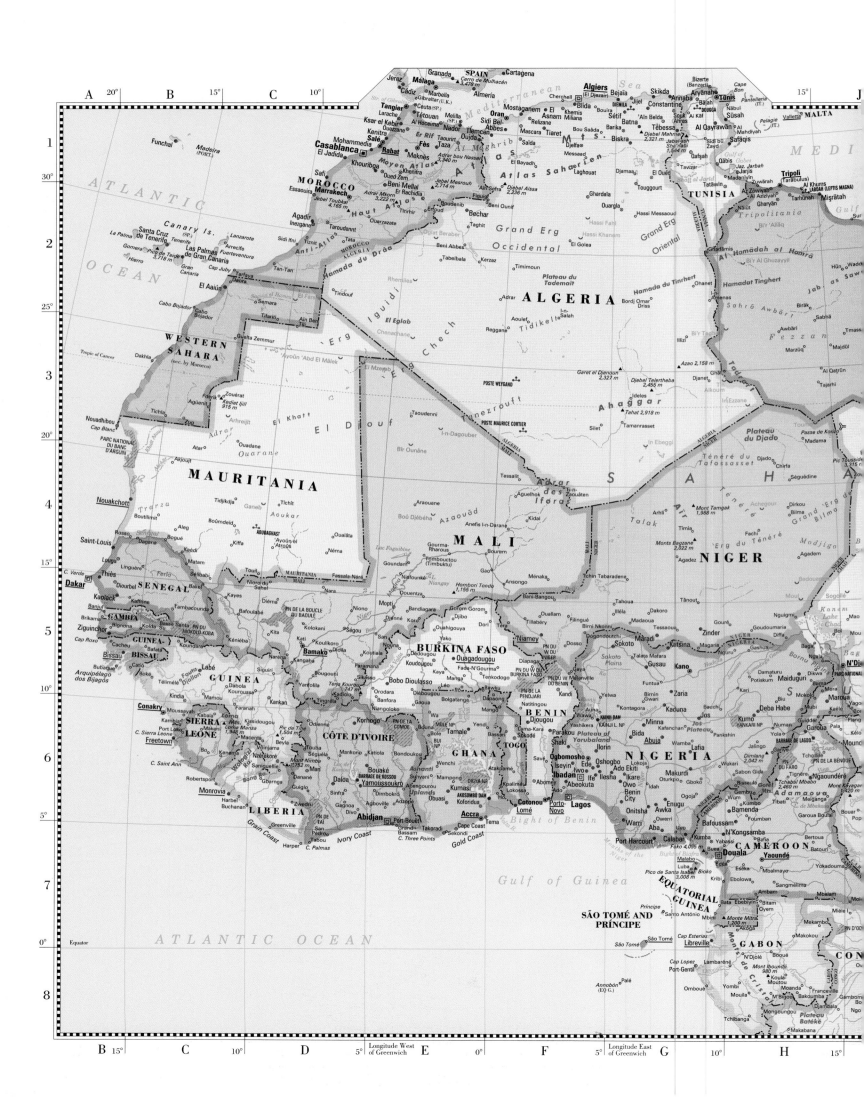

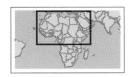

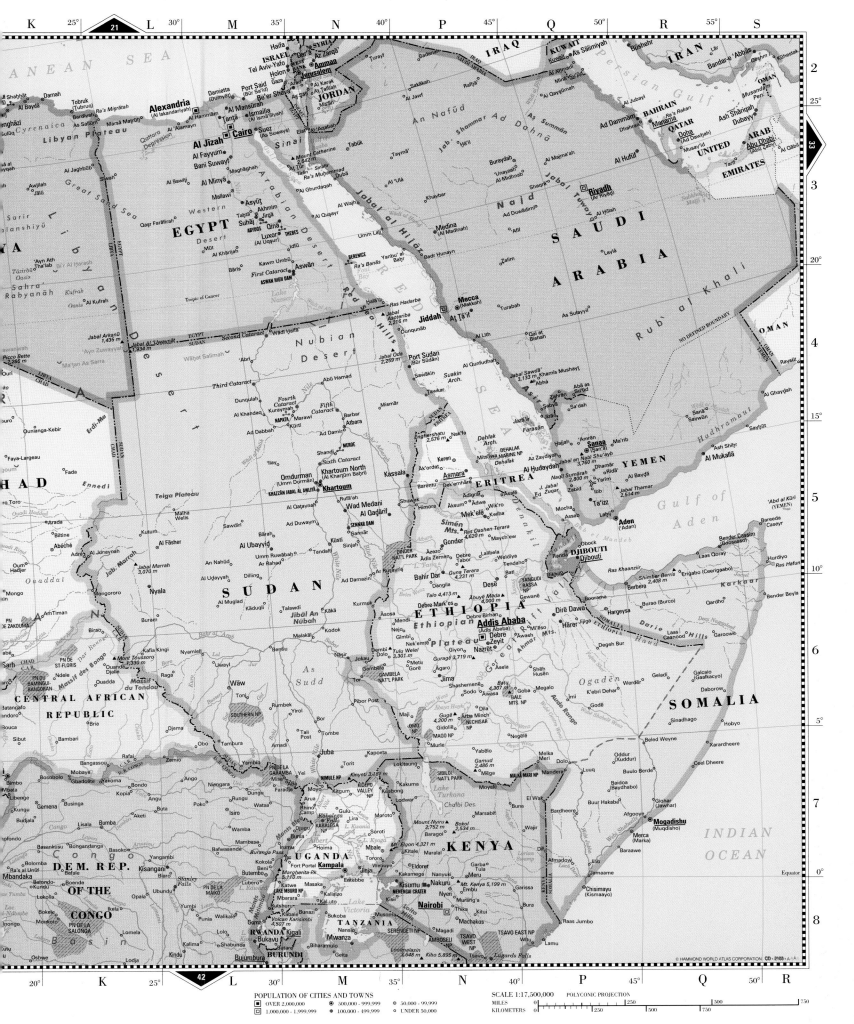

Southern Africa

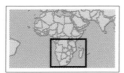

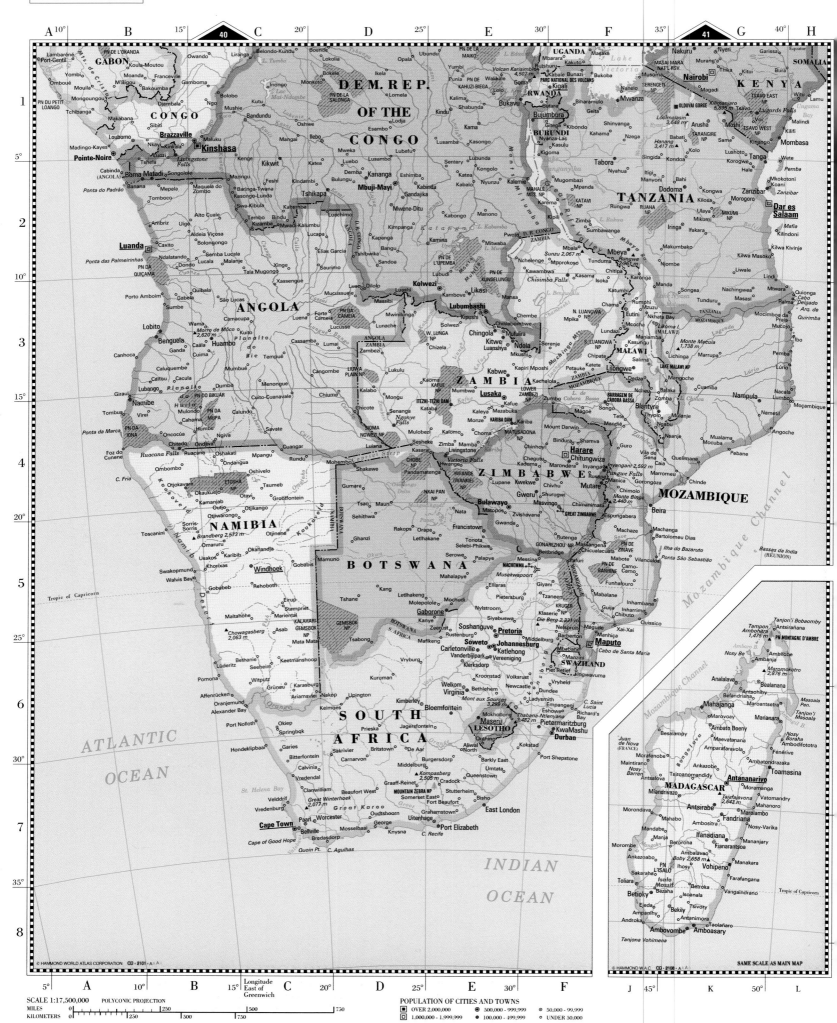

SCALE 1:17,500,000   POLYCONIC PROJECTION

MILES 0 _____ 250 _____ 500 _____ 750
KILOMETERS 0 ___ 250 ___ 500 ___ 750

POPULATION OF CITIES AND TOWNS

■ OVER 2,000,000   ● 500,000 - 999,999   ◎ 50,000 - 99,999
□ 1,000,000 - 1,999,999   ● 100,000 - 499,999   ○ UNDER 50,000

SAME SCALE AS MAIN MAP

Antarctica

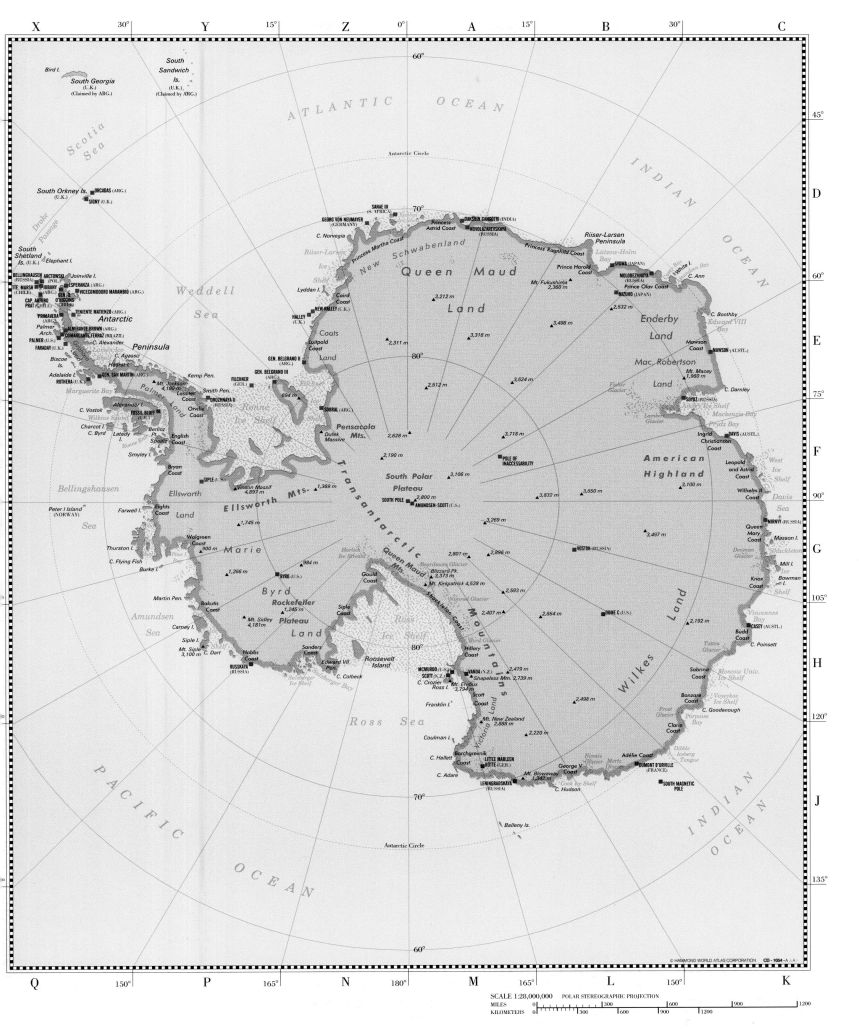

SCALE 1:28,000,000 POLAR STEREOGRAPHIC PROJECTION

MILES 0   300   600   900   1200

KILOMETERS 0   300   600   900   1200

© HAMMOND WORLD ATLAS CORPORATION   CD - 1054 - A - A - A

Australia, New Zealand - Physical

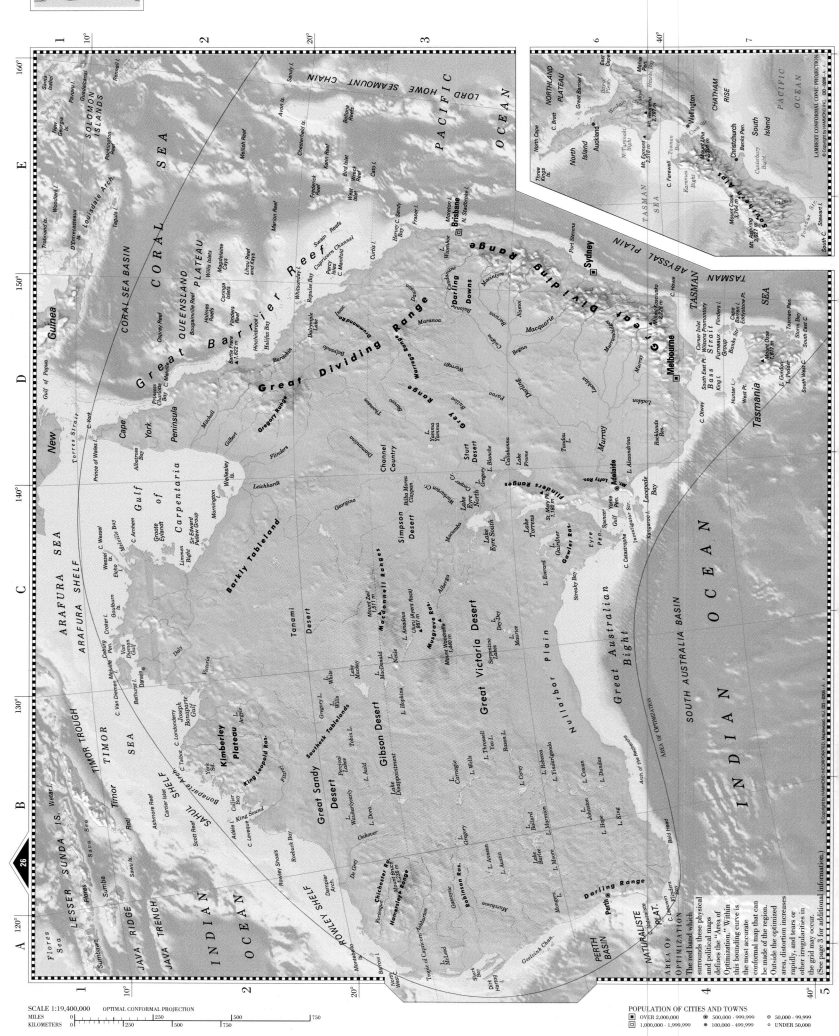

SCALE 1:19,400,000   OPTIMAL CONFORMAL PROJECTION

MILES   0   250   500   750
KILOMETERS   0   250   500   750

POPULATION OF CITIES AND TOWNS
- OVER 2,000,000
- 1,000,000 - 1,999,999
- 500,000 - 999,999
- 100,000 - 499,999
- 50,000 - 99,999
- UNDER 50,000

North America - Political

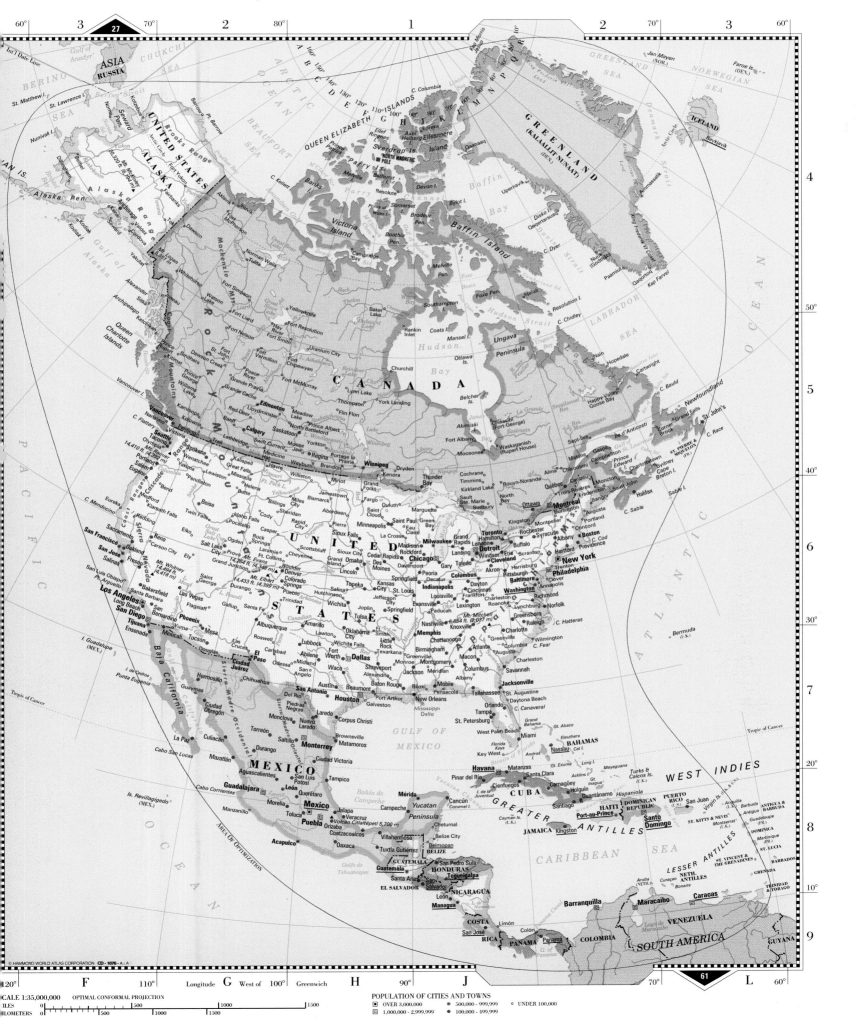

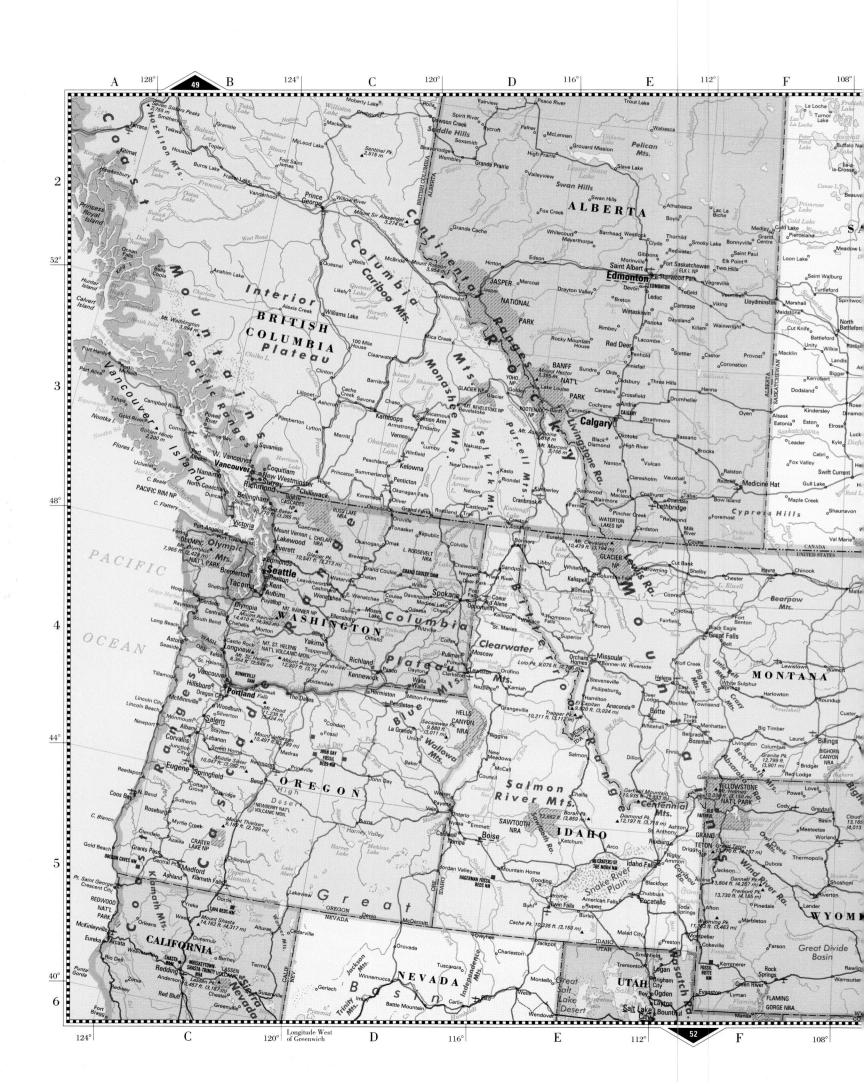

Southwestern Canada, Northwestern United States

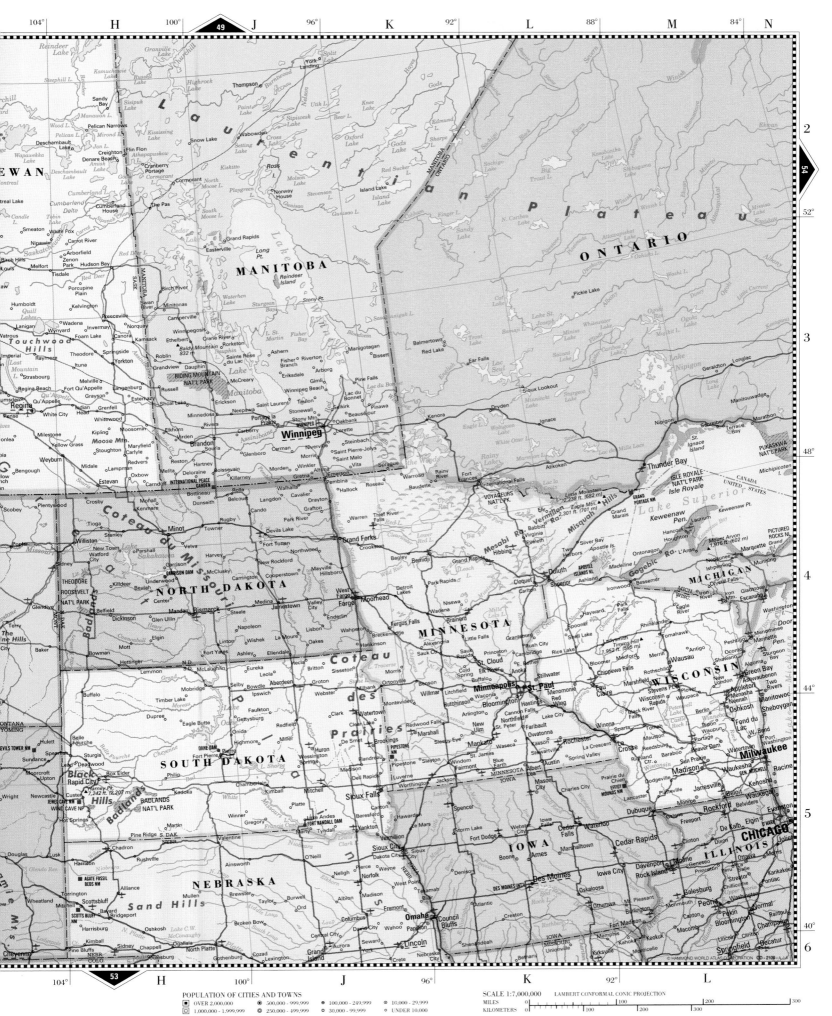

POPULATION OF CITIES AND TOWNS

SCALE 1:7,000,000   LAMBERT CONFORMAL CONIC PROJECTION

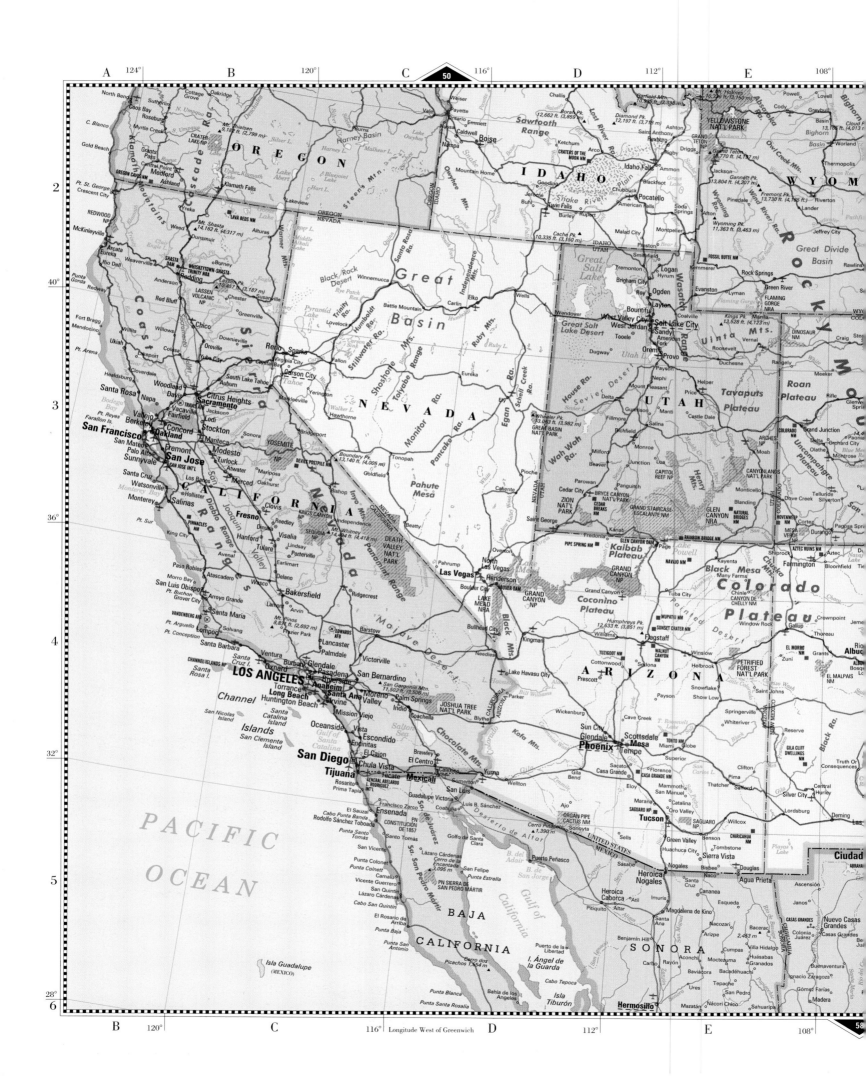

Southwestern United States

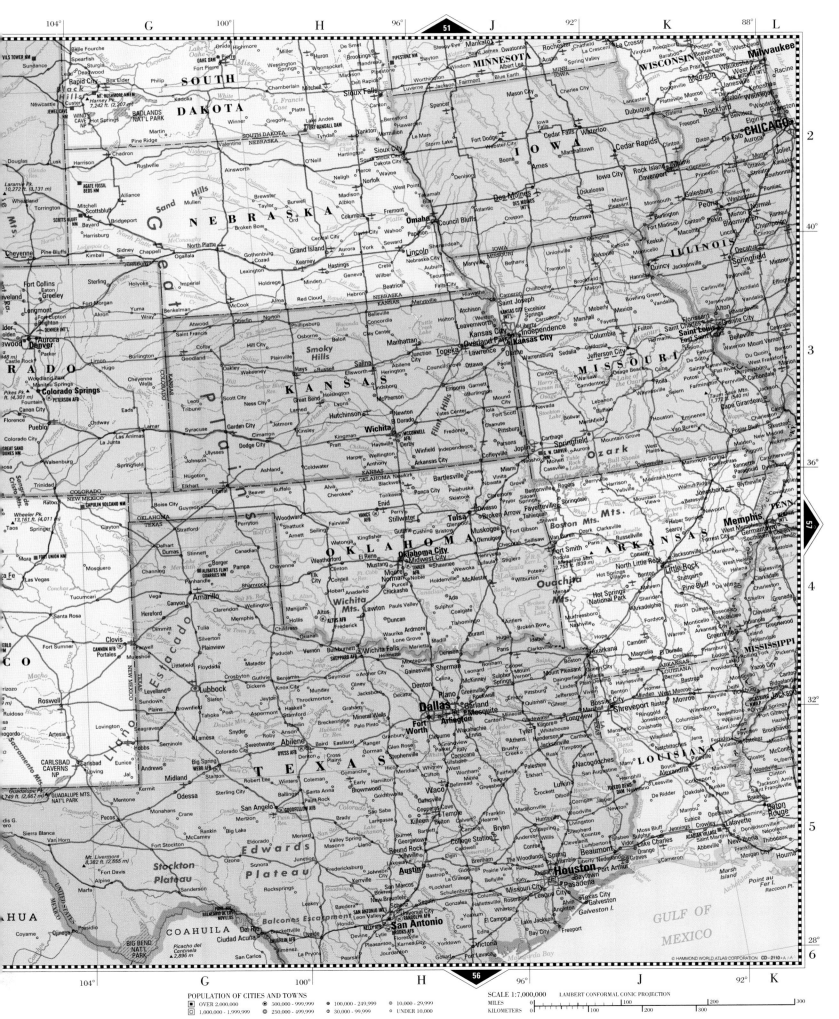

POPULATION OF CITIES AND TOWNS

■ OVER 2,000,000	● 500,000 - 999,999	● 100,000 - 249,999	● 10,000 - 29,999
◻ 1,000,000 - 1,999,999	● 250,000 - 499,999	● 30,000 - 99,999	○ UNDER 10,000

SCALE 1:7,000,000   LAMBERT CONFORMAL CONIC PROJECTION

MILES 0   100   200   300

KILOMETERS 0   100   200   300

© HAMMOND WORLD ATLAS CORPORATION   CD-2110-A-A

Southeastern Canada, Northeastern United States

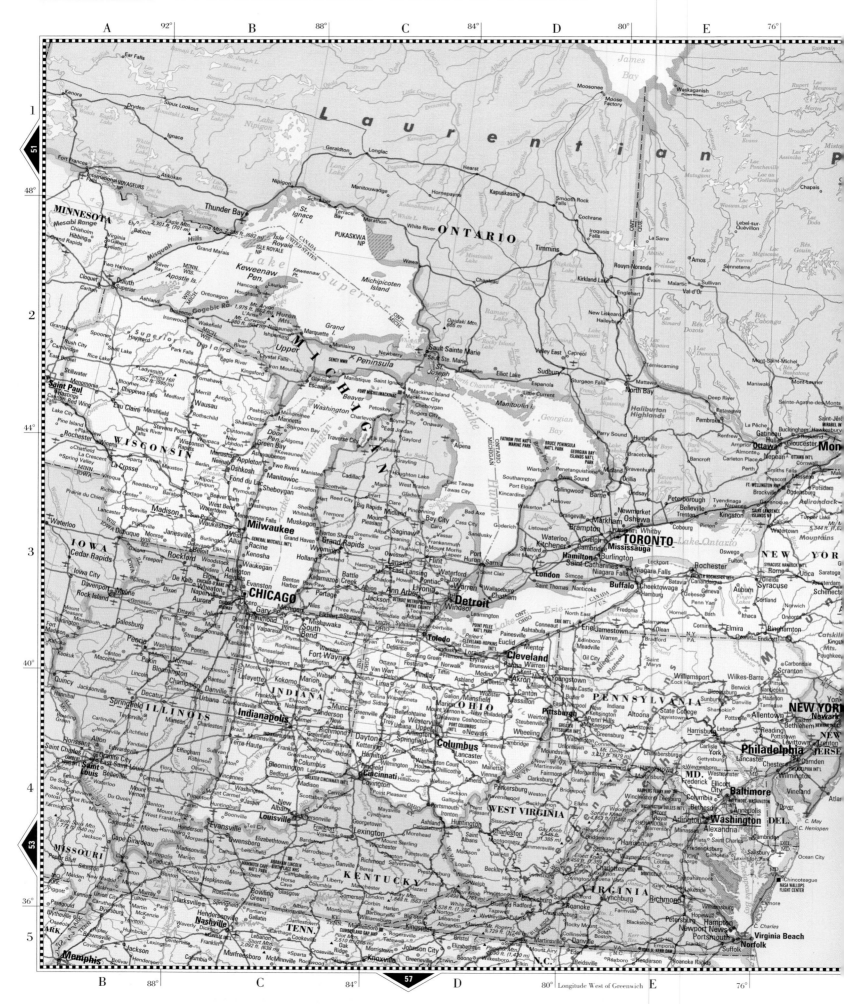

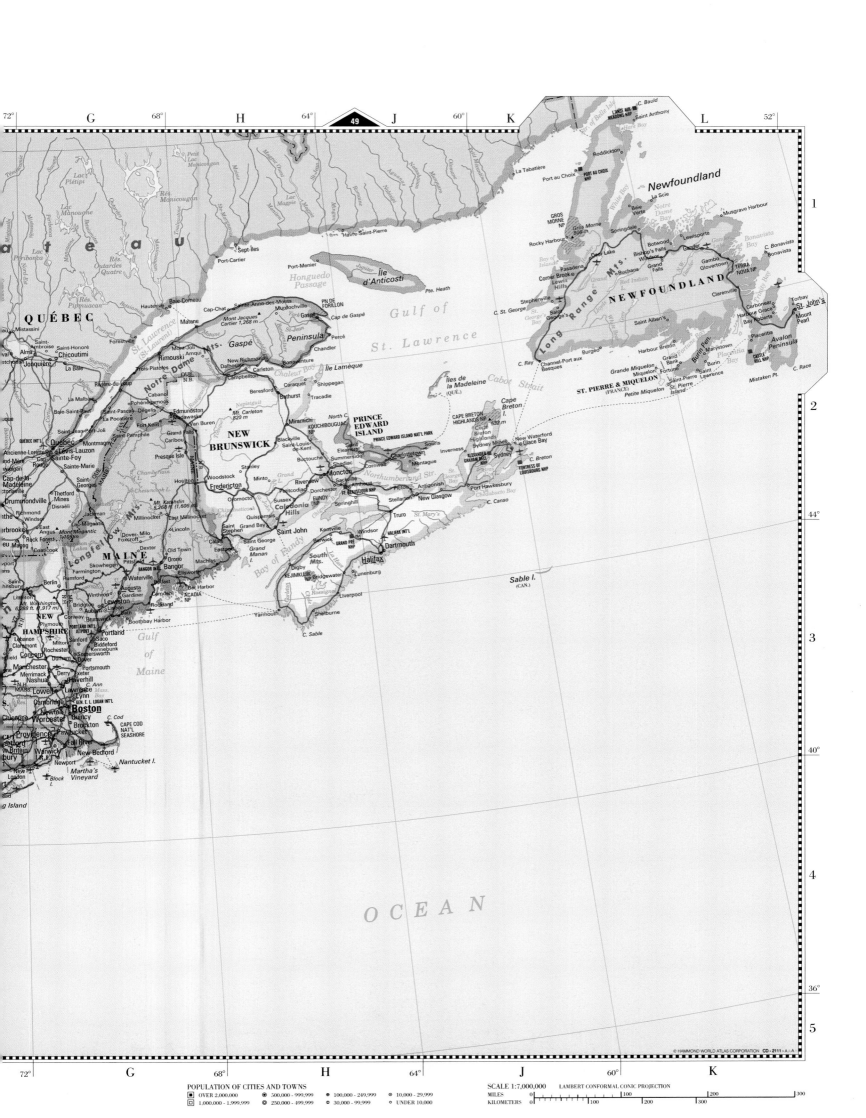

QUÉBEC

Plateau

Lac Plétipi

Lac Manouane

Rés. Manicougan

Petit Lac Manicougan

Maniquagan Riv

Magpie Qui

Lac Magpie

Natashquan

Rivière St-Augustin

Newfoundland

C. Bauld
CAPE ADE.
MEADOWS NP
Saint Anthony
Str. of Belle Isle

Roddickton

La Tabatière
Port au Choix
PORT AU CHOIX
NHP
La Scie

La Belle

Newfoundland

GROS
MORNE
NP
Gros
Morne
806 m
Springdale

Baie
Verte

Notre
Dame
Bay

Musgrave Harbour

Havre-Saint-Pierre
Sept-Îles
Port-Cartier

Port-Menier

Honguedo
Passage

Île d'Anticosti

Pte. Heath

Rocky Harbour
Deer Lake
Pasadena
Corner Brook
Lewis
Hills

Bay of
Islands

Bishop's Falls
Windsor

Grand
Falls

Botwood
Lewisporte
Gander

Red Indian L.

Gambo
Gloverton

Bonavista Bay

C. Bonavista
Bonavista

TERRA
NOVA NP

Hauterive
Baie-Comeau
Cap-Chat
Sainte-Anne-des-Monts
Murdochville
PN DE
FORILLON

Gulf of
St. Lawrence

Stephenville
Saint Alban's

Grand
Range Mts.

NEWFOUNDLAND
Clarenville

Carbonear
Harbour Grace
Bay Roberts

St. John's
Mount
Pearl

Saint-Fabien
Mont-Joli
Rimouski
Amqui
Gaspé
Cap de Gaspé
Percé
Chandler

C. St. George
St.
George's
Bay

Saint
George's

Long
Burgeo

Harbour Breton

Grand
Bank
Burin

Placentia
CASTLE
HILL NHP

Avalon
Peninsula

*Gaspé
Peninsula*

Notre Dame Mts.

Trois-Pistoles
Rivière-du-Loup

New Richmond
Dalhousie
Carleton

Bonaventure
Campbellton

Îles de
la Madeleine
(QUE.)

C. Ray
Channel-Port aux
Basques

Grande Miquelon
Miquelon

Placentia Bay

C. Race

La Malbaie

Chaleur Bay

Caraquet
Beresford
Bathurst

Île Lamèque

Cabot Strait

Petite Miquelon

St-Pierre
Lawrence

Mistaken Pt.

Baie-Saint-Paul
Saint-Pascal
Dégelis

Shippegan
Tracadie

Cape
Breton
I.

ST. PIERRE & MIQUELON
(FRANCE)

St. Pierre
Island

Saint-Jean-Port-Joli
Edmundston
Madawaska
Van Buren

Miramichi
KOUCHIBOUGUAC
NP

CAPE BRETON
HIGHLANDS NP

Cape
Breton
532 m

Fort Kent
Grand Falls
Caribou

North C.

PRINCE
EDWARD
ISLAND

Cape
Breton
Highlands

New Waterford
Glace Bay

Montmagny
QUÉBEC INT'L
Québec
Lévis-Lauzon
Sainte-Foy

NEW
BRUNSWICK

Blackville
Saint-Louis-
de-Kent

Saint
Eleanors
Summerside

PRINCE EDWARD ISLAND NAT'L PARK

Charlottetown

Souris

Sydney Mines
Sydney

Mont
Mégantic
1105 m

Presque Isle

Stanley
Minto

Buctouche
Shediac

Montague

Inverness

ALEXANDER
GRAHAM BELL
NHP

C. Breton

Saint-Georges
Woodstock
Fredericton

Riverview
Moncton

Cornwall

Northumberland Str.

St.
George's
Bay

FORTRESS OF
LOUISBOURG NHP

Ancienne-Lorette
Cap-
Rouge

Houlton
Oromocto

Sackville
FT. BEAUSÉJOUR NHP

Pictou
Antigonish
New Glasgow

Port Hawkesbury

Chedabucto Bay

Sainte-Marie

Petitcodiac
Dorchester
Amherst

Stellarton

C. Canso

Drummondville
Victoriaville

Thetford
Mines

Mt. Katahdin
5,268 ft (1,606 m)

Sussex
Springhill

Truro

St. Mary's

Disraëli

East Millinocket

EUNDY
NP

Windsor

HALIFAX INT'L

Richmond
Windsor

Millinocket

Quispamsis

Caledonia
Hills

Berwick
Kentville

GRAND PRE
NHP

Dartmouth

Sherbrooke
East
Angus

Dover-Milo
Foxcroft

Saint John
Grand Bay

South
Mts.

Halifax

Lac-Mégantic

East Lincoln

Saint
Stephen

Saint George

Digby

Lunenburg

Magog
Coaticook

Dexter

Calais
Eastport

Grand Manan
I.

KEJIMKUJIK
NP
Bridgewater

Longfellow Mts.

Skowhegan

Old Town
Orono

Machias

Bay of Fundy

Liverpool

Sable I.
(CAN.)

MAINE

Farmington
Waterville
Bangor
Ellsworth

Lake
Rossignol

Shelburne

Rumford

Belfast

Bar Harbor

Berlin

Augusta
Gardiner

Camden
ACADIA
NP

Yarmouth

C. Sable

Mt. Washington
6,288 ft (1,917 m)

Winthrop
Lewiston
Auburn
Lisbon

Rockland

NEW
HAMPSHIRE

Bridgton
Conway

Brunswick

Bath
Bootbay Harbor

Littleton

Plymouth

PORTLAND INT'L
JETPORT

Portland

Lebanon
Milton

Sanford
Saco
Biddeford
Kennebunk

*Gulf of
Maine*

Claremont
Rochester
Dover
Somersworth

Concord
Durham

Portsmouth

Manchester
Derry
Exeter

Merrimack
Nashua

Haverhill

C. Ann
Mass.
Bay

Chicopee
N.H.

Lowell
Lawrence
Lynn

MASS.
Cambridge
Newton

Boston
Quincy

C. Cod

CAPE COD
NAT'L
SEASHORE

Worcester
Brockton

Providence
Pawtucket

Fall River

Hartford
New Britain
bury

Warwick
R.I.

New Bedford

Nantucket I.

New
London

Newport

Block
I.

*Martha's
Vineyard*

g Island

OCEAN

Southeastern United States

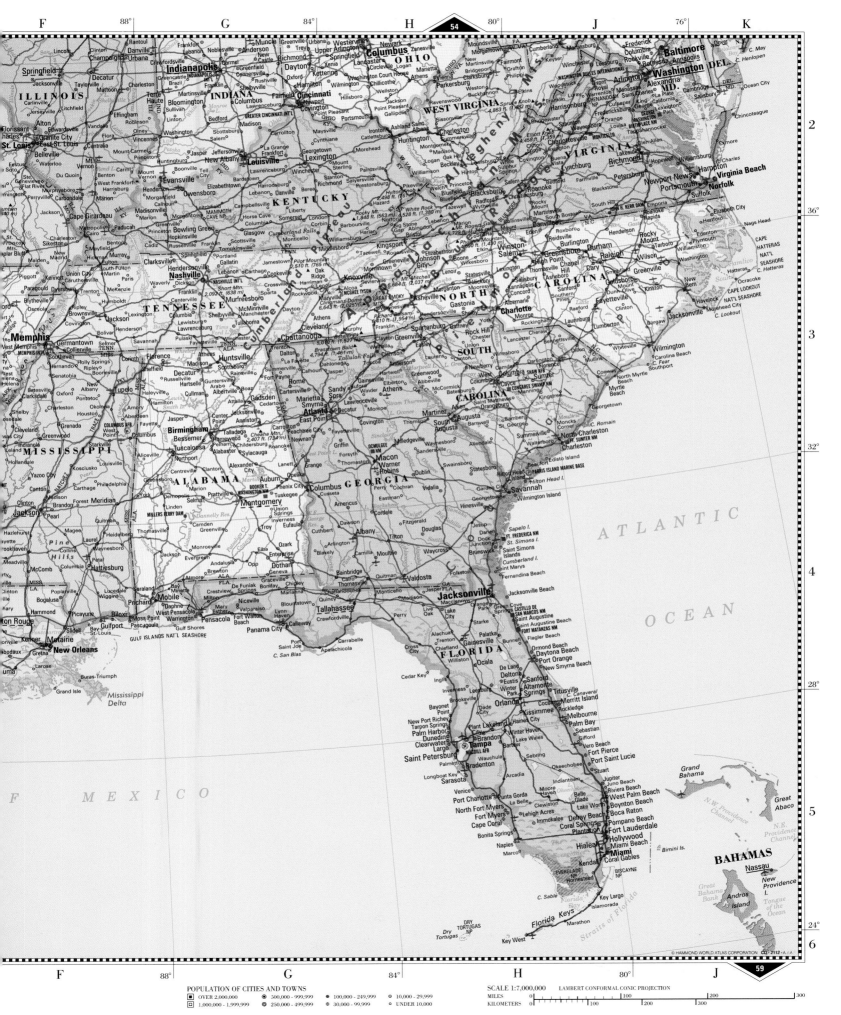

POPULATION OF CITIES AND TOWNS

- ■ OVER 2,000,000
- ● 500,000 - 999,999
- ● 100,000 - 249,999
- ◦ 10,000 - 29,999
- ▣ 1,000,000 - 1,999,999
- ● 250,000 - 499,999
- ● 30,000 - 99,999
- ◦ UNDER 10,000

SCALE 1:7,000,000   LAMBERT CONFORMAL CONIC PROJECTION

MILES   0   100   200   300

KILOMETERS   0   100   200   300

© HAMMOND WORLD ATLAS CORPORATION   CO - 2112 - A - A A

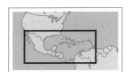

Middle America and Caribbean

South America - Physical

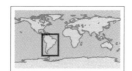

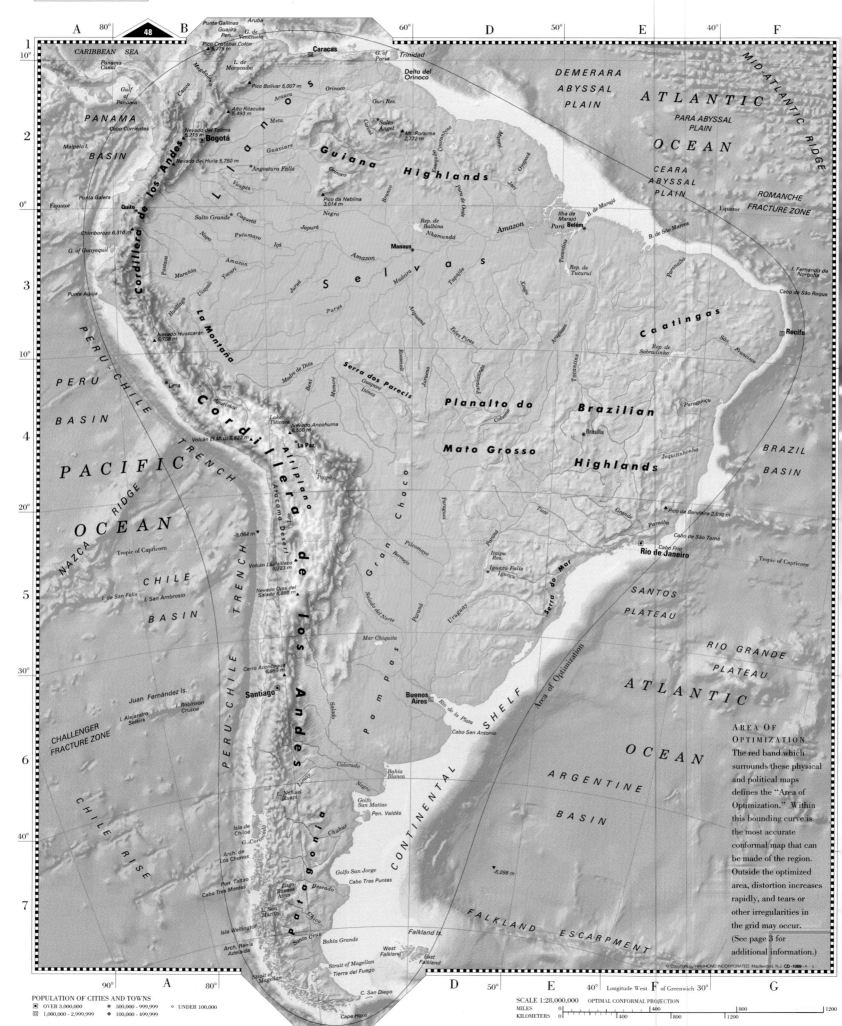

CARIBBEAN SEA

Panama Canal

Gulf of Panama

PANAMA

Cabo Corrientes

Malpelo I.

BASIN

Punta Galera

Equator

Quito

Chimborazo 6,310 m

G. of Guayaquil

Punta Aguja

PERU-CHILE

PERU

BASIN

PACIFIC

OCEAN

NAZCA

RIDGE

Tropic of Capricorn

CHILE

BASIN

Juan Fernández Is.

I. de San Félix

I. San Ambrosio

I. Alejandro Selkirk

I. Robinson Crusoe

CHALLENGER FRACTURE ZONE

CHILE RISE

Punta Gallinas

Guajira Pen.

Pico Cristóbal Colón 5,775 m

Aruba

G. de Venezuela

L. de Maracaibo

Pico Bolívar 5,007 m

Arauca

Magdalena

Cauca

Cordillera de los Andes

Nevado del Tolima 5,215 m

Bogotá

Nevado del Huila 5,750 m

Angostura Falls

Vaupés

Meta

Guaviare

La Montaña

Orinoco

Caquetá

Salto Grande

Napo

Putumayo

Marañón

Içá

Pastaza

Ucayali

Japurá

Negro

Amazon

Yavarí

Amazon

Madre de Diós

Juruá

Purus

Huallaga

Nevado Huascarán 6,768 m

Lima

Cordillera de los Andes

Apurímac

Beni

Mamoré

Guaporé

Iténez

Lake Titicaca

Nevado Ancohuma 6,550 m

La Paz

Altiplano

Atacama Desert

Volcán El Misti 5,822 m

-8,064 m

Volcán Llullaillaco 6,723 m

Nevado Ojos del Salado 6,880 m

L. Poopó

Cordillera de los Andes

PERU-CHILE TRENCH

Cerro Aconcagua 6,959 m

Santiago

Salado

Mar Chiquita

Río Colorado

L. Nahuel Huapi

Isla de Chiloé

G. Corcovado

Arch. de Los Chonos

Pen. Taitao

Cabo Tres Montes

Isla Wellington

Arch. Reina Adelaida

L. San Martín

Lago Buenos Aires

Santa Cruz

Bahía Grande

Strait of Magellan

Tierra del Fuego

Cape Horn

C. San Diego

Caracas

G. of Paria

Trinidad

Delta del Orinoco

Orinoco

Guri Res.

Salto Angel

Mt. Roraima 2,772 m

L l a n o s

Guiana Highlands

Pico da Neblina 3,014 m

Orinoco

Branco

Caroní

Essequibo

Courantyne

Jari

Puru de Oeste

Negro

Rep. de Balbina

Nhamundá

Amazon

Amazon

Manaus

S e l v a s

Madeira

Tapajós

Aripuanã

Teles Pires

Roosevelt

Telés Pires

Serra dos Parecis

Guaporé

Iténez

Xingu

Araguaia

Tocantins

Juruena

Planalto do

Mato Grosso

Coluene

Paranatinga

Gran Chaco

Bermejo

Pilcomayo

Paraguay

Salado del Norte

Paraná

Mar Chiquita

Pampas

Paraná

Uruguay

Río de la Plata

Buenos Aires

Cabo San Antonio

Bahía Blanca

Río Negro

Golfo San Matías

Pen. Valdés

Chubut

Golfo San Jorge

Deseado

Cabo Tres Puntas

Chico

PATAGONIA

DEMERARA ABYSSAL PLAIN

PARA ABYSSAL PLAIN

ATLANTIC

OCEAN

CEARA ABYSSAL PLAIN

ROMANCHE FRACTURE ZONE

Equator

MID-ATLANTIC RIDGE

Ilha de Marajó

B. de Marajó

Pará

Belém

B. de São Marcos

Rep. de Tucuruí

Parnaíba

I. Fernando de Noronha

Cabo de São Roque

Recife

São Francisco

Rep. de Sobradinho

C a a t i n g a s

Brazilian

Highlands

Brasília

Jequitinhonha

Paraguaçu

Pico da Bandeira 2,890 m

BRAZIL BASIN

Grande

Paraíba

Cabo de São Tomé

Cabo Frio

Rio de Janeiro

Tropic of Capricorn

Itaipu Res.

Iguazú Falls

Iguaçú

Paraná

Tietê

Serra do Mar

SANTOS PLATEAU

RIO GRANDE PLATEAU

ATLANTIC

OCEAN

CONTINENTAL SHELF

Area of Optimization

ARGENTINE

BASIN

-6,098 m

FALKLAND ESCARPMENT

Falkland Is.

West Falkland

East Falkland

AREA OF OPTIMIZATION

The red band which surrounds these physical and political maps defines the "Area of Optimization." Within this bounding curve is the most accurate conformal map that can be made of the region. Outside the optimized area, distortion increases rapidly, and tears or other irregularities in the grid may occur.

(See page 3 for additional information.)

© Copyright by HAMMOND INCORPORATED, Maplewood, N.J. CD-1069-A-1

POPULATION OF CITIES AND TOWNS

■ OVER 3,000,000   ● 500,000 - 999,999   ○ UNDER 100,000

□ 1,000,000 - 2,999,999   ● 100,000 - 499,999

SCALE 1:28,000,000   OPTIMAL CONFORMAL PROJECTION

MILES   0   400   800   1200

KILOMETERS   0   400   800   1200

Longitude West of Greenwich

South America - Political

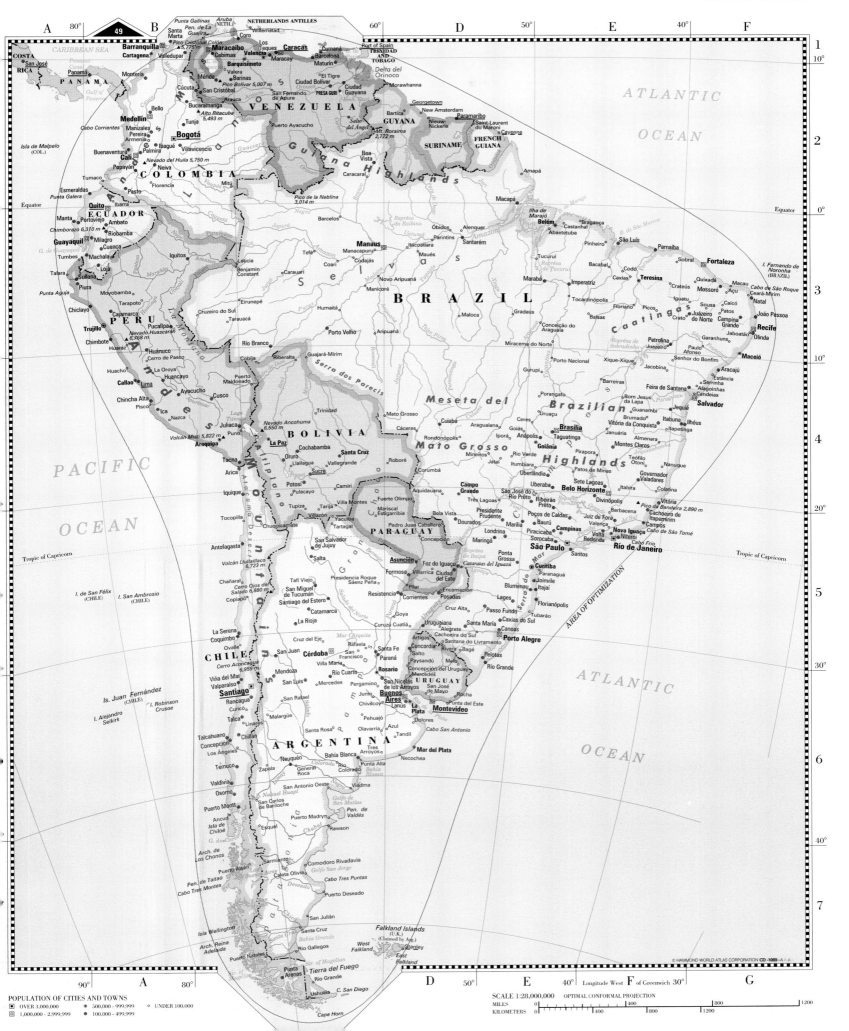

POPULATION OF CITIES AND TOWNS

- OVER 3,000,000
- 1,000,000 - 2,999,999
- 500,000 - 999,999
- 100,000 - 499,999
- UNDER 100,000

SCALE 1:28,000,000   OPTIMAL CONFORMAL PROJECTION

MILES   0   400   800   1200

KILOMETERS   0   400   800   1200

Northern South America

Southern South America

PACIFIC

OCEAN

BOLIVIA

PARAGUAY

BRAZIL

CHILE

ARGENTINA

URUGUAY

Buenos Aires

Montevideo

Pôrto Alegre

São Paulo

Rio de Janeiro

Santiago

Córdoba

Rosario

Mendoza

Mar del Plata

A T L A N T I C

O C E A N

Golfo de San Matías

Península de Valdés

Golfo de San Jorge

Patagonia

Falkland Islands
(Islas Malvinas)
(U.K. - CLAIMED BY ARGENTINA)
Mt. Adam 700 m   C. Dolphin   Port Howard
West Falkland   Stanley
Port Stephens   Mt. Usborne 705 m
C. Meredith   East Falkland

Bahía Grande

Punta Dungeness

Isla Grande de Tierra del Fuego

Cabo San Diego
Cabo San Juan
I. de los Estados

Ushuaia

I. Navarino

Cape Horn
Drake Passage

S. Georgia I.
(U.K.)

© HAMMOND WORLD ATLAS CORPORATION CD - 2105 - A - A

SCALE 1:15,000,000   LAMBERT CONFORMAL CONIC PROJECTION
MILES   0   200   400   600
KILOMETERS 0   200   400   600

POPULATION OF CITIES AND TOWNS
■ OVER 2,000,000   ● 500,000 - 999,999   ◉ 50,000 - 99,999
▣ 1,000,000 - 1,999,999 ● 100,000 - 499,999   ○ UNDER 50,000

Index of the World

This index is a comprehensive listing of the places and geographic features found in the atlas. Names are arranged in strict alphabetical order, without regard to hyphens or spaces. Every name is followed by the country or area to which it belongs. Except for cities, towns, countries and cultural areas, all entries include a reference to feature type, such as province, river, island, peak, and so on. The page number and alpha-numeric code appear in blue to the left of each listing. The page number directs you to the largest scale map on which the name can be found. The code refers to the grid squares formed by the horizontal and vertical lines

of latitude and longitude on each map. Following the letters from left to right and the numbers from top to bottom helps you to locate quickly the square containing the place or feature. Inset maps have their own alpha-numeric codes. Names that are accompanied by a point symbol are indexed to the symbol's location on the map. Other names are indexed to the initial letter of the name. When a map name contains a subordinate or alternate name, both names are listed in the index. To conserve space and provide room for more entries, many abbreviations are used in this index. The primary abbreviations are listed below.

Index Abbreviations

A			
Ab,Can	Alberta		
Abor.	Aboriginal		
Acad.	Academy		
ACT	Australian Capital Territory		
A.F.B.	Air Force Base		
Afld.	Airfield		
Afg.	Afghanistan		
Afr.	Africa		
Ak,US	Alaska		
Al,US	Alabama		
Alb.	Albania		
Alg.	Algeria		
Amm. Dep.	Ammunition Depot		
And.	Andorra		
Ang.	Angola		
Angu.	Anguilla		
Ant.	Antarctica		
Anti.	Antigua and Barbuda		
Ar,US	Arkansas		
Arch.	Archipelago		
Arg.	Argentina		
Arm.	Armenia		
Arpt.	Airport		
Aru.	Aruba		
ASam.	American Samoa		
Ash.	Ashmore and Cartier Islands		
Aus.	Austria		
Austl.	Australia		
Aut.	Autonomous		
Az,US	Arizona		
Azer.	Azerbaijan		
Azor.	Azores		
B			
Bahm.	Bahamas, The		
Bahr.	Bahrain		
Bang.	Bangladesh		
Bar.	Barbados		
BC,Can	British Columbia		
Bela.	Belarus		
Belg.	Belgium		
Belz.	Belize		
Ben.	Benin		
Berm.	Bermuda		
Bfld.	Battlefield		
Bhu.	Bhutan		
Bol.	Bolivia		
Bor.	Borough		
Bosn.	Bosnia and Herzegovina		
Bots.	Botswana		
Braz.	Brazil		
BrIn.	British Indian Ocean Territory		
Bru.	Brunei		
Bul.	Bulgaria		
Burk.	Burkina Faso		
Buru.	Burundi		
BVI	British Virgin Islands		
C			
Ca,US	California		
CAfr.	Central African Republic		
Camb.	Cambodia		
Camr.	Cameroon		
Can.	Canada		
Can.	Canal		

Canl.	Canary Islands
Cap.	Capital
Cap. Dist.	Capital District
Cap. Terr.	Capital Territory
Cay.	Cayman Islands
C.d'Iv.	Côte d'Ivoire
C.G.	Coast Guard
Chan.	Channel
Chl.	Channel Islands
Co.	County
Co,US	Colorado
Col.	Colombia
Com.	Comoros
Cont.	Continent
CpV.	Cape Verde Islands
CR	Costa Rica
Cr.	Creek
Cro.	Croatia
CSea.	Coral Sea Islands Territory
Ct,US	Connecticut
Ctr.	Center
Ctry.	Country
Cyp.	Cyprus
Czh.	Czech Republic
D	
DC,US	District of Columbia
De,US	Delaware
Den.	Denmark
Depr.	Depression
Dept.	Department
Des.	Desert
DF	Distrito Federal
Dist.	District
Djib.	Djibouti
Dom.	Dominica
Dpcy.	Dependency
D.R.Congo	Democratic Republic of the Congo
DRep.	Dominican Republic
E	
Ecu.	Ecuador
Emb.	Embankment
Eng.	Engineering
Eng,UK	England
EqG.	Equatorial Guinea
Erit.	Eritrea
ESal.	El Salvador
Est.	Estonia
Eth.	Ethiopia
Eur.	Europe
F	
Falk.	Falkland Islands
Far.	Faroe Islands
Fed. Dist.	Federal District
Fin.	Finland
Fl,US	Florida
For.	Forest
Fr.	France
FrAnt.	French Southern and Antarctic Lands
FrG.	French Guiana
FrPol.	French Polynesia
FYROM	Former Yugoslav Rep. of Macedonia
G	
Ga,US	Georgia
Galp.	Galapagos Islands

Gam.	Gambia, The
Gaza	Gaza Strip
GBis.	Guinea-Bissau
Geo.	Georgia
Ger.	Germany
Gha.	Ghana
Gib.	Gibraltar
Glac.	Glacier
Gov.	Governorate
Govt.	Government
Gre.	Greece
Grld.	Greenland
Gren.	Grenada
Grsld.	Grassland
Guad.	Guadeloupe
Guat.	Guatemala
Gui.	Guinea
Guy.	Guyana
H	
Har.	Harbor
Hi,US	Hawaii
Hist.	Historic(al)
Hon.	Honduras
Hts.	Heights
Hun.	Hungary
I	
Ia,US	Iowa
Ice.	Iceland
Id,US	Idaho
Il,US	Illinois
IM	Isle of Man
In,US	Indiana
Ind. Res.	Indian Reservation
Indo.	Indonesia
Int'l	International
Ire.	Ireland
Isl., Isls.	Island, Islands
Isr.	Israel
Isth.	Isthmus
It.	Italy
J	
Jam.	Jamaica
Jor.	Jordan
K	
Kaz.	Kazakhstan
Kiri.	Kiribati
Ks,US	Kansas
Kuw.	Kuwait
Ky,US	Kentucky
Kyr.	Kyrgyzstan
L	
La,US	Louisiana
Lab.	Laboratory
Lag.	Lagoon
Lakesh.	Lakeshore
Lat.	Latvia
Lcht.	Liechtenstein
Ldg.	Landing
Leb.	Lebanon
Les.	Lesotho
Libr.	Liberia
Lith.	Lithuania
Lux.	Luxembourg
M	
Ma,US	Massachusetts
Madg.	Madagascar
Madr.	Madeira
Malay.	Malaysia

Mald.	Maldives
Malw.	Malawi
Mart.	Martinique
May.	Mayotte
Mb,Can	Manitoba
Md,US	Maryland
Me,US	Maine
Mem.	Memorial
Mex.	Mexico
Mi,US	Michigan
Micr.	Micronesia, Federated States of
Mil.	Military
Mn,US	Minnesota
Mo,US	Missouri
Mol.	Moldova
Mon.	Monument
Mona.	Monaco
Mong.	Mongolia
Monts.	Montserrat
Mor.	Morocco
Moz.	Mozambique
Mrsh.	Marshall Islands
Mrta.	Mauritania
Mrts.	Mauritius
Ms,US	Mississippi
Mt.	Mount
Mt,US	Montana
Mtn., Mts.	Mountain, Mountains
Mun. Arpt.	Municipal Airport
N	
NAm.	North America
Namb.	Namibia
NAnt.	Netherlands Antilles
Nat'l	National
Nav.	Naval
NB,Can	New Brunswick
Nbrhd.	Neighborhood
NC,US	North Carolina
NCal.	New Caledonia
ND,US	North Dakota
Ne,US	Nebraska
Neth.	Netherlands
Nf,Can	Newfoundland
Nga.	Nigeria
NH,US	New Hampshire
NI,UK	Northern Ireland
Nic.	Nicaragua
NJ,US	New Jersey
NKor.	North Korea
NM,US	New Mexico
NMar.	Northern Mariana Isl.
Nor.	Norway
NP	National Park
NS,Can	Nova Scotia
Nv,US	Nevada
NW,Can	Northwest Territories
NWR	National Wildlife Refuge
NY,US	New York
NZ	New Zealand
O	
Obl.	Oblast
Oh,US	Ohio
Ok,US	Oklahoma
On,Can	Ontario
Or,US	Oregon
P	
Pa,US	Pennsylvania

PacUS	Pacific Islands, U.S.
Pak.	Pakistan
Pan.	Panama
Par.	Paraguay
Par.	Parish
PE,Can	Prince Edward Island
Pen.	Peninsula
Phil.	Philippines
Phys. Reg.	Physical Region
Pitc.	Pitcairn Islands
Plat.	Plateau
PN	National Park
PNG	Papua New Guinea
Pol.	Poland
Port.	Portugal
Poss.	Possession
Pkwy.	Parkway
PR	Puerto Rico
Pref.	Prefecture
Prov.	Province
Prsv.	Preserve
Pt.	Point
Q	
Qu,Can	Quebec
R	
Rec.	Recreation(al)
Ref.	Refuge
Reg.	Region
Rep.	Republic
Res.	Reservoir, Reservation
Reun.	Réunion
RI,US	Rhode Island
Riv.	River
Rom.	Romania
Rsv.	Reserve
Rus.	Russia
Rvwy.	Riverway
Rwa.	Rwanda
S	
SAfr.	South Africa
Sam.	Samoa
SAm.	South America
SaoT.	São Tomé and Príncipe
SAr.	Saudi Arabia
Sc,UK	Scotland
SC,US	South Carolina
SD,US	South Dakota
Seash.	Seashore
Sen.	Senegal
Sey.	Seychelles
SGeo.	South Georgia and Sandwich Islands
Sing.	Singapore
Sk,Can	Saskatchewan
SKor.	South Korea
SLeo.	Sierra Leone
Slov.	Slovenia
Slvk.	Slovakia
SMar.	San Marino
Sol.	Solomon Islands
Som.	Somalia
Sp.	Spain
Spr., Sprs.	Spring, Springs
SrL.	Sri Lanka
Sta.	Station
StH.	Saint Helena
Str.	Strait
StK.	Saint Kitts and Nevis

StL.	Saint Lucia
StP.	Saint Pierre and Miquelon
StV.	Saint Vincent and the Grenadines
Sur.	Suriname
Sval.	Svalbard
Swaz.	Swaziland
Swe.	Sweden
Swi.	Switzerland
T	
Tah.	Tahiti
Tai.	Taiwan
Taj.	Tajikistan
Tanz.	Tanzania
Ter.	Terrace
Terr.	Territory
Thai.	Thailand
Tn,US	Tennessee
Tok.	Tokelau
Trg.	Training
Trin.	Trinidad and Tobago
Trkm.	Turkmenistan
Trks.	Turks and Caicos Islands
Tun.	Tunisia
Tun.	Tunnel
Turk.	Turkey
Tuv.	Tuvalu
Twp.	Township
Tx,US	Texas
U	
UAE	United Arab Emirates
Ugan.	Uganda
UK	United Kingdom
Ukr.	Ukraine
Uru.	Uruguay
US	United States
USVI	U.S. Virgin Islands
Ut,US	Utah
Uzb.	Uzbekistan
V	
Va,US	Virginia
Val.	Valley
Van.	Vanuatu
VatC.	Vatican City
Ven.	Venezuela
Viet.	Vietnam
Vill.	Village
Vol.	Volcano
Vt,US	Vermont
W	
Wa,US	Washington
Wal,UK	Wales
Wall.	Wallis and Futuna
WBnk.	West Bank
Wi,US	Wisconsin
Wild.	Wildlife, Wilderness
WSah.	Western Sahara
WV,US	West Virginia
Wy,US	Wyoming
Y	
Yem.	Yemen
Yk,Can	Yukon Territory
Yugo.	Yugoslavia
Z	
Zam.	Zambia
Zim.	Zimbabwe

A

18/F4 Aachen, Ger.
40/G6 Aba, Nga.
32/D5 Abā as Su'ūd, SAr.
32/E2 Abadan, Iran
24/K4 Abakan, Rus.
40/F6 Abeokuta, Nga.
18/D2 Aberdeen, Sc,UK
51/J4 Aberdeen, SD,US
50/B4 Aberdeen, Wa,US
18/C3 Aberystwyth, Wal,UK
32/D5 Abhā, SAr.
40/E6 Abidjan, C.d'Iv.
53/H3 Abilene, Ks,US
53/H4 Abilene, Tx,US
54/D1 Abitibi (riv.), On,Can
23/F5 Abkhazia (reg.), Geo.
33/K2 Abottābād, Pak.
33/F4 Abu Dhabi (cap.), UAE
40/G6 Abuja (cap.), Nga.
62/E5 Abunã (Abuná) (riv.), Braz., Bol.
55/G2 Acadia Nat'l Pk., Me,US
58/B4 Acapulco, Mex.
62/G3 Acarai (mts.), Braz.
40/E6 Accra (cap.), Gha.
24/K4 Achinsk, Rus.
59/G3 Acklins (isl.), Bah.
64/C3 Aconcagua (mt.), Arg.
53/H4 Ada, Ok,US
40/H6 Adamaora (plat.), Camr., Nga.
47/M7 Adamstown (cap.), Pitc.
23/E6 Adana, Turk.
23/D5 Adapazarı, Turk.
32/D3 Ad Dahnā (des.), SAr.
32/F3 Ad Dammān, SAr.
41/N6 Addis Ababa (cap.), Eth.
45/C4 Adelaide, Austl.
41/Q5 Aden (gulf), Afr., Asia
32/D6 Aden, Yem.
21/F2 Adige (riv.), It.
54/F2 Adirondack (mts.), NY,US
23/E6 Adıyahman, Turk.
46/D5 Admiralty (isls.), PNG
54/C3 Adrian, Mi,US
21/G2 Adriatic (sea), Eur.
21/K4 Aegean (sea)
33/H2 Afghanistan
39/* Africa
40/D1 Agadir, Mor.
35/F3 Agartala, India
21/J1 Aggteleki Nat'l Park, Hun.
34/C2 Agra, India
21/G4 Agrigento, It.
21/J4 Agrínion, Gre.
62/E2 Aguaro-Guariquito Nat'l Park, Ven.
58/A3 Aguascalientes, Mex.
42/D7 Agulhas (cape), SAfr.
40/F3 Ahaggar (mts.), Alg.
36/B3 Ahmadabad, India
41/P6 Ahmar (mts.), Eth.
32/E2 Ahvaz, Iran
57/H3 Aiken, SC,US
40/G4 Aïr (plat.), Niger
20/E3 Aix-en-Provence, Fr.
21/F3 Ajaccio, Fr.
34/B2 Ajmer, India
29/M4 Akita, Japan
34/C3 Akola, India
54/D3 Akron, Oh,US
23/D6 Akşehir, Turk.
35/F3 Akyab, Myanmar
57/G3 Alabama (state), US
57/G4 Alabama (riv.), Al,US
63/L6 Alagoinhas, Braz.
53/F4 Alamogordo, NM,US
53/F3 Alamosa, Co,US
22/G3 Aland (isls.), Fin.
49/B3 Alaska (state), US
49/C4 Alaska (gulf), Ak,US
49/B4 Alaska (pen.), Ak,US
49/B3 Alaska (range), Ak,US
20/C4 Albacete, Sp.
21/H3 Albania
49/J4 Albany (riv.), On,Can
57/G4 Albany, Ga,US
54/F3 Albany (cap.), NY,US
50/C4 Albany, Or,US
32/E2 Al Başrah, Iraq
41/M7 Albert (lake), Afr.
50/E2 Alberta (prov.), Can.
51/K5 Albert Lea, Mn,US
64/B7 Alberto de Agostini Nat'l Park, Chile
20/C5 Alborán (isl.), Sp.
18/G2 Alborg, Den.
52/F4 Albuquerque, NM,US
20/C3 Alcalá de Henares, Sp.
20/B4 Alcántara (res.), Sp.
25/N4 Aldan (plat.), Rus.
25/P3 Aldan (riv.), Rus.
18/D4 Alderney (isl.), Chl.
32/C1 Aleppo, Syria
64/B5 Alerces Nat'l Park, Arg.
49/A4 Aleutian (isls.), Ak,US
49/D4 Alexander (arch.), Ak,US
41/L1 Alexandria, Egypt
56/E4 Alexandria, La,US
54/E4 Alexandria, Va,US
M2/41 Al Fayyum, Egypt
21/H2 Alfold, Great (plain), Hun.
33/G3 Al Fujayrah, UAE
40/F2 Algeria
40/F1 Algiers (cap.), Alg.
32/D6 Al Ḩudaydah, Yem.
32/E3 Al Hufūf, SAr.
20/C4 Alicante, Sp.
45/C3 Alice Springs, Austl.
36/C2 Aligarh, India
41/M2 Al Jīzah, Egypt
33/G4 Al Khābūrah, Oman
32/F3 Al Khobar, SAr.
40/H1 Al Khums, Libya
32/E2 Al Kūt, Iraq
36/D2 Allahabad, India
54/D4 Allegheny (mts.), US
54/F3 Allentown, Pa,US
34/C6 Alleppey, India
54/D3 Alliance, Oh,US
40/E1 Al Maghrib (reg.), Alg., Mor.
32/B2 Al Mahallah al Kubrá, Egypt
41/M1 Al Mansūra, Egypt
63/J6 Almas (riv.), Braz.
24/H5 Almaty (cap.), Kaz.
18/F3 Almelo, Neth.
20/C4 Almería, Sp.
41/M2 Al Minyā, Egypt
32/E3 Al Mubarraz, SAr.
32/E6 Al Mukallā, Yem.
63/J5 Alpercatas (mts.), Braz.
20/E2 Alps (mts.), Eur.
20/E2 Alsace (reg.), Fr.
28/B2 Altai (mts.), Asia
62/E7 Altiplano (plat.), Bol., Peru
54/B4 Alton, Il,US
54/E3 Altoona, Pa,US
28/C4 Altun (mts.), China
53/H4 Altus, Ok,US
41/L5 Al Ubayyiḑ, Sudan
62/D4 Amacayacú, Col.
20/A4 Amadora, Port.
29/M5 Amagasaki, Japan
29/K5 Amakusa (sea), Japan
62/F4 Amaña (lake), Braz.
53/G4 Amarillo, Tx,US
63/H4 Amazon (riv.), SAm.
63/G4 Amazônia Nat'l Park, Braz.
33/L2 Ambāla, India
62/C4 Ambato, Ecu.
37/G4 Ambon, Indo.
63/J8 Americana, Braz.
52/E2 American Fork, Ut,US
47/J6 American Samoa
57/G3 Americus, Ga,US
53/J2 Ames, Ia,US
55/H2 Amherst, NS,Can
20/D1 Amiens, Fr.
32/C2 Amman (cap.), Jor.
32/F1 Āmol, Iran
34/C3 Amravati, India
33/K2 Amritsar, India
18/F3 Amsterdam (cap.), Neth.
54/F3 Amsterdam, NY,US
24/G6 Amudar'ya (riv.), Asia
43/S Amundsen (sea), Ant.
48/E2 Amundsen (gulf), Can.
29/M1 Amur (riv.), Asia
50/E4 Anaconda, Mt,US
25/T3 Anadyr', Rus.
25/R3 Anadyr (gulf), Rus.
25/T3 Anadyr' (range), Rus.
52/C4 Anaheim, Ca,US
63/J7 Anápolis, Braz.
23/C6 Anatolia (reg.), Turk.
49/C3 Anchorage, Ak,US
21/G3 Ancona, It.
64/B5 Ancud (gulf), Chile
20/B4 Andalusia (reg.), Sp.
35/F5 Andaman (sea), Asia
35/F5 Andaman (isls.), India
54/C3 Anderson, In,US
57/H3 Anderson, SC,US
61/B3 Andes (mts.), SAm.
24/H5 Andijon, Uzb.
20/D3 Andorra
20/D3 Andorra la Vella (cap.), And.
59/F3 Andros (isl.), Bahm.
21/K4 Ándros (isl.), Gre.
59/J4 Anegada Passage (chan.), West Indies
20/D3 Aneto (peak), Sp.
64/B1 Angamos (pt.), Chile
25/L4 Angara (riv.), Rus.
28/E1 Angarsk, Rus.
62/F2 Angel (falls), Ven.
20/C2 Angers, Fr.
18/C3 Anglesea (isl.), Wal,UK
42/C3 Angola
59/J4 Anguilla (isl.), UK
23/D6 Ankara (cap.), Turk.
55/G3 Ann (cape), Ma,US
40/G1 Annaba, Alg.
32/C3 An Nafūd (des.), SAr.
32/D2 An Najaf, Iraq
35/J4 Annamitique (mts.), Laos, Viet.
54/E4 Annapolis (cap.), Md,US
34/D2 Annapurna (mtn.), Nepal
54/D3 Ann Arbor, Mi,US
57/G3 Anniston, Al,US
30/C1 Anqing, China
29/J3 Anshan, China
23/E6 Antakya (Antioch), Turk.
23/D6 Antalya, Turk.
42/K10 Antananarivo (cap.), Madg.
43/V Antarctic (pen.), Ant.
43/* Antarctica
20/E3 Antibes, Fr.
55/J1 Anticosti (isl.), Qu,Can
59/J4 Antigua and Barbuda
23/E6 Antioch (Antakya), Turk.
64/B1 Antofagasta, Chile
42/K9 Antsiranana, Madg.
64/B4 Antuco (vol.), Chile
18/F4 Antwerp, Belg.
28/G4 Anyang, China
24/J4 Anzhero-Sudzhensk, Rus.
29/N3 Aomori, Japan
20/E2 Aosta, It.
18/F3 Apeldoorn, Neth.
21/G3 Apennines (mts.), It.
47/S9 Apia (cap.), Sam.
63/G6 Apiacás (mts.), Braz.
49/J6 Appalachian (mts.), US
54/B2 Appleton, Wi,US
62/E2 Apure (riv.), Ven.
32/B3 Aqaba (gulf), Asia
24/F5 Aqtaū, Kaz.
24/F4 Aqtöbe, Kaz.
32/D4 Arabian (pen.), Asia
33/H5 Arabian (sea), Asia
32/B3 Arabian (des.), Egypt
63/L6 Aracaju, Braz.
63/H8 Araçatuba, Braz.
21/J2 Arad, Rom.
46/C5 Arafura (sea)
20/C3 Aragón (reg.), Sp.
63/J5 Araguaia (riv.), Braz.
63/H6 Araguaia Nat'l Park, Braz.
32/E3 Arāk, Iran
35/F3 Arakan (mts.), Myanmar
24/G5 Aral (sea), Asia
18/B3 Aran (isls.), Ire.
23/F6 Ararat (mt.), Turk.
23/G6 Aras (riv.), Asia
24/E3 Archangel'sk, Rus.
52/E3 Arches Nat'l Pk., Ut,US
14/A1 Arctic (ocean)
29/K2 Arda, China
23/G6 Ardabil, Iran
18/F4 Ardennes (for.), Belg.
53/H4 Ardmore, Ok,US
62/D7 Arequipa, Peru
64/C4 Argentina
21/K2 Arges (riv.), Rom.
21/J4 Argos, Gre.
18/G2 Arhus, Den.
62/D7 Arica, Chile
62/F5 Aripuanā (riv.), Braz.
52/D4 Arizona (state), US
53/J4 Arkadelphia, Ar,US
53/K4 Arkansas (riv.), US
56/E3 Arkansas (state), US
24/H2 Arkticheskiy Institut (isls.), Rus.
20/E3 Arles, Fr.
56/D3 Arlington, Tx,US
54/E4 Arlington, Va,US
18/C3 Armagh, NI,UK
23/F5 Armavir, Rus.
23/F5 Armenia
62/C3 Armenia, Col.
F4/18 Arnhem, Neth.
45/C2 Arnhem Land (reg.), Austl.
21/F3 Arno (riv.), It.
18/C3 Arran (isl.), Sc,UK
21/J4 Arta (gulf), Gre.
20/D1 Arras (reg.), Fr.
37/H5 Aru (isls.), Indo.
59/H5 Aruba (isl.), Neth.
41/K7 Aruwimi (riv.), D.R. Congo
23/F2 Arzamas, Rus.
29/N3 Asahikawa, Japan
34/E3 Asansol, India
14/J6 Ascension (isl.), StH.
40/E6 Ashanti (reg.), Gha.
57/H3 Asheville, NC,US
33/G1 Ashgabat (cap.), Trkm.
57/H2 Ashland, Ky,US
50/C5 Ashland, Or,US
45/B2 Ashmore and Cartier Is. (terr.), Austl.
33/G3 Ash Shāriqah, UAE
53/D3 Ashtabula, Oh,US
27/* Asia
32/D5 'Asīr, (mts.), SAr., Yem.
32/C5 Asmara (cap.), Erit.
52/F3 Aspen, Co,US
45/G7 Aspiring (mtn.), NZ
32/E3 As Sālimīyah, Kuw.
35/F2 Assam (state), India
18/F3 Assen, Neth.
41/M6 As Sudd (reg.), Sudan
31/B1 Astana (cap.), Kaz.
50/C4 Astoria, Or,US
23/G4 Astrakhan', Rus.
64/E2 Asunción (cap.), Par.
32/B4 Aswān, Egypt
32/B3 Asyūt, Egypt
64/C1 Atacama (des.), Arg.
62/E7 Atacama (des.), Chile
23/E6 Ataturk (res.), Turk.
41/M4 'Atbarah, Nahr (riv.), Sudan
53/J3 Atchison, Ks,US
49/F3 Athabasca (lake), Can.
21/J4 Athens (cap.), Gre.
57/H3 Athens, Ga,US
54/D4 Athens, Oh,US
21/K3 Athos (mt.), Gre.
25/U4 Atka (isl.), Ak,US
57/G3 Atlanta (cap.), Ga,US
14/G3 Atlantic (ocean)
54/F4 Atlantic City, NJ,US
40/E1 Atlas (mts.), Afr.
40/F1 Atlas Saharien (mts.), Alg., Mor.
32/D4 Aţ Ţā'if, SAr.
25/T5 Attu (isl.), Ak,US
64/C4 Atuel (riv.), Arg.
57/G3 Auburn, Al,US
55/G2 Auburn, Me,US
54/E3 Auburn, NY,US
45/H6 Auckland, NZ
41/P6 Audo (range), Eth.
18/G4 Augsburg, Ger.
57/H3 Augusta, Ga,US
55/G2 Augusta (cap.), Me,US
34/C4 Aurangabad, India
53/F3 Aurora, Co,US
56/D4 Austin (cap.), Tx,US
45/* Australia
45/D4 Australian Cap. Terr., Austl.
21/G2 Austria
62/D6 Auzangate (mtn.), Peru
55/L2 Avalon (pen.), Nf,Can
20/E3 Avignon, Fr.
21/J3 Axios (riv.), Gre.
23/C6 Aydın, Turk.
45/C3 Ayers Rock (mt.), Austl.
35/F4 Ayeyarwaddy (riv.), Myanmar
25/S3 Ayon (isl.), Rus.
18/C3 Ayr, Sc,UK
40/E4 Azaouād (reg.), Mali
23/G5 Azerbaijan
14/H4 Azores (isls.), Port.
23/E4 Azov (sea), Eur.
59/E6 Azuero (pen.), Pan.
32/B2 Az Zagāzig, Egypt
32/C2 Az Zarqā', Jor.

B

41/P5 Bab el Mandeb (str.)
32/F1 Bābol, Iran
19/M3 Babruysk, Bela.
32/D2 Babylon (ruins), Iraq
21/K2 Bacău, Rom.
30/D5 Bacolod, Phil.
20/D3 Badalona, Sp.
20/F1 Baden-Baden, Ger.
51/H5 Badlands Nat'l Pk., SD,US
49/K2 Baffin (isl.), NW,Can
49/L2 Baffin (bay), NAm.
32/D2 Baghdad (cap.), Iraq
33/J1 Baghlān, Afg.
40/J5 Baguirmi (reg.), Chad
59/F2 Bahamas
33/K3 Bahawalpur, Pak.
58/D4 Bahia (isls.), Hon.
64/D4 Bahía Blanca, Arg.
64/C7 Bahía Grande (bay), Arg.
33/G4 Bahlah, Oman
32/F3 Bahrain
41/L6 Bahr al 'Arab (riv.), Sudan
21/J2 Baia Mare, Rom.
29/J2 Baicheng, China
28/E4 Baiyin, China
21/H2 Baja, Hun.
59/L8 Baja California (pen.), Mex.
47/H4 Baker (isl.), PacUS
52/C4 Bakersfield, Ca,US
32/E2 Bakhtarān, Iran
23/G5 Baku (cap.), Azer.
62/E6 Bala (mts.), Bol.
23/G3 Balakovo, Rus.
21/H2 Balaton (lake), Hun.
62/F4 Balbina (riv.), Braz.
20/D4 Balearic (isls.), Sp.
63/L7 Baleia (pt.), Braz.
36/D5 Bali (isl.), Indo.
36/D5 Bali (sea), Indo.
23/C6 Balıkesir, Turk.
37/E4 Balikpapan, Indo.
21/J3 Balkan (mts.), Bulg.
31/B2 Balkhash (lake), Kaz.
19/L5 Bălţi, Mol.
19/J2 Baltic (sea), Eur.
54/E4 Baltimore, Md,US
40/D5 Bamako (cap.), Mali
18/G4 Bamberg, Ger.
41/J6 Bamingui-Bangoran Nat'l Park, CAfr.
46/F5 Banaba (isl.), Kiri.
63/H6 Bananal (isl.), Braz.
37/G5 Banda (sea), Indo.
36/A2 Banda Aceh, Indo.
33/G3 Bandar-e 'Abbās, Iran
32/F3 Bandar-e Būshehr, Iran
36/D3 Bandar Seri Begawan (cap.), Bru.
63/K8 Bandeira (peak), Braz.
36/C5 Bandung, Indo.
50/E2 Banff Nat'l Pk., Ab,Can
34/C5 Bangalore, India
37/F4 Banggai (isls.), Indo.
36/C4 Bangka (isl.), Indo.
35/H5 Bangkok (cap.), Thai.
34/E3 Bangladesh
18/C3 Bangor, NI,UK
55/G2 Bangor, Me,US
41/J7 Bangui (cap.), CAfr.
41/L2 Banī Suwayf, Egypt
21/H2 Banja Luka, Bosn.
36/D4 Banjarmasin, Indo.
40/B5 Banjul (cap.), Gam.
49/E2 Banks (isl.), Can.
19/J4 Banská Bystrica, Slvk.
36/A3 Banyak (isls.), Indo.
28/H4 Baoding, China
28/F5 Baoji, China
28/G3 Baotou, China
36/E4 Barabai, Indo.
20/C3 Baracaldo, Sp.
19/L3 Baranavichy, Bela.
59/K5 Barbados
54/D3 Barberton, Oh,US
20/D3 Barcelona, Sp.
62/F1 Barcelona, Ven.
34/C2 Bareilly, India
17/H1 Barents (sea), Eur.
55/G2 Bar Harbor, Me,US
21/H3 Bari, It.
62/D2 Barinas, Ven.
34/F3 Barisāl, Bang.
36/B4 Barisan (mts.), Indo.
36/D4 Barito (riv.), Indo.
57/G2 Barkley (lake), Ky,Tn,US
45/C2 Barkly Tableland (plat.), Austl.
24/J4 Barnaul, Rus.
34/B3 Baroda, India
62/E1 Barquisimeto, Ven.
62/D2 Barrancabermeja, Col.
62/D1 Barranquilla, Col.
54/E2 Barrie, On,Can
49/B2 Barrow (pt.), Ak,US
18/D3 Barrow-in-Furness, Eng,UK
52/C4 Barstow, Ca,US
53/H3 Bartlesville, Ok,US
19/M3 Barysaw, Bela.
20/E2 Basel, Swi.
30/D3 Bashi (chan.), Phil., Tai.
18/D4 Basingstoke, Eng,UK
45/D4 Bass (str.), Austl.
35/F4 Bassein, Myanmar
59/J4 Basse-Terre (cap.), Guad.
59/J4 Basse-Terre (isl.), Guad.
59/J4 Basseterre (cap.), StK.
21/F3 Bastia, Fr.
56/F3 Bastrop, La,US
58/E3 Batabanó (gulf), Cuba
33/L2 Batāla, India
40/H8 Batéké (plat.), Congo
18/D4 Bath, Eng,UK
49/G2 Bathurst (isl.), Can.
55/H2 Bathurst, NB,Can
23/F6 Batman, Turk.
40/G1 Batna, Alg.
57/F4 Baton Rouge (cap.), La,US
54/C3 Battle Creek, Mi,US
36/B3 Batu (bay), Malay.
23/F5 Batumi, Geo.
63/J8 Baurú, Braz.
59/F3 Bayamo, Cuba
59/H4 Bayamón, PR
28/D5 Bayan Har (mts.), China
54/D3 Bay City, Mi,US
24/G3 Baydaratskaya (bay), Rus.
28/F1 Baykal (lake), Rus.
25/L4 Baykal (mts.), Rus.
24/G5 Baykonyr, Kaz.
20/C2 Bayonne, Fr.
18/G4 Bayreuth, Ger.
56/E4 Baytown, Tx,US
23/G5 Bazardyuzyu, Gora (mt.), Azer.
52/E2 Bear (lake), US
50/F3 Bearpaw (mts.), Mt,US
53/H2 Beatrice, Ne,US
49/C2 Beaufort (sea), NAm.
57/H3 Beaufort, SC,US
56/E4 Beaumont, Tx,US
40/E1 Bechar, Alg.
54/D4 Beckley, WV,US
18/D3 Bedford, Eng,UK
32/B2 Beersheba, Isr.
25/M2 Begichev (isl.), Rus.
63/H3 Béhague (pt.), FrG.
35/J3 Beihai, China
28/H4 Beijing (Peking) (cap.), China
29/J3 Beipiao, China
32/C2 Beirut (cap.), Leb.
40/G1 Bejaïa, Alg.
36/C5 Bekasi, Indo.
19/L3 Belarus
63/J4 Belém, Braz.
18/C3 Belfast (cap.), NI,UK
55/G2 Belfast, Me,US
34/B4 Belgaum, India
18/E4 Belgium
23/E3 Belgorod, Rus.
21/J2 Belgrade (cap.), Yugo.
36/C4 Belitung (isl.), Indo.
58/D4 Belize
58/D4 Belize City, Belz.
25/P2 Bel'kovskiy (isl.), Rus.
34/C4 Bellary, India
54/E2 Belleville, On,Can
54/B4 Belleville, Il,US
50/C3 Bellingham, Wa,US
43/U Bellingshausen (sea), Ant.
62/C2 Bello, Col.
58/D4 Belmopan (cap.), Belz.
63/K7 Belo Horizonte, Braz.
54/B3 Beloit, Wi,US
24/J5 Belovo, Rus.
23/E1 Beloye (lake), Rus.
24/G2 Belyy (isl.), Rus.
51/K4 Bemidji, Mn,US
34/D2 Benares (Varanasi), India
50/C4 Bend, Or,US
34/E4 Bengal (bay), Asia
29/H5 Bengbu, China
41/K1 Benghazi, Libya
42/B3 Benguela, Ang.
62/E6 Beni (riv.), Bol.
40/F5 Benin
40/F6 Benin (bight), Afr.
40/G6 Benin City, Nga.
18/C2 Ben Nevis (mt.), Sc,UK
55/F3 Bennington, Vt,US
53/J4 Benton, Ar,US
54/C3 Benton Harbor, Mi,US
40/G6 Benue (riv.), Nga.
29/J3 Benxi, China
29/L5 Beppu, Japan
21/J3 Berat, Alb.
37/H4 Berau (bay), Indo.
19/H5 Berchtesgaden Nat'l Park, Ger.
54/C4 Berea, Ky,US
19/M3 Berezina (riv.), Bela.
23/J2 Berezniki, Rus.
21/F2 Bergamo, It.
22/C3 Bergen, Nor.
34/D4 Berhampur, India
25/T4 Bering (sea)
25/V3 Bering (str.)
25/S4 Bering (isl.), Rus.
52/B3 Berkeley, Ca,US
19/H3 Berlin (cap.), Ger.
55/G2 Berlin, NH,US
64/D2 Bermejo (riv.), Arg.
49/L6 Bermuda (isl.), UK
20/E2 Bern (cap.), Swi.
64/B6 Bernardo O'Higgins Nat'l Park, Chile
20/E2 Besançon, Fr.
57/G3 Bessemer, Al,US
54/F3 Bethlehem, Pa,US
23/D6 Beyşehir, Turk.
34/E2 Bhagalpur, India
34/E2 Bhaktapur, Nepal
33/L2 Bhatinda, India
34/E3 Bhātpāra, India
34/B3 Bhavnagar, India
34/D3 Bhilai, India
34/C3 Bhopal, India
34/E3 Bhubaneswar, India
34/E2 Bhutan
40/G7 Biafra (bight), Afr.
37/J4 Biak (isl.), Indo.
19/K3 Bialystok, Pol.
55/G3 Biddeford, Me,US
42/C3 Bie (plat.), Ang.
18/G3 Bielefeld, Ger.
19/J4 Bielsko-Biala, Pol.
35/J5 Bien Hoa, Viet.
56/C4 Big Bend Nat'l Pk., Tx,US
50/G4 Bighorn (riv.), US
50/F4 Bighorn (mts.), Wy,US
56/C3 Big Spring, Tx,US
40/B5 Bijagós (arch.), GBis.
34/B2 Bikaner, India
46/F3 Bikini (atoll), Mrsh.
42/C4 Bikuar Nat'l Park, Ang.
34/D3 Bilāspur, India
23/D4 Bila Tserkva, Ukr.
35/G5 Bilaukraung (range), Myanmar, Thai.
20/C4 Bilbao, Sp.
50/F4 Billings, Mt,US
57/F4 Biloxi, Ms,US
59/F2 Biminis (isls.), Bahm.
54/F3 Binghamton, NY,US
64/B4 Bio-Bio (riv.), Chile
18/D3 Birmingham, Eng,UK
57/G3 Birmingham, Al,US
52/E5 Bisbee, Az,US
20/B2 Biscay (bay), Eur.
57/H5 Biscayne Nat'l Pk., Fl,US
31/B3 Bishkek (cap.), Kyr.
42/E7 Bisho, SAfr.
40/F1 Biskra, Alg.
46/D5 Bismarck (arch.), PNG
51/H4 Bismarck (cap.), ND,US
40/B5 Bissau (cap.), GBis.
21/J3 Bitola, FYROM
50/E4 Bitterroot (range), US
37/G3 Bitung, Indo.
24/J4 Biysk, Rus.
40/G1 Bizerte, Tun.
23/D5 Black (sea)
18/G5 Black (for.), Ger.
50/E5 Blackfoot, Id,US
51/H5 Black Hills (mts.), US
18/D3 Blackpool, Eng,UK
57/H2 Blacksburg, Va,US
40/E5 Black Volta (riv.), Afr.
21/J3 Blagoevgrad, Bul.
29/K1 Blagoveshchensk, Rus.
20/E2 Blanc (mt.), Eur.
62/C5 Blanca (mts.), Peru
62/B4 Blanco (cape), Ecu.
42/F4 Blantyre, Malw.
41/L7 Bleu (mts.), D.R. Congo
40/F1 Blida, Alg.
55/G3 Block (isl.), RI,US
42/E6 Bloemfontein, SAfr.
54/B3 Bloomington, Il,US
54/C4 Bloomington, In,US
51/K4 Bloomington, Mn,US
50/D4 Blue (mts.), Or,US
57/H2 Bluefield, WV,US
41/M5 Blue Nile (riv.), Afr.
57/H2 Blue Ridge (mts.), US
64/G2 Blumenau, Braz.
53/K4 Blytheville, Ar,US
63/J5 Boa Esperança (res.), Braz.
40/E5 Bobo-Dioulasso, Burk.
57/H5 Boca Raton, Fl,US
22/E2 Bodø, Nor.
57/F4 Bogalusa, La,US
28/B3 Bogda Feng (mtn.), Mong.
36/C5 Bogor, Indo.
62/D3 Bogotá (cap.), Col.
28/H4 Bo Hai (gulf), China
19/H4 Bohemia (reg.), Czh.
50/D5 Boise (cap.), Id,US
62/D2 Bolívar (mt.), Ven.
62/D2 Bolívar (peak), Ven.
62/F7 Bolivia
21/F2 Bologna, It.
25/L2 Bol'shevik (isl.), Rus.
25/Q2 Bol'shoy Lyakhovskiy (isl.), Rus.
21/F2 Bolzano, It.
37/H4 Bomberai (pen.), Indo.
63/K5 Bom Jesus do Gurgueia (mts.), Braz.
40/H1 Bon (cape), Tun.
59/H5 Bonaire (isl.), NAnt.
45/B2 Bonaparte (arch.), Austl.
37/F4 Bone (gulf), Indo.
42/K10 Bongolava (uplands), Madg.
41/K6 Bongos, Massif des (plat.), CAfr.
21/F3 Bonifacio (str.), Eur.
46/D2 Bonin (isls.), Japan
18/F4 Bonn, Ger.
50/C4 Bonneville (dam), US
37/E5 Bonthain, Indo.
53/J2 Boone, Ia,US
47/K6 Bora Bora (isl.), FrPol.
50/E4 Borah (peak), Id,US
63/L5 Borborema (plat.), Braz.
20/C2 Bordeaux, Fr.
56/C3 Borger, Tx,US
37/E3 Borneo (isl.), Asia
22/E5 Bornholm (isl.), Den.
40/H5 Bornu (plains), Nga.
32/E2 Borūjerd, Iran
21/H3 Bosnia and Herzegovina
23/C5 Bosporus (str.), Turk.
52/E3 Bossier City, La,US
55/G3 Boston (cap.), Ma,US
22/F3 Bothnia (gulf), Eur.
21/K2 Botoşani, Rom.
28/H4 Botou, China
42/D5 Botswana
40/E6 Bouaké, C.d'Iv.
40/D5 Boucle du Baoulé Nat'l Park, Mali
46/E5 Bougainville (isl.), PNG
53/F2 Boulder, Co,US
52/D4 Boulder City, Nv,US
20/D1 Boulogne-sur-Mer, Fr.
52/E2 Bountiful, Ut,US
20/D2 Bourges, Fr.
18/D4 Bournemouth, Eng,UK
15/K8 Bouvet (isl.), Nor.
57/G2 Bowling Green, Ky,US
54/D3 Bowling Green, Oh,US
57/H5 Boynton Beach, Fl,US
50/F4 Bozeman, Mt,US
21/H3 Brač (isl.), Cro.
57/H5 Bradenton, Fl,US
18/D3 Bradford, Eng,UK
20/A3 Braga, Port.
35/F2 Brahmaputra (riv.), Asia
21/K2 Brăila, Rom.
62/F4 Branco (riv.), Braz.
54/D3 Brantford, On,Can
63/J7 Brasília (cap.), Braz.
63/J7 Brasília Nat'l Park, Braz.
21/K2 Braşov, Rom.
19/J4 Bratislava (cap.), Slvk.
25/L4 Bratsk, Rus.
55/F3 Brattleboro, Vt,US
18/G3 Braunschweig, Ger.
62/F7 Bravo (mtn.), Bol.
61/D3 Brazil
56/D4 Brazos (riv.), Tx,US
42/C1 Brazzaville (cap.), Congo
18/D4 Brecon Beacons Nat'l Park, Wal,UK
18/F4 Breda, Neth.
18/G3 Bremen, Ger.
18/G3 Bremerhaven, Ger.
50/C4 Bremerton, Wa,US
21/F2 Brescia, It.
19/K3 Brest, Bela.
20/B1 Brest, Fr.
55/F3 Bridgeport, Ct,US
59/K5 Bridgetown (cap.), Bar.
52/D2 Brigham City, Ut,US
18/D4 Brighton, Eng,UK
21/J3 Brindisi, It.
45/E3 Brisbane, Austl.
18/C4 Bristol (chan.), UK
18/D4 Bristol, Eng,UK
49/A4 Bristol (bay), Ak,US
57/H2 Bristol, Tn,US
57/H2 Bristol, Va,US
50/C3 British Columbia (prov.), Can.
27/G10 British Indian Ocean Terr., UK
20/C2 Brittany (reg.), Fr.
19/J4 Brno, Czh.
55/G3 Brockton, Ma,US
53/J3 Broken Arrow, Ok,US
45/D4 Broken Hill, Austl.
51/J4 Brookings, SD,US
49/B3 Brooks (range), Ak,US
56/D5 Brownsville, Tx,US
56/D4 Brownwood, Tx,US
18/E4 Brugge, Belg.
36/D2 Brunei
64/B7 Brunswick (pen.), Chile
57/H4 Brunswick, Ga,US
55/G3 Brunswick, Me,US
18/F4 Brussels (cap.), Belg.
56/D4 Bryan, Tx,US
23/D3 Bryansk, Rus.
52/D3 Bryce Canyon Nat'l Pk., Ut,US
62/D2 Bucaramanga, Col.
21/K2 Bucharest (cap.), Rom.
21/H2 Budapest (cap.), Hun.
62/C3 Buenaventura, Col.
64/E3 Buenos Aires (cap.), Arg.
64/B6 Buenos Aires (lake), Arg., Chile
54/E3 Buffalo, NY,US
19/K3 Bug (riv.), Eur.
42/E1 Bujumbura (cap.), Buru.
42/E1 Bukavu, D.R. Congo
24/G6 Bukhoro, Uzb.
21/J2 Bükki Nat'l Park, Hun.
42/E5 Bulawayo, Zim.
21/K3 Bulgaria
28/D2 Bulnayn (mts.), Mong.
37/F5 Bulukumba, Indo.
32/D3 Buraydah, SAr.
52/C4 Burbank, Ca,US
34/E3 Burdwan, India
K3/21 Burgas, Bulg.
20/C3 Burgos, Sp.
20/E2 Burgundy (reg.), Fr.
40/E5 Burkina Faso
54/E3 Burlington, On,Can
53/K2 Burlington, Ia,US
57/J2 Burlington, NC,US
55/F2 Burlington, Vt,US
23/C5 Bursa, Turk.
37/G4 Buru (isl.), Indo.
42/E1 Burundi
54/E3 Butler, Pa,US
30/E6 Butuan, Phil.
37/F5 Butung (isl.), Indo.
21/K2 Buzău, Rom.
19/J3 Bydgoszcz, Pol.
24/K2 Byrranga (mts.), Rus.
19/J3 Bytom, Pol.

C

63/K5 Caatingas (reg.), Braz.
62/D1 Cabimas, Ven.
42/B2 Cabinda, Ang.
64/C7 Cabo de Hornos Nat'l Park, Chile
54/E2 Cabonga (res.), Qu,Can
63/H3 Cabo Orange Nat'l Park, Braz.
42/F4 Cabora Bassa (lake), Moz.
55/J2 Cabot (str.), Can.
21/J3 Čačak, Yugo.
63/G5 Cachimbo (mts.), Braz.
20/B4 Cádiz, Sp.
20/B4 Cádiz (gulf), Sp.
20/C1 Caen, Fr.
30/D6 Cagayan de Oro, Phil.
21/F4 Cagliari, It.
59/H4 Caguas, PR
63/H7 Caiapó (mts.), Braz.
59/G3 Caicos (isls.), Trks.
45/D2 Cairns, Austl.
32/B3 Cairo (cap.), Egypt
54/B4 Cairo, Il,US
40/G7 Calabar, Nga.
21/H4 Calabria (reg.), It.
20/D1 Calais, Fr.
55/H2 Calais, Me,US
64/C2 Calalaste (mts.), Arg.
34/E3 Calcutta, India
50/D5 Caldwell, Id,US
50/E3 Calgary, Ab,Can
62/C3 Cali, Col.
34/C5 Calicut (Kozhikode), India
59/M8 California (gulf), Mex.
52/B3 California (state), US
62/C6 Callao, Peru
59/F3 Camagüey, Cuba
59/F3 Camagüey (arch.), Cuba
34/B3 Cambay (gulf), India
35/H5 Cambodia
18/D3 Cambrian (mts.), Wal,UK
18/E3 Cambridge, Eng,UK
55/G3 Cambridge, Ma,US
54/E4 Cambridge, Md,US
53/J4 Camden, Ar,US
55/F4 Camden, NJ,US
57/H3 Camden, SC,US
42/D3 Cameia Nat'l Park, Ang.
40/H7 Cameroon
64/B4 Campanario (mtn.), Arg.
58/C4 Campeche, Mex.
58/C4 Campeche (bay), Mex.
63/L5 Campina Grande, Braz.
64/G1 Campinas, Braz.
63/H8 Campo Grande, Braz.
63/K8 Campos, Braz.
35/J5 Cam Ranh, Viet.
49/G4 Canada
53/G3 Canadian (riv.), US
62/F2 Canaima Nat'l Park, Ven.
40/B2 Canary (isls.), Sp.
45/D4 Canberra (cap.), Austl.
58/D3 Cancún, Mex.
64/C2 Candado (mtn.), Arg.
28/H4 Cangzhou, China
20/E3 Cannes, Fr.
64/F2 Canoas, Braz.
20/B3 Cantabrica, Cordillera (range), Sp.
45/H7 Canterbury (bight), NZ
18/E4 Canterbury, Eng,UK
35/J6 Can Tho, Viet.
47/H5 Canton (isl.), Kiri.
54/D3 Canton, Oh,US
30/B3 Canton (Guangzhou), China

67
Canyo – Fürth

52/E3 Canyonlands Nat'l Pk., Ut,US
55/J2 Cape Breton (isl.), NS,Can
57/H5 Cape Coral, Fl,US
57/F2 Cape Girardeau, Mo,US
42/C7 Cape Town (cap.), SAfr.
14/H5 Cape Verde
45/D2 Cape York (pen.), Austl.
59/G4 Cap-Haïtien, Haiti
63/J4 Capim (riv.), Braz.
52/E3 Capitol Reef Nat'l Pk., Ut,US
63/H8 Capivara (res.), Braz.
42/D4 Caprivi Strip (reg.), Namb.
62/D4 Caquetá (riv.), Col.
62/E1 Caracas (cap.), Ven.
63/H5 Carajás (mts.), Braz.
54/B4 Carbondale, Il,US
20/D3 Carcassonne, Fr.
18/D4 Cardiff (cap.), Wal,UK
18/C3 Cardigan (bay), Wal,UK
59/G4 Caribbean (sea)
50/C2 Cariboo (mts.), BC,Can
55/G2 Caribou, Me,US
18/D3 Carlisle, Eng,UK
54/E3 Carlisle, Pa,US
18/C3 Carlow, Ire.
53/F4 Carlsbad, NM,US
53/F4 Carlsbad Caverns Nat'l Pk., NM,US
59/H4 Carolina, PR
46/D4 Caroline (isls.), Micr.
19/J4 Carpathians (mts.), Eur.
45/C2 Carpentaria (gulf), Austl.
21/F2 Carrara, It.
52/C3 Carson (sink), Nv,US
52/C3 Carson City (cap.), Nv,US
62/C1 Cartagena, Col.
20/C4 Cartagena, Sp.
58/E6 Cartago, CR
40/D1 Casablanca, Mor.
52/E4 Casa Grande, Az,US
50/C5 Cascade (range), US
64/F1 Cascavel, Braz.
50/G5 Casper, Wy,US
24/F6 Caspian (sea)
20/D3 Castellón de la Plana, Sp.
59/J5 Castries (cap.), StL.
20/D3 Catalonia (reg.), Sp.
21/G4 Catania, It.
21/H4 Catanzaro, It.
32/B3 Catherine (mt.), Egypt
55/F3 Catskill (mts.), NY,US
23/F5 Caucasus (mts.), Eur.
63/J3 Caviana (isl.), Braz.
34/D2 Cawnpore (Kanpur), India
63/K4 Caxias, Braz.
64/F2 Caxias do Sul, Braz.
62/C3 Cayambe (mtn.), Ecu.
63/H3 Cayenne (cap.), FrG.
58/E4 Cayman Islands, UK
30/D5 Cebu, Phil.
52/D3 Cedar City, Ut,US
53/J2 Cedar Falls, Ia,US
53/K2 Cedar Rapids, Ia,US
59/L8 Cedros (isl.), Mex.
37/F3 Celebes (sea), Asia
37/F4 Celebes (isl.), Indo.
18/C4 Celtic (sea), Eur.
37/H4 Cenderawasih (bay), Indo.
41/J6 Central African Republic
62/C5 Central, Cordillera (mts.), SAm.
54/B4 Centralia, Il,US
50/C4 Centralia, Wa,US
33/H3 Central Makrān (mts.), Pak.
63/J7 Central, Planalto (plat.), Braz.
25/L2 Central Siberian (plat.), Rus.
37/G4 Ceram (isl.), Indo.
37/G4 Ceram (sea), Indo.
64/C4 Cerro Colorados (res.), Arg.
19/H4 České Budějovice, Czh.
20/B5 Ceuta, Sp.
34/D6 Ceylon (isl.)
64/D1 Chaco Austral (reg.), Arg.
62/G8 Chaco Boreal (reg.), Par.
64/D1 Chaco Central (reg.), Arg.
64/D2 Chaco, Gran (reg.), SAm.
64/E2 Chaco Nat'l Park, Arg.
41/J4 Chad
40/H5 Chad (lake), Afr.
27/G10 Chagos (arch.), Brln.
54/E4 Chambersburg, Pa,US
42/F3 Chambeshi (riv.), Zam.
20/E1 Champagne (reg.), Fr.
54/B3 Champaign, Il,US
54/F2 Champlain (lake), NAm.
62/C5 Chan Chan (ruins), Peru
33/L2 Chandigarh, India
34/C3 Chandrapur, India
29/K3 Changchun, China
30/D3 Changhua, Tai.
27/L6 Chang Jiang (Yangtze) (riv.), China
35/K2 Changsha, China
28/G4 Changzhi, China
29/H5 Changzhou, China
64/C1 Chañi (mtn.), Arg.
52/C4 Channel (isls.), Ca,US
45/D3 Channel Country (reg.), Austl.
18/D4 Channel Islands, UK
63/K6 Chapada Diamantina Nat'l Park, Braz.
63/J6 Chapada dos Veadeiros Nat'l Park, Braz.
57/J3 Chapel Hill, NC,US
40/J5 Chari (riv.), Afr.
24/G6 Chärjew, Trkm.
18/F4 Charleroi, Belg.
57/J3 Charleston, SC,US
54/D4 Charleston (cap.), WV,US
57/H3 Charlotte, NC,US
59/J4 Charlotte Amalie (cap.), USVI
57/J2 Charlottesville, Va,US
55/J2 Charlottetown (cap.), PE,Can
20/D1 Chartres, Fr.
55/H2 Chatham, NB,Can
57/G4 Chattahoochee (riv.), US
57/G4 Chattahoochee, Fl,US
57/G3 Chattanooga, Tn,US
25/T3 Chaunskaya (bay), Rus.
23/D2 Cheboksary, Rus.
54/C2 Cheboygan, Mi,US
40/E2 Chech, Erg (des.), Alg.
54/E3 Cheektowaga, NY,US
50/C4 Chehalis, Wa,US
29/K5 Cheju, SKor.
29/K5 Cheju (isl.), SKor.
29/K5 Cheju (str.), SKor.
50/C4 Chelan (lake), Wa,US
18/D4 Cheltenham, Eng,UK
24/G4 Chelyabinsk, Rus.
25/L2 Chelyuskina (cape), Rus.
34/D5 Chennai (Madras), India
19/H4 Chemnitz, Ger.
29/H3 Chengde, China
28/E5 Chengdu (Chengtu), China
20/C1 Cherbourg, Fr.
23/E2 Cherepovets, Rus.
23/D4 Cherkasy, Ukr.
23/F5 Cherkessk, Rus.
23/D3 Chernihiv, Ukr.
23/C4 Chernivtsi, Ukr.
23/D4 Cherry Hill, NJ,US
25/Q3 Cherskiy (range), Rus.
54/E4 Chesapeake (bay), US
18/D3 Chester, Eng,UK
58/D4 Chetumal, Mex.
53/F2 Cheyenne (riv.), US
53/F2 Cheyenne (cap.), Wy,US
35/G4 Chiang Mai, Thai.
30/D3 Chiayi, Tai.
29/N4 Chiba, Japan
54/C3 Chicago, Il,US
58/D3 Chichén-Itzá (ruins), Mex.
45/A3 Chichester (range), Austl.
53/H4 Chickasha, Ok,US
62/C5 Chiclayo, Peru
64/C5 Chico (riv.), Arg.
52/B3 Chico, Ca,US
54/F3 Chicopee, Ma,US
55/G1 Chicoutimi, Qu,Can
29/H3 Chifeng, China
63/K7 Chifre (mts.), Braz.
59/N8 Chihuahua, Mex.
61/B6 Chile
64/B4 Chillán, Chile
54/D4 Chillicothe, Oh,US
64/A5 Chiloé (isl.), Chile
62/C4 Chimborazo (mt.), Ecu.
62/C5 Chimbote, Peru
27/J6 China, People's Rep. of
30/D3 China, Rep. of (Taiwan)
33/K2 Chiniot, Pak.
24/G5 Chirchiq, Uzb.
58/E6 Chiriquí (gulf), Pan.
19/M5 Chişinău (cap.), Mold.
28/G1 Chita, Rus.
35/F3 Chittagong, Bang.
42/D4 Chobe Nat'l Park, Bots.
35/H5 Chon Buri, Thai.
29/K3 Chŏngjin, NKor.
29/K4 Chongju, SKor.
30/A2 Chongqing (Chungking), China
29/K4 Chŏnju, SKor.
64/A6 Chonos (arch.), Arg.
34/D3 Chota Nagur (plat.), India
28/G2 Choybalsan, Mong.
45/H7 Christchurch, NZ
27/K11 Christmas (isl.), Austl.
64/C5 Chubut (riv.), Arg.
25/U3 Chukchi (pen.), Rus.
25/U3 Chukchi (sea), Rus.
52/C4 Chula Vista, Ca,US
24/J4 Chulym (riv.), Rus.
29/K4 Ch'unch'ŏn, SKor.
49/H4 Churchill, Can.
49/H4 Churchill (riv.), Can.
36/C5 Ciamis, Indo.
36/C5 Cianjur, Indo.
59/E3 Cienfuegos, Cuba
36/C5 Cilacap, Indo.
53/G3 Cimarron (riv.), US
54/C4 Cincinnati, Oh,US
21/F3 Cinto (mt.), Fr.
36/C5 Cirebon, Indo.
58/B4 Citlaltépetl (mt.), Mex.
62/F2 Ciudad Bolívar, Ven.
62/F2 Ciudad Guayana, Ven.
59/N7 Ciudad Juárez, Mex.
58/B3 Ciudad Madero, Mex.
59/N8 Ciudad Obregón, Mex.
20/B4 Ciudad Real, Sp.
58/B3 Ciudad Victoria, Mex.
55/F3 Claremont, NH,US
53/J3 Claremore, Ok,US
54/D4 Clarksburg, WV,US
57/F3 Clarksdale, Ms,US
57/G2 Clarksville, Tn,US
18/B4 Clear (cape), Ire.
57/H5 Clearwater, Fl,US
50/D4 Clearwater (mts.), Id,US
20/D2 Clermont-Ferrand, Fr.
55/D3 Cleveland, Oh,US
57/G3 Cleveland, Tn,US
53/K2 Clinton, Ia,US
14/D5 Clipperton (isl.), Fr.
52/C3 Clovis, Ca,US
53/G4 Clovis, NM,US
21/J2 Cluj-Napoca, Rom.
18/C3 Clyde, Firth of (inlet), Sc,UK
50/A2 Coast (mts.), Can.
49/E5 Coast (ranges), US
57/H4 Coastal (plain), US
62/E7 Cochabamaba, Bol.
34/C6 Cochin, India
58/E5 Coco (riv.), Hon., Nic.
27/J11 Cocos (isls.), Austl.
55/G3 Cod (cape), Ma,US
50/F4 Cody, Wy,US
50/D4 Coeur d'Alene, Id,US
53/J3 Coffeyville, Ks,US
34/C5 Coimbatore, India
21/A3 Coimbra, Port.
62/E2 Cojedes (riv.), Ven.
59/P10 Colima, Mex.
56/D4 College Station, Tx,US
20/E1 Colmar, Fr.
18/F4 Cologne (Köln), Ger.
62/D3 Colombia
34/C6 Colombo (cap.), SrL.
59/F6 Colón, Pan.
64/D4 Colorado (riv.), Arg.
52/E3 Colorado (plat.), US
52/D4 Colorado (riv.), US
52/F3 Colorado (state), US
56/D4 Colorado (riv.), Tx,US
53/F3 Colorado Springs, Co,US
50/C2 Columbia (mts.), BC,Can
50/C4 Columbia (riv.), NAm.
53/J3 Columbia, Mo,US
50/D4 Columbia (plat.), Or,Wa,US
57/H3 Columbia (cap.), SC,US
57/G3 Columbia, Tn,US
57/G3 Columbus, Ga,US
54/C4 Columbus, In,US
57/F3 Columbus, Ms,US
54/D4 Columbus (cap.), Oh,US
21/F2 Como (lake), It.
64/C6 Comodoro Rivadavia, Arg.
40/E6 Comoe Nat'l Park, C.d'Iv.
34/C6 Comorin (cape), India
39/G6 Comoros
21/D1 Compiègne, Fr.
41/C6 Conakry (cap.), Gui.
62/F7 Concepción (lake), Bol.
64/B4 Concepción, Chile
52/B3 Concord, Ca,US
55/G3 Concord (cap.), NH,US
57/H3 Concord, NC,US
30/B3 Conghua, China
39/E5 Congo, Dem. Rep. of the
39/D4 Congo, Rep. of the
39/D5 Congo (riv.), Afr.
41/K7 Congo (basin), D.R. Congo
18/B3 Connacht (reg.), Ire.
55/G2 Connecticut (riv.), US
55/F3 Connecticut (state), US
18/G5 Constance (lake), Eur.
21/L2 Constanta, Rom.
41/G1 Constantine, Alg.
63/K7 Contagem, Braz.
50/C2 Continental (ranges), Ab,BC,Can
53/J4 Conway, Ar,US
45/G7 Cook (mt.), NZ
45/H7 Cook (str.), NZ
47/J6 Cook Islands, NZ
50/B5 Coos Bay, Or,US
19/H2 Copenhagen (cap.), Den.
46/E6 Coral (sea)
57/H5 Coral Gables, Fl,US
45/E2 Coral Sea Is. (terr.), Austl.
57/H5 Coral Springs, Fl,US
62/D3 Cordillera de los Picachos Nat'l Park, Col.
64/D3 Córdoba, Arg.
64/D3 Córdoba (mts.), Arg.
20/B4 Córdoba, Sp.
21/H4 Corfu (Kérkira), Gre.
21/J4 Corinth, Gre.
21/J4 Corinth (gulf), Gre.
18/B4 Cork, Ire.
55/K1 Corner Brook, Nf,Can
54/E3 Corning, NY,US
54/F2 Cornwall, On,Can
62/E1 Coro, Ven.
34/D5 Coromandel (coast), India
58/E6 Coronado (bay), CR
62/D7 Coropuna (mtn.), Peru
56/D5 Corpus Christi, Tx,US
64/E2 Corrientes, Arg.
21/F3 Corsica (isl.), Fr.
56/D3 Corsicana, Tx,US
54/E3 Cortland, NY,US
23/D5 Çorum, Turk.
63/J7 Corumba (riv.), Braz.
50/C4 Corvallis, Or,US
21/G3 Cosenza, It.
54/D3 Coshocton, Oh,US
58/E5 Costa Rica
40/D6 Côte d'Ivoire
20/C1 Cotentin (pen.), Fr.
40/F6 Cotonou, Benin
19/H4 Cottbus, Ger.
53/J2 Council Bluffs, Ia,US
18/D3 Coventry, Eng,UK
54/C4 Covington, Ky,US
58/D3 Cozumel (isl.), Mex.
21/J2 Craiova, Rom.
50/E3 Cranbrook, BC,Can
50/C5 Crater Lake Nat'l Pk., Or,US
54/C3 Crawfordsville, In,US
21/G2 Cres (isl.), Cro.
21/K5 Crete (isl.), Gre.
21/K4 Crete (sea), Gre.
23/D4 Crimea (pen.), Ukr.
40/H8 Cristal (mts.), Gabon
62/D1 Cristóbal Colón (peak), Col.
21/G2 Croatia
37/E3 Crocker (range), Malay.
56/E4 Crowley, La,US
42/C2 Cuango (riv.), Ang.
42/B2 Cuanza (riv.), Ang.
59/F3 Cuba
42/C4 Cubango (riv.), Ang.
62/D2 Cucuta, Col.
62/C4 Cuenca, Ecu.
58/B4 Cuernavaca, Mex.
63/G7 Cuiabá, Braz.
63/H6 Culene (riv.), Braz.
45/D3 Culgoa (riv.), Austl.
59/N9 Culiacán, Mex.
57/G3 Cullman, Al,US
62/F1 Cumaná, Ven.
57/G3 Cumberland (plat.), US
57/G2 Cumberland (riv.), US
54/E4 Cumberland, Md,US
18/D3 Cumbrian (mts.), Eng,UK
59/H5 Curaçao (isl.), NAnt.
64/G2 Curitiba, Braz.
62/D6 Cusco, Peru
34/E3 Cuttack, India
21/K4 Cyclades (isls.), Gre.
32/B1 Cyprus
41/K1 Cyrenaica (reg.), Libya
19/H4 Czech Republic
19/J4 Czestochowa, Pol.

D

21/G3 D'Abruzzo Nat'l Park, It.
34/E4 Dacca (Dhaka) (cap.), Bang.
18/G4 Dachau, Ger.
35/J2 Dafang, China
29/J2 Da Hinggang (mts.), China
46/C2 Daito (isls.), Japan
40/B5 Dakar (cap.), Sen.
35/J5 Da Lat, Viet.
55/H1 Dalhousie, NB,Can
29/J4 Dalian, China
56/D3 Dallas, Tx,US
21/G2 Dalmatia (reg.), Cro.
45/D3 Dalrymple (lake), Austl.
57/G3 Dalton, Ga,US
34/B3 Damān, India
32/B2 Damanhur, Egypt
32/C2 Damascus (cap.), Syria
32/F1 Damavand (mt.), Iran
32/B2 Damietta, Egypt
37/H4 Dampier (str.), Indo.
41/P5 Danakil (reg.), Djib., Eth.
35/E2 Da Nang, Viet.
29/J3 Dandong, China
21/L2 Danube (riv.), Eur.
55/C3 Danville, Il,US
54/E4 Danville, Va,US
29/K2 Daqing, China
34/E2 Darbhanga, India
23/C6 Dardanelles (str.), Turk.
42/G2 Dar es Salaam (cap.), Tanz.
28/F2 Darhan, Mong.
41/Q6 Darie (hills), Som.
59/F6 Darien Nat'l Park, Pan.
34/E2 Darjiling, India
45/A4 Darling (range), Austl.
45/D4 Darling (riv.), Austl.
45/D3 Darling Downs (ridge), Austl.
18/D3 Darlington, Eng,UK
18/G4 Darmstadt, Ger.
18/C4 Dartmoor Nat'l Park, Eng,UK
55/J2 Dartmouth, NS,Can
45/C2 Darwin, Austl.
64/B7 Darwin (mts.), Chile
41/N5 Dashen Terara, Ras (peak), Eth.
24/F5 Dashhowuz, Trkm.
33/F2 Dasht-e Kavīr (des.), Iran
33/G2 Dasht-e Lūt (des.), Iran
28/G3 Datong, China
19/L2 Daugava (Western Dvina) (riv.), Lat.
19/L3 Daugavpils, Lat.
30/E6 Davao, Phil.
53/K2 Davenport, Ia,US
58/E6 David, Pan.
43/F Davis (sea), Ant.
49/M3 Davis (str.), NAm.
52/B3 Davis, Ca,US
49/D3 Dawson, Can.
50/C2 Dawson Creek, BC,Can
28/F5 Daxian, China
54/C4 Dayton, Oh,US
57/H4 Daytona Beach, Fl,US
32/C2 Dead (sea), Asia
52/C3 Death Valley Nat'l Mon., Ca,Nv,US
21/J2 Debrecen, Hun.
57/G3 Decatur, Al,US
57/G3 Decatur, Ga,US
54/B4 Decatur, Il,US
34/C5 Deccan (plat.), India
54/C3 Defiance, Oh,US
33/L2 Dehra Dun, India
54/B3 De Kalb, Il,US
57/H4 De Land, Fl,US
54/F4 Delaware (bay), US
54/F3 Delaware (riv.), US
54/F4 Delaware (state), US
54/D3 Delaware, Oh,US
21/J4 Delfoi (ruins), Gre.
64/D5 Delgada (pt.), Arg.
34/C2 Delhi, India
21/F2 Dello Stelvio Nat'l Park, It.
57/H5 Delray Beach, Fl,US
56/C4 Del Rio, Tx,US
41/P5 Denakil (reg.), Erit., Eth.
18/F3 Den Helder, Neth.
23/C6 Denizli, Turk.
18/G3 Denmark
14/A2 Denmark (str.)
56/D3 Denton, Tx,US
53/F3 Denver (cap.), Co,US
33/J3 Dera Ghāzi Khān, Pak.
23/G5 Derbent, Rus.
18/D3 Derby, Eng,UK
18/B3 Derg, Lough (lake), Ire.
56/E4 De Ridder, La,US
55/G3 Derry, NH,US
64/C6 Deseado (riv.), Arg.
53/J2 Des Moines (cap.), Ia,US
23/D3 Desna (riv.), Eur.
64/A7 Desolación (isl.), Chile
18/H4 Dessau, Ger.
54/D3 Detroit, Mi,US
63/H2 Devil's (isl.), FrG.
49/J2 Devon (isl.), Can.
32/E2 Dezfūl, Iran
25/T3 Dezhnaya (cape), Rus.
28/H4 Dezhou, China
32/E3 Dhahran, SAr.
34/E3 Dhaka (Dacca) (cap.), Bang.
34/E3 Dhānbād, India
32/F5 Dhofar (reg.), Oman
34/B3 Dhulia, India
63/K6 Diamantina (uplands), Braz.
51/H4 Dickinson, ND,US
27/G10 Diego Garcia (isls.), Brln.
35/H3 Dien Bien Phu, Viet.
20/D1 Dieppe, Fr.
37/J5 Digul (riv.), Indo.
20/E2 Dijon, Fr.
37/G5 Dili, Indo.
25/P2 Dimitriya Lapteva (str.), Rus.
21/H2 Dinaric Alps (mts.), Eur.
41/N5 Dinder Nat'l Park, Sudan
18/B3 Dingle (bay), Ire.
52/E2 Dinosaur Nat'l Mon., Co,Ut,US
41/P6 Dire Dawa, Eth.
63/J8 Divinópolis, Braz.
62/D5 Divisor (mts.), Braz.
54/B3 Dixon, Il,US
23/F6 Diyarbakir, Turk.
40/H3 Djado (plat.), Niger
36/C5 Djakarta (Jakarta), Indo.
41/P5 Djibouti
41/P5 Djibouti (cap.), Djib.
36/D5 Djokjakarta (Yogyakarta), Indo.
23/D4 Dnipro (riv.), Eur.
23/D4 Dniprodzerzhyns'k, Ukr.
23/D4 Dnipropetrovs'k, Ukr.
23/C4 Dnister (riv.), Eur.
37/H4 Doberai (pen.), Indo.
63/K7 Doce (riv.), Braz.
23/C6 Dodecanese (isls.), Gre.
53/G3 Dodge City, Ks,US
23/E5 Dogukaradeniz (mts.), Turk.
32/F3 Doha (cap.), Qatar
63/K5 Dois Irmãos (mts.), Braz.
64/C1 Domeyko (mts.), Chile
59/J4 Dominica
59/H4 Dominican Republic
23/F4 Don (riv.), Rus.
34/D6 Dondra (head), SrL.
18/B3 Donegal (bay), Ire.
23/E4 Donets (riv.), Ukr.
23/E4 Donets'k, Ukr.
30/B3 Dongguan, China
29/H4 Dongying, China
21/D2 Dordogne (riv.), Fr.
18/F4 Dortmund, Ger.
57/G4 Dothan, Al,US
40/G7 Douala, Camr.
18/C3 Douglas (cap.), IM,UK
52/E5 Douglas, Az,US
20/B3 Douro (riv.), Port.
18/E4 Dover (str.), Eur.
18/E4 Dover, Eng,UK
54/F4 Dover (cap.), De,US
55/G3 Dover, NH,US
64/C8 Drake (passage)
42/E6 Drakensburg (range), SAfr.
21/H2 Dráva (riv.), Eur.
19/H4 Dresden, Ger.
21/H2 Drina (riv.), Bosn.
45/D3 Drummond (range), Austl.
33/G3 Dubayyi (Dubai), UAE
18/C3 Dublin (cap.), Ire.
57/H3 Dublin, Ga,US
21/H3 Dubrovnik, Cro.
53/K2 Dubuque, Ia,US
24/J3 Dudinka, Rus.
20/E2 Dufourspitze (mt.), Eur.
62/E3 Duida Marahuaca Nat'l Park, Ven.
18/F4 Duisburg, Ger.
51/L4 Duluth, Mn,US
18/D3 Dumfries, Sc,UK
53/H4 Duncan, Ok,US
18/C3 Dundalk, Ire.
18/D2 Dundee, Sc,UK
45/H7 Dunedin, NZ
57/H4 Dunedin, Fl,US
20/D1 Dunkirk (Dunkerque), Fr.
59/P9 Durango, Mex.
52/F3 Durango, Co,US
53/H4 Durant, Ok,US
42/F6 Durban, SAfr.
34/E3 Durgapur, India
18/D3 Durham, Eng,UK
57/J3 Durham, NC,US
55/G3 Durham, NH,US
21/H3 Durrës, Alb.
24/G6 Dushanbe (cap.), Taj.
18/F4 Düsseldorf, Ger.
17/J2 Dvina, Northern (Dvina Severnaya) (riv.), Rus.
23/C2 Dvina, Western (Dvina Zapadnaya) (riv.), Bela.
23/F2 Dzerzhinsk, Rus.
25/P4 Dzhugdzhur (range), Rus.

E

56/C4 Eagle Pass, Tx,US
27/M6 East China (sea), Asia
47/Q7 Easter (isl.), Chile
34/C5 Eastern Ghats (mts.), India
64/E7 East Falkland (isl.), Falk.
18/F3 East Frisian (isls.), Ger.
54/C3 East Lansing, Mi,US
54/D3 East Liverpool, Oh,US
42/E7 East London, SAfr.
57/G3 East Point, Ga,US
25/S2 East Siberian (sea), Rus.
54/B4 East St. Louis, Il,US
54/B2 Eau Claire, Wi,US
20/D3 Ebro (riv.), Sp.
58/B4 Ecatepec, Mex.
20/E2 Écrins Nat'l Park, Fr.
62/C4 Ecuador
57/J2 Eden, NC,US
57/J2 Edenton, NC,US
56/D5 Edinburg, Tx,US
18/D3 Edinburgh (cap.), Sc,UK
23/C5 Edirne, Turk.
50/C4 Edmonds, Wa,US
50/E2 Edmonton (cap.), Ab,Can
55/G2 Edmundston, NB,Can
23/C6 Edremit, Turk.
56/C4 Edwards (plat.), Tx,US
54/B4 Edwardsville, Il,US
52/B3 Eel (riv.), Ca,US
54/B4 Effingham, Il,US
21/G4 Egadi (isls.), It.
45/H6 Egmont (mt.), NZ
41/L2 Egypt
18/F4 Eifel (plat.), Ger.
18/F4 Eindhoven, Neth.
40/F1 El Asnam, Alg.
32/B3 Elat (Elath), Isr.
23/E6 Elazig, Turk.
21/F3 Elba (isl.), It.
18/G3 Elbe (riv.), Ger.
52/F3 Elbert (mt.), Co,US
19/J3 Elblag, Pol.
23/F5 El'brus (mt.), Rus.
32/E1 Elburz (mts.), Iran
52/C4 El Cajon, Ca,US
52/D4 El Centro, Ca,US
62/D2 El Cocuy Nat'l Park, Col.
40/D3 El Djouf (des.), Mrta.
53/J4 El Dorado, Ar,US
17/H3 Elektrostal', Rus.
59/F2 Eleuthera (isl.), Bahm.
54/B3 Elgin (mt.), Il,US
41/M7 Elgon (mt.), Ugan.
57/J2 Elizabeth City, NC,US
54/C3 Elkhart, In,US
40/C3 El Khatt (escarp.), Mrta.
50/C4 Ellensburg, Wa,US
49/J2 Ellesmere (isl.), Can.
43/U Ellsworth Land (reg.), Ant.
54/E3 Elmira, NY,US
62/D7 El Misti (vol.), Peru
64/C4 El Nevado (mtn.), Arg.
56/A4 El Paso, Tx,US
52/H4 El Reno, Ok,US
58/D5 El Salvador
62/E2 El Tuparro Nat'l Park, Col.
62/D2 El Viejo (mtn.), Col.
54/D3 Elyria, Oh,US
63/H7 Emas Nat'l Park, Braz.
18/F3 Emden, Ger.
18/F3 Emmen, Neth.
53/H3 Emporia, Ks,US
18/F3 Ems (riv.), Eur.
43/D Enderby Land (reg.), Ant.
54/E3 Endicott, NY,US
46/F3 Enewetak (atoll), Mrsh.
23/G3 Engel's, Rus.
18/D3 England, UK
18/B3 English (chan.), Eur.
53/H3 Enid, Ok,US
41/K4 Ennedi (plat.), Chad
18/C3 Enniskillen, NI,UK
18/F3 Enschede, Neth.
59/L7 Ensenada, Mex.
41/M8 Entebbe, Ugan.
40/G6 Enugu, Nga.
32/E1 Enzeli (Bandar-e Anzali), Iran
20/E1 Épinal, Fr.
40/G7 Equatorial Guinea
28/E2 Erdenet, Mong.
63/G4 Erepecu (lake), Braz.
18/G4 Erfurt, Ger.
40/D3 Erg Chech (des.), Alg., Mali
40/D2 Erg Iguidi (des.), Alg., Mrta.
54/D3 Erie (lake), NAm.
54/D3 Erie, Pa,US
32/C5 Eritrea
18/G4 Erlangen, Ger.
34/C5 Erode, India
18/B3 Erris Head (pt.), Ire.
19/H4 Erzgebirge (mts.), Eur.
23/F6 Erzurum, Turk.
22/H3 Esbo (Espoo), Fin.
54/C2 Escanaba, Mi,US
52/C4 Escondido, Ca,US
32/F2 Esfahān, Iran
23/D6 Eskişehir, Turk.
62/C3 Esmeraldas, Ecu.
63/K7 Espinhaço (mts.), Braz.
46/F6 Espiritu Santo (isl.), Van.
22/H3 Espoo (Esbo), Fin.
18/F4 Essen, Ger.
62/G2 Essequibo (riv.), Guy.
64/D7 Estados (isl.), Arg.
19/L2 Estonia
20/A3 Estrella (mts.), Port.
63/J5 Estrondo (mts.), Braz.
41/N5 Ethiopia
41/N6 Ethiopian (plat.), Eth.
21/G4 Etna (vol.), It.
42/C4 Etosha Nat'l Park, Namb.
21/K4 Euboea (Évvoia) (isl.), Gre.
54/D3 Euclid, Oh,US
50/C4 Eugene, Or,US
56/E4 Eunice, La,US
27/D6 Euphrates (riv.), Asia
52/A2 Eureka, Ca,US
17/* Europe
53/F3 Evans (mt.), Co,US
54/C3 Evanston, Il,US
54/C4 Evansville, In,US
34/E2 Everest (mt.), Asia
50/C3 Everett, Wa,US
57/H5 Everglades Nat'l Pk., Fl,US
20/B4 Évora, Port.
21/K4 Évvoia (isl.), Gre.
18/D4 Exeter, Eng,UK
55/G3 Exeter, NH,US
18/D4 Exmoor Nat'l Park, Eng,UK
45/C3 Eyre (lake), Austl.
45/C4 Eyre (pen.), Austl.

F

49/C3 Fairbanks, Ak,US
54/C4 Fairfield, Oh,US
50/D4 Fairmont, WV,US
33/K2 Faisalabad, Pak.
56/D5 Falcon (res.), NAm.
18/C3 Falkirk, Sc,UK
64/D7 Falkland Islands, UK
55/G3 Fall River, Ma,US
18/C4 Falmouth, Eng,UK
32/B1 Famagusta, Cyp.
42/K11 Fandriana, Madg.
47/K4 Fanning (Tabuaeran) (isl.), Kiri.
52/B3 Farallon (isls.), Ca,US
31/B3 Farghona, Uzb.
51/J4 Fargo, ND,US
51/K5 Faribault, Mn,US
34/C2 Farīdābād, India
52/E3 Farmington, NM,US
20/B4 Faro, Port.
17/D2 Faroe (isls.), Den.
53/J3 Fayetteville, Ar,US
57/J3 Fayetteville, NC,US
18/G3 Fehmarn (isl.), Ger.
29/J3 Fengcheng, China
51/K4 Fergus Falls, Mn,US
21/F2 Ferrara, It.
64/C3 Fertil (val.), Arg.
40/E1 Fès, Mor.
40/H2 Fezzan (reg.), Libya
42/K11 Fianarantsoa, Madg.
63/L6 Fiera de Santana, Braz.
46/G6 Fiji
21/K3 Filippoi (ruins), Gre.
54/D3 Findlay, Oh,US
20/A3 Finisterre (cape), Sp.
22/H2 Finland
22/H4 Finland (gulf), Eur.
21/F3 Firenze (Florence), It.
33/K2 Firozpur, India
21/G2 Fiume (Rijeka), Cro.
52/E4 Flagstaff, Az,US
52/E2 Flaming Gorge (res.), US
50/B3 Flattery (cape), Wa,US
18/G3 Flensburg, Ger.
45/D4 Flinders (isl.), Austl.
45/C4 Flinders (ranges), Austl.
54/D3 Flint, Mi,US
57/G3 Florence, Al,US
57/J3 Florence, SC,US
21/F3 Florence (Firenze), It.
37/F5 Flores (isl.), Indo.
37/E5 Flores (sea), Indo.
64/G2 Florianópolis, Braz.
58/E3 Florida (str.), Cuba, Fl,US
57/H4 Florida (state), US
57/H5 Florida (bay), Fl,US
53/K3 Florissant, Mo,US
21/G3 Foggia, It.
54/B3 Fond du Lac, Wi,US
58/D5 Fonseca (gulf), NAm.
20/D1 Fontainebleau, Fr.
30/C2 Foochow (Fuzhou), China
21/G2 Forlì, It.
63/G6 Formosa (mts.), Braz.
63/L4 Fortaleza, Braz.
52/F2 Ft. Collins, Co,US
59/J5 Ft.-de-France (cap.), Mart.
53/J2 Ft. Dodge, Ia,US
18/D2 Forth (firth), Sc,UK
18/D2 Forth, Firth of (inlet), Sc,UK
57/H5 Ft. Lauderdale, Fl,US
50/E3 Ft. Macleod, Ab,Can
53/K2 Ft. Madison, Ia,US
49/F4 Ft. McMurray, Can
57/H5 Ft. Myers, Fl,US
50/G4 Ft. Peck Lake (res.), Mt,US
57/H5 Ft. Pierce, Fl,US
49/F4 Ft. Smith, NW,Can
53/J4 Ft. Smith, Ar,US
57/G4 Ft. Walton Beach, Fl,US
54/C3 Ft. Wayne, In,US
18/C2 Fort William, Sc,UK
56/D3 Ft. Worth, Tx,US
30/B3 Foshan, China
54/D3 Fostoria, Oh,US
40/C5 Fouta Djallon (reg.), Gui.
45/G7 Foveaux (str.), NZ
49/J3 Foxe (basin), Can
62/F7 Frailes (mts.), Bol.
63/J8 França, Braz.
20/D2 France
51/J5 Francis Case (lake), SD,US
42/E5 Francistown, Bots.
54/C3 Frankfort, In,US
54/C4 Frankfort (cap.), Ky,US
18/G4 Frankfurt am Main, Ger.
19/H3 Frankfurt an der Oder, Ger.
50/D3 Franklin D. Roosevelt (lake), Wa,US
24/F2 Franz Josef Land (isls.), Rus.
50/C3 Fraser (riv.), BC,Can
22/D5 Fredericia, Den.
54/E4 Frederick, Md,US
54/E4 Fredericksburg, Va,US
55/H2 Fredericton (cap.), NB,Can
22/D4 Frederikshavn, Den.
59/F2 Freeport, Bah.
54/B3 Freeport, Il,US
40/C6 Freetown (cap.), SLeo.
18/F5 Freiburg, Ger.
50/B3 Fremont, Ca,US
53/H2 Fremont, Ne,US
63/H3 French Guiana
47/M6 French Polynesia
52/C3 Fresno, Ca,US
20/E2 Fribourg, Swi.
45/D4 Frome (lake), Austl.
53/F2 Front (range), Co,US
57/J2 Front Royal, Va,US
29/M4 Fukui, Japan
29/L5 Fukuoka, Japan
29/N4 Fukushima, Japan
33/J2 Fūlādī (mt.), Afg.
53/K3 Fulton, Mo,US
46/G5 Funafuti (cap.), Tuv.
40/B1 Funchal, Port.
55/H2 Fundy (bay), NAm.
55/H2 Fundy Nat'l Pk., NB,Can
63/J8 Furnas (res.), Braz.
45/D4 Furneaux Group (isls.), Austl.
18/G4 Fürth, Ger.

68

Fushu – Kielc

29/J3 Fushun, China
29/J3 Fuxin, China
30/C2 Fuzhou, China

G

40/H7 Gabon
42/E5 Gaborone (cap.), Bots.
57/G3 Gadsden, Al,US
21/G3 Gaeta (gulf), It.
57/H3 Gaffney, SC,US
57/H4 Gainesville, Fl,US
57/H3 Gainesville, Ga,US
45/C4 Gairdner (lake), Austl.
14/E6 Galápagos (isls.), Ecu.
21/K2 Galaţi, Rom.
54/B3 Galesburg, Il,US
57/G2 Gallatin, Tn,US
34/D6 Galle, SrL.
64/B7 Gallegos (riv.), Arg.
62/D1 Gallinas (pt.), Col.
23/C5 Gallipoli, Turk.
52/E4 Gallup, NM,US
52/E4 Galveston, Tx,US
18/B3 Galway, Ire.
41/M6 Gambela Nat'l Park, Eth.
40/B5 Gambia
40/B5 Gambia (riv.), Gam., Sen.
47/M7 Gambier (isls.), FrPol.
23/G5 Gäncä, Azer.
55/L1 Gander, Nf,Can
34/B3 Gandhinagar, India
31/D5 Gangdise (mts.), China
27/H7 Ganges (riv.), Asia
34/E3 Ganges, Mouths of the (delta), Bang., India
34/E2 Gangtok, India
30/C2 Ganzhou, China
20/E2 Gap, Fr.
24/F5 Garabogazköl (gulf), Trkm.
41/L7 Garamba Nat'l Park, D.R. Congo
21/F2 Garda (lake), It.
53/G3 Garden City, Ks,US
52/D3 Garland, Tx,US
21/F2 Garmisch-Partenkirchen, Ger.
20/D2 Garonne (riv.), Fr.
54/C3 Gary, In,US
36/C4 Gaspar (str.), Indo.
55/H1 Gaspé (pen.), Qu,Can
57/H3 Gastonia, NC,US
35/F2 Gauhāti, India
45/C4 Gawler (range), Austl.
34/E3 Gaya, India
32/B2 Gaza, Gaza
32/B2 Gaza Strip
23/E6 Gaziantep, Turk.
19/J3 Gdańsk, Pol.
19/J3 Gdańsk (gulf), Pol.
19/J3 Gdynia, Pol.
45/D4 Geelong, Austl.
35/H3 Gejiu, China
42/D6 Gemsbok Nat'l Park, Bots.
64/B6 General Carrera (lake), Chile
20/E2 Geneva, Swi.
54/E3 Geneva, NY,US
20/E2 Geneva (Léman) (lake), Eur.
21/F2 Genoa (Genova), It.
21/F2 Genova (gulf), It.
58/E4 George Town (cap.), Cay.
62/G2 Georgetown (cap.), Guy.
36/B2 George Town (Pinang), Malay.
23/F5 Georgia
50/C3 Georgia (str.), BC,Can
57/G3 Georgia (state), US
54/D2 Georgian (bay), On,Can
18/H4 Gera, Ger.
63/J6 Geral de Goias (mts.), Braz.
18/G4 Germany
54/E4 Gettysburg, Pa,US
40/E6 Ghana
34/C2 Ghaziābād, India
33/J2 Ghazni, Afg.
18/E4 Ghent, Belg.
20/B5 Gibraltar (str.)
20/B4 Gibraltar, UK
45/B3 Gibson (des.), Austl.
29/M4 Gifu, Japan
20/B3 Gijón, Sp.
52/D4 Gila (riv.), US
46/G5 Gilbert Is. (Kiribati)
50/G4 Gillette, Wy,US
20/D3 Girona (Gerona), Sp.
20/C2 Gironde (riv.), Fr.
25/R3 Gizhiga (bay), Rus.
55/K2 Glace Bay, NS,Can
64/B6 Glaciares Nat'l Park, Arg.
50/D2 Glacier Nat'l Pk., BC,Can
50/E3 Glacier Nat'l Pk., Mt,US
18/C3 Glasgow, Sc,UK
52/D4 Glendale, Az,US
52/C4 Glendale, Ca,US
55/F3 Glens Falls, NY,US
18/D4 Gloucester, Eng,UK
34/B4 Goa (dist.), India
63/J7 Goânia, Braz.
28/E3 Gobi (des.), Asia
34/D4 Godavari (riv.), India
64/C3 Godoy Cruz, Arg.
49/M3 Godthåb (Nuuk) (cap.), Grld.
33/L1 Godwin Austen (K2) (mt.), Asia
63/J7 Goiânia, Braz.
45/E3 Gold Coast, Austl.
40/E7 Gold Coast (reg.), Gha.
53/F3 Golden, Co,US
57/J3 Goldsboro, NC,US
59/G4 Gonâve (gulf), Haiti
41/N5 Gonder, Eth.
42/C7 Good Hope (cape), SAfr.
52/B2 Goose (lake), US
49/L4 Goose Bay-Happy Valley, Nf,Can
34/D2 Gorakhpur, India
33/F2 Gorgān, Iran
23/F2 Gor'kiy (res.), Rus.
23/F2 Gor'kiy (Nizhniy Novgorod), Rus.
37/F3 Gorontalo, Indo.
23/C4 Goryn (riv.), Ukr.
19/H4 Gorzow Wielkopolski, Pol.
21/J3 Gostivar, FYROM
22/D4 Göteborg, Swe.
22/F4 Gotland (isl.), Swe.
18/G4 Göttingen, Ger.
19/L4 Goverla, Gora (mt.), Ukr.
63/K7 Governador Baladares, Braz.
28/D3 Govi Altayn (mts.), Mong.
24/G1 Graham Bell (isl.), Rus.
40/D6 Grain Coast (reg.), Libr.
18/C2 Grampian (mts.), Sc,UK
20/C4 Granada, Sp.
64/C6 Gran Altiplanicie Central (plat.), Arg.
64/C6 Gran Bajo Oriental (val.), Arg.
40/B2 Gran Canaria (isl.), Sp.
64/D2 Gran Chaco (reg.), SAm.
59/F2 Grand Bahama (isl.), Bahm.
52/D3 Grand Canyon Nat'l Pk., Az,US
58/E4 Grand Cayman (isl.), Cay.
62/F7 Grande (riv.), Bol.
63/J7 Grande (riv.), Braz.
63/K6 Grande (riv.), Braz.
50/D2 Grande Prairie, Ab,Can
40/H4 Grand 'Erg de Bilma (des.), Niger
40/E1 Grand Erg Occidental (des.), Alg.
40/G1 Grand Erg Oriental (des.), Alg., Tun.
56/C4 Grande, Rio (riv.), NAm.
59/J4 Grande-Terre (isl.), Guad.
51/J4 Grand Forks, ND,US
53/H2 Grand Island, Ne,US
52/E3 Grand Junction, Co,US
55/H2 Grand Manan (isl.), NB,Can
54/C3 Grand Rapids, Mi,US
50/F5 Grand Teton Nat'l Pk., Wy,US
59/G3 Grand Turk (cap.), Trks.
57/F2 Granite City, Il,US
62/F2 Gran Sabana, La (plain), Ven.
52/F4 Grants, NM,US
50/C5 Grants Pass, Or,US
62/C5 Gran Vilaya (ruins), Peru
20/F3 Grasse, Fr.
21/G2 Graz, Aus.
59/F2 Great Abaco (isl.), Bahm.
45/B4 Great Australian (bight), Austl.
45/D2 Great Barrier (reef), Austl.
50/C2 Great Basin (basin), US
52/D3 Great Basin Nat'l Park, Nv,US
49/E3 Great Bear (lake), Can.
53/H3 Great Bend, Ks,US
18/D2 Great Britain (isl.), UK
45/D4 Great Dividing (range), Austl.
59/F3 Greater Antilles (isls.), NAm.
36/C4 Greater Sunda (isls.), Indo.
59/F3 Great Exuma (isl.), Bahm.
50/F4 Great Falls, Mt,US
59/G3 Great Inagua (isl.), Bahm.
34/B2 Great Indian (Thar) (des.), India
42/D7 Great Karoo (reg.), SAfr.
53/G2 Great Plains (plains), US
42/F2 Great Rift (val.), Afr.
41/N6 Great Rift (val.), Djib., Eth.
52/D2 Great Salt (lake), Ut,US
41/K2 Great Sand Sea (des.), Afr.
45/B2 Great Sandy (des.), Austl.
49/F3 Great Slave (lake), NW,Can
57/H3 Great Smoky Mts. Nat'l Pk., NC,Tn,US
45/B3 Great Victoria (des.), Austl.
28/F4 Great Wall, China
21/J4 Greece
53/F2 Greeley, Co,US
52/E3 Green (riv.), US
55/F3 Green (mts.), Vt,US
54/B2 Green Bay, Wi,US
57/H2 Greeneville, Tn,US
55/F3 Greenfield, Ma,US
49/R2 Greenland (sea)
49/N2 Greenland, Den.
18/C3 Greenock, Sc,UK
57/J2 Greensboro, NC,US
54/E3 Greensburg, Pa,US
57/F3 Greenville, Ms,US
57/J3 Greenville, NC,US
57/H3 Greenville, SC,US
57/F3 Greenwood, Ms,US
57/H3 Greenwood, SC,US
45/D2 Gregory (range), Austl.
59/J5 Grenada
20/E2 Grenoble, Fr.
57/F4 Gretna, La,US
45/D3 Grey (range), Austl.
57/G3 Griffin, Ga,US
18/D3 Grimsby, Eng,UK
18/F3 Groningen, Neth.
45/C2 Groote Eylandt (isl.), Austl.
21/G2 Grossglockner (mt.), Aus.
23/G5 Groznyy, Rus.
59/F3 Guacanaybo (gulf), Cuba
58/A3 Guadalajara, Mex.
20/C3 Guadalajara, Sp.
46/E6 Guadalcanal (isl.), Sol.
20/B4 Guadalquivir (riv.), Sp.
58/B2 Guadalupe, Mex.
56/B3 Guadalupe (mts.), US
56/B4 Guadalupe Mts. Nat'l Pk., Tx,US
20/B3 Guadarrama (mts.), Sp.
59/J4 Guadeloupe, Fr.
59/J4 Guadeloupe Passage (chan.), West Indies
20/B4 Guadiana (riv.), Eur.
64/B5 Guafo (str.), Chile
62/E3 Guainiá (riv.), Col.
62/D1 Guajira (pen.), SAm.
64/C5 Gualicho (marsh), Arg.
46/D3 Guam
28/F5 Guangyuan, China
30/B3 Guangzhou (Canton), China
59/F3 Guantánamo, Cuba
62/F6 Guaporé (Iténez) (riv.), Braz.
62/E2 Guárico (res.), Ven.
58/C4 Guatemala
58/C5 Guatemala (cap.), Guat.
62/E3 Guaviare (riv.), Col.
62/B4 Guayaquil, Ecu.
62/B4 Guayaquil (gulf), Ecu.
59/M8 Guaymas, Mex.
19/H3 Guben (Wilhelm-Pieck-Stadt), Ger.
54/D3 Guelph, On,Can
18/D4 Guernsey (isl.), Chl.
62/F2 Guiana Highlands (mts.), SAm.
30/B2 Guilin, China
40/C5 Guinea
40/F7 Guinea (gulf), Afr.
40/B5 Guinea-Bissau
35/J2 Guiyang, China
35/K2 Gujranwala, Pak.
33/K2 Gujrāt, Pak.
34/C4 Gulbarga, India
56/D5 Gulf Coastal (plain), Tx,US
57/F4 Gulfport, Ms,US
23/F6 Güneydogu Toroslar (mts.), Turk.
34/D4 Guntur, India
64/F2 Gural (mts.), Braz.
62/F2 Guri (res.), Ven.
63/H4 Gurupá, Grande de (isl.), Braz.
63/J4 Gurupi (mts.), Braz.
63/J4 Gurupi (riv.), Braz.
23/H4 Gur'yev, Kaz.
53/H4 Guthrie, Ok,US
62/G3 Guyana
34/C2 Gwalior, India
42/E4 Gweru, Zim.
24/H2 Gyda (pen.), Rus.
21/H2 Győr, Hun.
23/F5 Gyumri, Arm.

H

18/F3 Haarlem, Neth.
32/E5 Hadhramaut (reg.), Yem.
29/K4 Haeju, NKor.
46/D3 Hagåtña (cap.), Guam
54/E4 Hagerstown, Md,US
18/F3 Hague, The (cap.), Neth.
29/J3 Haicheng, China
32/B2 Haifa, Isr.
30/B3 Haikou, China
30/B4 Hainan (isl.), China
29/J5 Haining, China
35/J3 Haiphong, Viet.
59/G4 Haiti
29/N3 Hakodate, Japan
32/C1 Halab (Aleppo), Syria
45/D2 Halifax (bay), Austl.
55/J2 Halifax (cap.), NS,Can
18/G4 Halle, Ger.
37/G3 Halmahera (isl.), Indo.
37/G4 Halmahera (sea), Indo.
22/E4 Hälsingborg, Swe.
32/E2 Hamadan, Iran
32/C1 Hamāh, Syria
29/M5 Hamamatsu, Japan
18/G3 Hamburg, Ger.
45/A3 Hamersley (range), Austl.
29/K3 Hamgyong (mts.), NKor.
29/K3 Hamhung, NKor.
54/E3 Hamilton, On,Can
45/H6 Hamilton, NZ
54/C4 Hamilton, Oh,US
18/F3 Hamm, Ger.
22/G1 Hammerfest, Nor.
54/C3 Hammond, In,US
57/F4 Hammond, La,US
54/E4 Hampton, Va,US
40/H3 Hamrā, Al Hamādah al (upland), Libya
29/K4 Han (riv.), SKor.
28/G4 Handan, China
52/C3 Hanford, Ca,US
28/D2 Hangayn (mts.), Mong.
30/D1 Hangzhou (Hangchow), China
53/K3 Hannibal, Mo,US
18/G3 Hannover, Ger.
35/J3 Hanoi (cap.), Viet.
55/F3 Hanover, NH,US
28/F5 Hanzhong, China
42/F4 Harare (cap.), Zim.
29/K2 Harbin, China
41/P6 Hargeysa, Som.
56/D5 Harlingen, Tx,US
54/E3 Harrisburg (cap.), Pa,US
54/E4 Harrisonburg, Va,US
54/C4 Harrodsburg, Ky,US
55/F3 Hartford (cap.), Ct,US
18/D3 Hartlepool, Eng,UK
18/G4 Harz (mts.), Ger.
53/H2 Hastings, Ne,US
57/F4 Hattiesburg, Ms,US
41/Q6 Haud (reg.), Eth.
58/E3 Havana (cap.), Cuba
52/D4 Havasu (lake), US
55/G3 Haverhill, Ma,US
50/F3 Havre, Mt,US
47/K2 Hawaii (state), US
47/K3 Hawaii (isl.), Hi,US
47/H2 Hawaiian (isls.), US
32/E3 Ḩawallī, Kuw.
49/F3 Hay River, NW,Can
53/H3 Hays, Ks,US
50/A2 Hazleton (mts.), BC,Can
54/F3 Hazleton, Pa,US
28/G4 Hebi, China
18/C2 Hebrides, Inner (isls.), Sc,UK
18/B2 Hebrides, Outer (isls.), Sc,UK
29/H5 Hefei, China
29/L2 Hegang, China
18/G4 Heidelberg, Ger.
18/G4 Heilbronn, Ger.
29/J1 Heilong (riv.), China
22/N7 Hekla (mt.), Ice.
28/F4 Helan (mts.), China
50/F4 Helena (cap.), Mt,US
33/H2 Helmand (riv.), Afg.
22/H3 Helsinki (cap.), Fin.
57/G2 Henderson, Ky,US
57/J2 Henderson, NC,US
52/D3 Henderson, Nv,US
35/G2 Hengduan (mts.), China
30/B2 Hengyang, China
33/H2 Herat, Afg.
59/M8 Hermosillo, Mex.
57/H5 Hialeah, Fl,US
51/K4 Hibbing, Mn,US
57/H3 Hickory, NC,US
57/H3 High Point, NC,US
19/K2 Hiiumaa (isl.), Est.
32/C3 Ḩijāz, Jabal al (mts.), SAr.
50/C4 Hillsboro, Or,US
47/K3 Hilo, Hi,US
27/G6 Himalaya (mts.), Asia
32/C2 Ḩimş, Syria
33/J1 Hindu Kush (mts.), Asia
29/N3 Hirosaki, Japan
29/L5 Hiroshima, Japan
59/G4 Hispaniola (isl.), NAm.
29/N4 Hitachi, Japan
45/D5 Hobart, Austl.
53/G4 Hobbs, NM,US
35/J5 Ho Chi Minh City (Saigon), Viet.
21/F2 Hohe Tauern (range), Aus.
28/G3 Hohhot, China
29/N3 Hokkaidō (isl.), Japan
59/F3 Holguín, Cuba
54/C3 Holland, Mi,US
57/H5 Hollywood, Fl,US
18/C3 Holyhead, Wal,UK
55/F3 Holyoke, Ma,US
57/H5 Homestead, Fl,US
19/M3 Homyel', Bela.
58/D4 Honduras
58/D4 Honduras (gulf), NAm.
30/B3 Hong Kong, China
46/E5 Honiara (cap.), Sol.
47/K2 Honolulu (cap.), Hi,US
29/M5 Honshu (isl.), Japan
50/C4 Hood (mt.), Or,US
52/D3 Hoover (dam), US
56/E3 Hope, Ar,US
54/E4 Hopewell, Va,US
54/B4 Hopkinsville, Ky,US
23/E4 Horlivka, Ukr.
33/G3 Hormuz (str.), Asia
64/C8 Horn (cape), Chile
54/E3 Hornell, NY,US
21/J2 Hortobágyi Nat'l Park, Hun.
56/E3 Hot Springs Nat'l Park, Ar,US
57/F4 Houma, La,US
56/E4 Houston, Tx,US
28/E1 Hövsgöl (lake), Mong.
47/H4 Howland (isl.), PacUS
34/E3 Howrah, India
19/H4 Hradec Králové, Czh.
19/K3 Hrodna, Bela.
30/D3 Hsinchu, Tai.
28/H5 Huaibei, China
30/B2 Huaihua, China
29/H5 Huainan, China
42/C3 Huambo, Ang.
62/C6 Huancayo, Peru
62/E8 Huanchaca (peak), Bol.
29/H4 Huang He (Yellow) (riv.), China
30/C2 Huangshi, China
62/C5 Huascarán (mt.), Peru
62/C5 Huascarán Nat'l Park, Peru
62/E6 Huatunas (lake), Bol.
28/F5 Huaying, China
34/C4 Hubli-Dharwar, India
18/D3 Huddersfield, Eng,UK
49/J3 Hudson (bay), Can.
49/K3 Hudson (str.), Can.
54/F3 Hudson (riv.), US
35/J4 Hue, Viet.
20/B4 Huelva, Sp.
42/B4 Huila (plat.), Ang.
62/C3 Huila (peak), Col.
54/F2 Hull, Qu,Can
18/D3 Hull, Eng,UK
28/H2 Hulun (lake), China
52/E4 Humphreys (peak), Az,US
21/H2 Hungary
29/K4 Hŭngnam, NKor.
29/K3 Hunjiang, China
54/C3 Huntington, In,US
54/D4 Huntington, WV,US
52/C4 Huntington Beach, Ca,US
57/G3 Huntsville, Al,US
56/E4 Huntsville, Tx,US
54/D2 Huron (lake), NAm.
51/J4 Huron, SD,US
53/H3 Hutchinson, Ks,US
29/J5 Huzhou, China
42/E4 Hwange Nat'l Park, Zim.
34/C4 Hyderabad, India
33/J3 Hyderabad, Pak.
20/E3 Hyères (isls.), Fr.

I

21/K2 Iaşi, Rom.
40/F6 Ibadan, Nga.
62/C3 Ibagué, Col.
64/E2 Iberá (marsh), Arg.
20/C3 Iberica, Sistema (range), Sp.
20/D4 Ibiza (isl.), Sp.
62/E4 Iça (riv.), Braz.
22/N7 Iceland
28/G5 Ichang (Yichang), China
50/E5 Idaho (state), US
50/E5 Idaho Falls, Id,US
40/F6 Ife, Nga.
40/F3 Iforas, Ardar des (mts.), Alg., Mali
64/F2 Iguaçu (riv.), Braz.
64/F2 Iguazú (falls), SAm.
64/F2 Iguazu Nat'l Park, Arg.
40/D2 Iguidi, Èrg (des.), Alg.
21/K4 Ikaria (isl.), Gre.
47/X15 Iles du Vent (isls.), FrPol.
40/F6 Ilesha, Nga.
63/H7 Ilha Salteira (res.), Braz.
62/E7 Illimani (mtn.), Bol.
54/B4 Illinois (state), US
54/B3 Illinois (riv.), Il,US
23/D2 Il'men (lake), Rus.
30/D5 Iloilo, Phil.
40/F6 Ilorin, Nga.
63/J5 Imperatriz, Braz.
35/F3 Imphal, India
29/K4 Inch'ŏn, SKor.
53/J3 Independence, Ks,US
53/J3 Independence, Mo,US
27/G7 India
54/C3 Indiana (state), US
54/E3 Indiana, Pa,US
54/C4 Indianapolis (cap.), In,US
15/N6 Indian Ocean
25/Q3 Indigirka (riv.), Rus.
52/C4 Indio, Ca,US
35/C1 Indochina (reg.), Asia
36/E4 Indonesia
34/C3 Indore, India
27/F7 Indus (riv.), Asia
62/C4 Ingapirca (ruins), Ecu.
18/G4 Ingolstadt, Ger.
21/G1 Inn (riv.), Eur.
18/C2 Inner Hebrides (isls.), Sc,UK
28/G3 Inner Mongolia (reg.), China
21/F2 Innsbruck, Aus.
35/G4 Insein, Myanmar
50/B2 Interior (plat.), BC,Can
51/H3 International Peace Garden, NAm.
49/D3 Inuvik, Can.
45/G6 Invercargill, NZ
18/C2 Inverness, Sc,UK
42/B4 Iona Nat'l Park, Ang.
21/H4 Ionian (sea), Eur.
21/H4 Ionian (isls.), Gre.
53/J2 Iowa (state), US
53/K2 Iowa City, Ia,US
63/K7 Ipatinga, Braz.
36/B3 Ipoh, Malay.
18/E3 Ipswich, Eng,UK
49/L3 Iqaluit, Can.
62/D8 Iquique, Chile
62/D4 Iquitos, Peru
21/K5 Iráklion, Gre.
27/E6 Iran
58/A3 Irapuato, Mex.
32/D2 Iraq
32/D1 Irbil, Iraq
18/B3 Ireland
18/C3 Ireland, Northern, UK
37/J4 Irian Jaya (reg.), Indo.
63/H4 Iriri (riv.), Braz.
18/C3 Irish (sea), Eur.
28/E1 Irkutsk, Rus.
21/J2 Iron Gate (gorge), Rom.
54/D4 Ironton, Oh,US
35/F4 Irrawaddy, Mouths of the (delta), Myanmar
24/G4 Irtysh (riv.), Rus.
52/C4 Irvine, Ca,US
53/H4 Irving, Tx,US
42/J11 Isala Massif (mts.), Madg.
18/G4 Isar (riv.), Ger.
20/E2 Isère (riv.), Fr.
40/F6 Iseyin, Nga.
62/E7 Isiboro Securé Nat'l Park, Bol.
23/E6 Iskenderun, Turk.
21/J3 Iskŭr (riv.), Bul.
33/K2 Islamabad (cap.), Pak.
64/B5 Isla Magdalena Nat'l Park, Chile
18/C3 Isle of Man, UK
54/B1 Isle Royale (isl.), Mi,US
54/B1 Isle Royale Nat'l Pk., Mi,US
32/B2 Ismailia, Egypt
31/B4 Ismail Samani (peak), Taj.
23/D6 Isparta, Turk.
32/B2 Israel
23/C5 Istanbul, Turk.
21/G2 Istria (pen.), Cro.
63/L6 Itabuna, Braz.
64/E1 Itaipu (res.), Braz., Par.
21/F3 Italy
63/K7 Itambé (peak), Braz.
63/L6 Itapicuru (riv.), Braz.
62/F6 Iténez (Guaporé) (riv.), Bol.
54/E3 Ithaca, NY,US
23/B4 Ivano-Frankivs'k, Ukr.
23/F2 Ivanovo, Rus.
40/D7 Ivory Coast (reg.), C.d'Iv.
57/N4 Iwaki, Japan
46/D2 Iwo Jima (isl.), Japan
23/H2 Izhevsk, Rus.
33/G4 Izkī, Oman
23/C6 Izmir, Turk.
23/C5 Izmit, Turk.

J

34/C3 Jabalpur, India
54/C3 Jackson, Mi,US
57/F3 Jackson (cap.), Ms,US
57/F3 Jackson, Tn,US
56/E3 Jacksonville, Ar,US
57/H4 Jacksonville, Fl,US
54/B4 Jacksonville, Il,US
57/J3 Jacksonville, NC,US
20/C4 Jaén, Sp.
34/C6 Jaffna, SrL.
34/C2 Jaipur, India
36/C5 Jakarta (cap.), Indo.
33/K2 Jalālābād, Afg.
58/B4 Jalapa, Mex.
34/C3 Jalgaon, India
59/F4 Jamaica
59/F4 Jamaica (chan.), Haiti, Jam.
63/G5 Jamanxim (riv.), Braz.
36/B4 Jambi, Indo.
49/J4 James (bay), Can.
54/E4 James (riv.), Va,US
51/J4 Jamestown, ND,US
54/E3 Jamestown, NY,US
33/K2 Jammu, India
34/B3 Jamnagar, India
34/E3 Jamshedpur, India
63/J3 Janaucu (isl.), Braz.
54/B3 Janesville, Wi,US
17/D1 Jan Mayen (isl.), Nor.
29/M4 Japan
29/L3 Japan (sea), Asia
29/M4 Japanese Alps (mts.), Japan
62/E4 Japurá (riv.), Braz.
63/H3 Jari (riv.), Braz.
47/J5 Jarvis (isl.), Pacific
63/H4 Jauaru (mts.), Braz.
62/F3 Jaua Sarisarinama Nat'l Park, Ven.
36/C5 Java (isl.), Indo.
36/D5 Java (sea), Indo.
37/K4 Jayapura, Indo.
53/J3 Jefferson City (cap.), Mo,US
54/C4 Jeffersonville, In,US
36/D5 Jember, Indo.
18/G4 Jena, Ger.
63/K7 Jequitinhonha (riv.), Braz.
20/B4 Jerez de la Frontera, Sp.
18/D4 Jersey (isl.), Chl.
32/D2 Jerusalem (cap.), Isr.
55/N6 Jésus (isl.), Qu,Can
21/H3 Jezerce (mt.), Alb.
33/K2 Jhang Sadar, Pak.
34/C2 Jhansi, India
33/K2 Jhelum, Pak.
29/L2 Jiamusi, China
30/D2 Jiaojiang, China
28/G4 Jiaozuo, China
29/J5 Jiaxing, China
32/C4 Jiddah, SAr.
29/K3 Jilin, China
29/H4 Jinan (Tsinan), China
30/C2 Jingdezhen, China
28/G5 Jingmen, China
30/C2 Jinhua, China
28/G3 Jining, China
29/J3 Jinzhou, China
30/C2 Jiujiang, China
29/L2 Jixi, China
32/D5 Jīzān, SAr.
63/M5 João Pessoa, Braz.
34/B2 Jodhpur, India
42/E6 Johannesburg, SAfr.
50/C4 John Day (riv.), Or,US
57/H2 Johnson City, Tn,US
47/J3 Johnston (atoll), PacUS
54/E3 Johnstown, Pa,US
36/B3 Johor Baharu, Malay.
64/G2 Joinvile, Braz.
54/B3 Joliet, Il,US
57/F3 Jonesboro, Ar,US
22/E4 Jönköping, Swe.
55/G1 Jonquière, Qu,Can
53/J3 Joplin, Mo,US
32/C2 Jordan
32/C2 Jordan (riv.), Asia
40/G6 Jos (plat.), Nga.
45/B2 Joseph Bonaparte (gulf), Austl.
50/B3 Juan de Fuca (str.), NAm.
61/A6 Juan Fernández (isls.), Chile
63/L5 Juazeiro do Norte, Braz.
20/C4 Júcar (riv.), Sp.
63/K8 Juiz de Fora, Braz.
63/G3 Juliana Top (peak), Sur.
33/L2 Jullundur, India
53/H3 Junction City, Ks,US
63/J8 Jundiaí, Braz.
49/D4 Juneau (cap.), Ak,US
20/F2 Jungfrau (mt.), Swi.
20/E2 Jura (mts.), Eur.
62/E4 Juruá (riv.), Braz.
58/E3 Juventud (isl.), Cuba

K

33/L1 K2 (mt.), Asia
41/M7 Kabalega Nat'l Park, Ugan.
33/J2 Kabul (cap.), Afg.
42/E3 Kabwe, Zam.
40/G5 Kaduna, Nga.
29/K4 Kaesŏng, NKor.
42/E4 Kafue (riv.), Zam.
42/E3 Kafue Nat'l Park, Zam.
29/L5 Kagoshima, Japan
23/E6 Kahramanmaras, Turk.
37/H5 Kai (isls.), Indo.
28/G5 Kaifeng, China
18/G4 Kaiserslautern, Ger.
35/H3 Kaiyuan, China
34/D4 Kakinada, India
49/N2 Kalaallit Nunaat (Greenland), Den.
42/D5 Kalahari (des.), Afr.
42/C6 Kalahari-Gemsbok Nat'l Park, Bots.
54/C3 Kalamazoo, Mi,US
41/K2 Kalanshiyū, Sahīr (des.), Libya
28/G3 Kalgan (Zhangjiakou), China
36/D4 Kalimantan (reg.), Indo.
19/K3 Kaliningrad (Königsberg), Rus.
19/J4 Kalisz, Pol.
23/E3 Kaluga, Rus.
25/R3 Kalyma (riv.), Rus.
17/K3 Kama (riv.), Rus.
25/R4 Kamchatka (pen.), Rus.
24/G4 Kamensk-Ural'skiy, Rus.
50/C3 Kamloops, BC,Can
41/M7 Kampala (cap.), Ugan.
23/C4 Kam'yanets' Podil's'kyy, Ukr.
23/G3 Kamyshin, Rus.
42/D2 Kananga, D.R. Congo
29/M4 Kanazawa, Japan
34/E2 Kanchenjunga (mt.), Asia
34/D6 Kandy, SrL.
45/C4 Kangaroo (isl.), Austl.
35/F2 Kangto (peak), China, India
24/E3 Kanin (pen.), Rus.
54/C3 Kankakee, Il,US
57/H3 Kannapolis, NC,US
41/G5 Kano, Nga.
34/D2 Kānpur, India
52/D2 Kansas (state), US
53/H3 Kansas (riv.), Ks,US
53/J3 Kansas City, Ks,US
53/J3 Kansas City, Mo,US
24/K4 Kansk, Rus.
62/G3 Kanuku (mts.), Guy.
30/D3 Kaohsiung, Tai.
42/B4 Kaokoveld, Namb.
42/B4 Kaokoveld (mts.), Namb.
41/B5 Kaolack, Sen.
36/C4 Kapuas (riv.), Indo.
24/G2 Kara (sea), Rus.
23/D5 Karabük, Turk.
33/J4 Karachi, Pak.
25/S4 Karaginskiy (isl.), Rus.
32/F1 Karaj, Iran
33/K1 Karakoram (mts.), Asia
28/E2 Karakorum (ruins), Mong.
24/F5 Karakumy (des.), Trkm.
25/S4 Karanginskiy (bay), Rus.
42/E4 Kariba (lake), Afr.
36/C4 Karimata (str.), Indo.
41/L8 Karisimbi (vol.), D.R. Congo
41/Q6 Karkaar (mts.), Som.
23/D4 Karkinits'ka Zatoka (gulf), Ukr.
19/H4 Karlovy Vary, Czh.
18/G4 Karlsruhe, Ger.
23/C6 Kárpathos (isl.), Gre.
23/F5 Kars, Turk.
42/C1 Kasai (riv.), D.R. Congo
32/F2 Kashan, Iran
30/C4 Kashi (Kashgar), China
41/N4 Kassala, Sudan
18/G4 Kassel, Ger.
33/K2 Kasūr, Pak.
55/G2 Katahdin (mt.), Me,US
42/D2 Katanga (reg.), D.R. Congo
34/E2 Kathmandu (cap.), Nepal
19/J4 Katowice, Pol.
40/G5 Katsina, Nga.
22/D4 Kattegat (str.), Eur.
47/K2 Kauai (isl.), Hi,US
42/C5 Kaukaveld, Namb.
19/K3 Kaunas, Lith.
29/M4 Kawasaki, Japan
23/E6 Kayseri, Turk.
31/B2 Kazakh (uplands), Kaz.
24/G5 Kazakhstan
23/G2 Kazan', Rus.
53/H2 Kearney, Ne,US
21/J5 Kecskemét, Hun.
36/D5 Kediri, Indo.
30/D2 Keelung, Tai.
55/F3 Keene, NH,US
36/B3 Kelang, Malay.
50/D3 Kelowna, BC,Can
50/C4 Kelso, Wa,US
24/J4 Kemerovo, Rus.
57/H5 Kendall, Fl,US
40/D1 Kenitra, Mor.
57/F4 Kenner, La,US
50/D4 Kennewick, Wa,US
54/C3 Kenosha, Wi,US
54/D3 Kent, Oh,US
54/B4 Kentucky (lake), US
54/C4 Kentucky (state), US
39/F4 Kenya
41/M8 Kenya (Batian) (mt.), Kenya
53/K2 Keokuk, Ia,US
23/E4 Kerch, Ukr.
21/H4 Kérkira (Corfu) (isl.), Gre.
46/G7 Kermadec (isls.), NZ
33/G2 Kerman, Iran
52/D4 Kerrville, Tx,US
24/J4 Ket' (riv.), Rus.
24/K2 Keta (riv.), Rus.
49/D4 Ketchikan, Ak,US
54/C4 Kettering, Oh,US
54/B2 Keweenaw (pen.), Mi,US
54/C2 Keweenaw (pt.), Mi,US
57/H5 Key West, Fl,US
29/M2 Khabarovsk, Rus.
21/J3 Khalkhidhikhi (pen.), Gre.
21/J4 Khalkis, Gre.
32/D5 Khamīs Mushayţ, SAr.
29/L3 Khanka (lake), China, Rus.
24/G3 Khanty-Mansiysk, Rus.
34/E3 Kharagpur, India
23/E3 Kharkiv, Ukr.
41/M4 Khartoum (cap.), Sudan
41/M4 Khartoum North, Sudan
25/L2 Khatanga (gulf), Rus.
25/L2 Khatanga (riv.), Rus.
23/D4 Kherson, Ukr.
21/K4 Khíos (isl.), Gre.
23/C4 Khmel'nytskyy, Ukr.
23/F3 Khopër (riv.), Rus.
32/E2 Khorramabad, Iran
32/E2 Khorramshahr, Iran
35/H4 Kho Sawai (plat.), Thai.
34/E3 Khulna, Bang.
33/J3 Khuzdār, Pak.
23/G6 Khvoy, Iran
33/K2 Khyber (pass), Asia
40/F5 Kiānji (lake), Nga.
18/G3 Kiel, Ger.
19/K4 Kielce, Pol.
23/D3 Kiev (cap.), Ukr.
42/F1 Kigali (cap.), Rwa.
42/C2 Kikwit, D.R. Congo

69
Kiev – Munto

56/E3 Kilgore, Tx,US
42/G1 Kilimanjaro (mt.), Tanz.
18/C3 Kilkenny, Ire.
18/B3 Killarney, Ire.
56/D4 Killeen, Tx,US
45/B2 Kimberley (plat.), Austl.
42/D6 Kimberley, SAfr.
29/K3 Kimch'aek, NKor.
23/F2 Kineshma, Rus.
45/D4 King (isl.), Austl.
45/B2 King (sound), Austl.
45/B2 King Leopold (ranges), Austl.
52/D4 Kingman, Az,US
52/C3 Kings Canyon Nat'l Pk., Ca,US
57/H2 Kingsport, Tn,US
59/F4 Kingston (cap.), Jam.
54/F3 Kingston, NY,US
59/J5 Kingstown (cap.), StV.
56/D5 Kingsville, Tx,US
42/C1 Kinshasa (cap.), D.R. Congo
57/J3 Kinston, NC,US
18/C3 Kintyre (pen.), Sc,UK
46/H5 Kiribati
23/D6 Kırıkkale, Turk.
47/K4 Kiritimati (isl.), Kiri.
53/J2 Kirksville, Mo,US
32/D1 Kirkuk, Iraq
23/D4 Kirovohrad, Ukr.
41/L7 Kisangani, D.R. Congo
41/M8 Kisumu, Kenya
29/L5 Kitakyushu, Japan
54/D3 Kitchener, On,Can
21/J4 Kithira (isl.), Gre.
42/E3 Kitwe, Zam.
42/E1 Kivu (lake), Afr.
23/D5 Kizilirmak (riv.), Turk.
22/E2 Kjølen (Kölen) (mts.), Eur.
21/G2 Klagenfurt, Aus.
19/K3 Klaipeda, Lith.
52/B2 Klamath (mts.), Ca,Or,US
50/C5 Klamath Falls, Or,US
25/S4 Klyuchevskaya Sopka (mtn.), Rus.
57/H3 Knoxville, Tn,US
29/L5 Kobe, Japan
18/F4 Koblenz, Ger.
37/H5 Kobroor (isl.), Indo.
29/L5 Kochi, Japan
49/B4 Kodiak (isl.), Ak,US
19/L2 Kohtla-Järva, Est.
54/C3 Kokomo, In,US
24/G4 Kökshetaū, Kaz.
24/D3 Kola (pen.), Rus.
34/B4 Kolhāpur, India
18/F4 Köln (Cologne), Ger.
23/E2 Kolomna, Rus.
23/D2 Kolpino, Rus.
42/E3 Kolwezi, D.R. Congo
25/R2 Kolyma (lowland), Rus.
25/R3 Kolyma (range), Rus.
25/S4 Komandorskiye (isls.), Rus.
19/J5 Komárno, Slvk.
37/E5 Komodo (isl.), Indo.
40/E6 Komoé (riv.), C.d'Iv.
25/L1 Komsomolets (isl.), Rus.
25/M1 Komsomol'sk-na-Amure, Rus.
33/J1 Kondūz, Afg.
18/G5 Konstanz, Ger.
35/J5 Kon Tum, Viet.
23/D6 Konya, Turk.
50/D3 Kootenai (riv.), US
21/G2 Koper, Slov.
24/G4 Kopeysk, Rus.
21/H3 Korčula (isl.), Cro.
29/J4 Korea (bay), China, NKor.
29/K5 Korea (str.), Japan, SKor.
29/K3 Korea, North
29/K4 Korea, South
29/N4 Koriyama, Japan
31/E3 Korla, China
46/C4 Koror (cap.), Palau
25/T5 Koryak (range), Rus.
23/C6 Kos (isl.), Gre.
45/D4 Kosciusko (mt.), Austl.
19/K4 Košice, Slvk.
21/J3 Kosovo (reg.), Yugo.
41/D6 Kossou (lake), C.d'Iv.
23/F2 Kostroma, Rus.
19/J3 Koszalin, Pol.
34/C2 Kota, India
36/B2 Kota Baharu, Malay.
37/E2 Kota Kinabalu, Malay.
25/P2 Kotel'nyy (isl.), Rus.
34/C6 Kotte, SrL.
49/A3 Kotzebue, Ak,US
63/H2 Kourou, FrG.
23/F2 Kovrov, Rus.
30/B3 Kowloon, China
35/G6 Kra (isth.), Thai.
36/C5 Krakatau (isl.), Indon.
19/J4 Kraków, Pol.
23/E4 Kramators'k, Ukr.
23/E4 Krasnodar, Rus.
24/K4 Krasnoyarsk, Rus.
35/H5 Kravanh (mts.), Camb.
23/D4 Kremenchuk, Ukr.
23/D4 Kremenchuts'ke (res.), Ukr.
25/T3 Kresta (gulf), Rus.
22/C4 Kristiansand, Nor.
21/G2 Krk (isl.), Cro.
42/F5 Kruger Nat'l Park, SAfr.
35/H5 Krung Thep (Bangkok), Thai.
23/D4 Kryvyy Rih, Ukr.
36/B3 Kuala Lumpur (cap.), Malay.
36/B2 Kuala Terengganu, Malay.
36/B3 Kuantan, Malay.
23/E4 Kuban (riv.), Rus.
36/D3 Kuching, Malay.
41/K3 Kufrah (oasis), Libya
23/G5 Kuma (riv.), Rus.
29/L5 Kumamoto, Japan
21/J3 Kumanovo, FYROM
40/E6 Kumasi, Gha.
35/G2 Kumon (range), Myanmar
42/E3 Kundelungu Nat'l Park, D.R. Congo
36/C5 Kuningan, Indo.
31/C4 Kunlun (mts.), Asia
35/H3 Kunming, China
29/K4 Kunsan, SKor.
37/F6 Kupang, Indo.
23/G6 Kura (riv.), Asia
32/D1 Kurdistan (reg.), Asia
21/K3 Kurdzhali, Bul.
24/K3 Kureyka (riv.), Rus.
24/G4 Kurgan, Rus.
25/Q5 Kuril (isls.), Rus.
34/C4 Kurnool, India
23/E3 Kursk, Rus.
28/B3 Kuruktag (mts.), China
29/L5 Kurume, Japan
29/N3 Kushiro, Japan
23/F5 K'ut'aisi, Geo.
34/A3 Kutch (gulf), India
34/A3 Kutch (reg.), India
34/A3 Kutch, Rann of (salt marsh), India
32/E3 Kuwait
32/E3 Kuwait (cap.), Kuw.
23/G2 Kuybyshev (res.), Rus.
23/H3 Kuybyshev (Samara), Rus.
46/F4 Kwajalein (atoll), Mrsh.
29/K4 Kwangju, SKor.
42/C1 Kwango (riv.), Ang., D.R. Congo
42/N7 Kyoga (lake), Ugan.
29/K4 Kyŏngju, SKor.
29/M4 Kyoto, Japan
31/B3 Kyrgyzstan
29/L5 Kyushu (isl.), Japan
28/C1 Kyzyl, Rus.

L

58/E6 La Amistad Int'l Park, CR
40/C2 Laayoune, WSah.
49/M4 Labrador (sea), Can.
49/L4 Labrador (reg.), Nf,Can
34/B5 Laccadive (sea), India
34/B5 Laccadive (Cannanore) (isls.), India
58/D4 La Ceiba, Hon.
45/C4 Lacepede (bay), Austl.
55/G3 Laconia, NH,US
20/A3 La Coruña, Sp.
54/B3 La Crosse, Wi,US
33/L2 Ladakh (mts.), Asia
24/D3 Ladoga (lake), Rus.
46/D5 Lae, PNG
54/C3 Lafayette, In,US
56/E4 Lafayette, La,US
64/F2 Lages, Braz.
40/F6 Lagos, Nga.
50/D4 La Grande, Or,US
57/G3 La Grange, Ga,US
33/K2 Lahore, Pak.
56/E4 Lake Charles, La,US
52/D4 Lake Havasu City, Az,US
57/H4 Lakeland, Fl,US
50/D3 Lake Louise, Ab,Can
50/F3 Lakewood, Ca,US
57/H5 Lake Worth, Fl,US
34/B5 Lakshadweep (isls.), India
20/C4 La Mancha (reg.), Sp.
40/H8 Lambaréné, Gabon
21/J4 Lamía, Gre.
47/K2 Lanai (isl.), Hi,US
18/D3 Lancaster, Eng,UK
52/C4 Lancaster, Ca,US
54/D4 Lancaster, Oh,US
54/E3 Lancaster, Pa,US
18/C4 Land's End (prom.), Eng,UK
29/H4 Langfang, China
20/E2 Langres (plat.), Fr.
54/C3 Lansing (cap.), Mi,US
30/C2 Lanxi, China
29/E4 Lanzhou (Lanchow), China
35/C2 Laos
62/E7 La Paz (cap.), Bol.
59/M9 La Paz, Mex.
29/N2 La Pérouse (str.), Asia
22/F1 Lapland (reg.), Eur.
54/C3 La Porte, In,US
25/M2 Laptev (sea), Rus.
50/G5 Laramie (mts.), US
50/G5 Laramie, Wy,US
56/D5 Laredo, Tx,US
57/H5 Largo, Fl,US
21/J4 Lárisa, Gre.
33/J3 Lārkāna, Pak.
20/C2 La Rochelle, Fr.
59/H4 La Romana, DRep.
52/F4 Las Cruces, NM,US
40/B2 Las Palmas de Gran Canaria, Sp.
21/F2 La Spezia, It.
52/B2 Lassen Volcanic Nat'l Pk., Ca,US
53/F4 Las Vegas, NM,US
52/C3 Las Vegas, Nv,US
32/C1 Latakia, Syria
21/G3 Latina, It.
19/L2 Latvia
62/E7 Lauca Nat'l Park, Chile
45/D5 Launceston, Austl.
57/F4 Laurel, Ms,US
54/C1 Laurentian (plat.), Can.
21/E2 Lausanne, Swi.
37/E4 Laut (isl.), Indo.
55/F2 Laval, Qu,Can
53/J3 Lawrence, Ks,US
55/G3 Lawrence, Ma,US
53/H4 Lawton, Ok,US
53/J3 Leavenworth, Ks,US
32/C2 Lebanon
54/E3 Lebanon, Pa,US
21/H4 Lecce, It.
18/D3 Leeds, Eng,UK
18/F3 Leeuwarden, Neth.
59/J4 Leeward (isls.), NAm.
19/J4 Legnica, Pol.
20/D2 Le Havre, Fr.
18/D3 Leicester, Eng,UK
18/F3 Leiden, Neth.
18/C3 Leinster (reg.), Ire.
19/H4 Leipzig, Ger.
30/A3 Leizhou (pen.), China
20/D1 Le Mans, Fr.
25/N3 Lena (riv.), Rus.
63/K4 Lençóis Maranhenses Nat'l Park, Braz.
30/B2 Lengshuijiang, China
30/B2 Lengshuitan, China
31/B4 Lenina (peak), Kyr., Taj.
24/J4 Leninsk-Kuznetskiy, Rus.
20/D1 Lens, Fr.
58/A3 León, Mex.
58/D5 León, Nic.
20/B3 León, Sp.
20/F2 Lepontine Alps (mts.), It., Swi.
20/D3 Lérida (Lleida), Sp.
35/H2 Leshan, China
21/J3 Leskovac, Yugo.
42/E6 Lesotho
59/H4 Lesser Antilles (isls.), NAm.
50/E2 Lesser Slave (lake), Ab,Can
21/K4 Lésvos (isl.), Gre.
37/G5 Leti (isls.), Indo.
18/C2 Lewis (isl.), Sc,UK
50/E3 Lewis (range), Mt,US
18/C2 Lewis, Butt of (prom.), Sc,UK
50/D4 Lewiston, Id,US
55/G2 Lewiston, Me,US
54/C4 Lexington, Ky,US
57/H3 Lexington, NC,US
30/D5 Leyte (isl.), Phil.
31/F6 Lhasa, China
20/D3 L'Hospitalet, Sp.
29/H5 Lianyungang, China
28/H4 Liaocheng, China
29/J3 Liaodong (gulf), China
29/K3 Liaoyuan, China
53/G3 Liberal, Ks,US
19/H4 Liberec, Czh.
40/D6 Liberia
40/G7 Libreville (cap.), Gabon
41/J2 Libya
41/K2 Libyan (des.), Afr.
41/K1 Libyan (plat.), Afr.
28/F5 Lichuan, China
21/G3 Lido di Ostia, It.
21/F2 Liechtenstein
18/F4 Liège, Belg.
19/K2 Liepāja, Lat.
20/F3 Ligurian (sea), It.
42/E3 Likasi, D.R. Congo
20/D1 Lille, Fr.
22/D3 Lillehammer, Nor.
42/F3 Lilongwe (cap.), Malw.
62/C6 Lima (cap.), Peru
54/C3 Lima, Oh,US
32/B2 Limassol, Cyp.
64/C4 Limay (riv.), Arg.
63/J8 Limeira, Braz.
18/B3 Limerick, Ire.
21/K4 Límnos (isl.), Gre.
20/D2 Limoges, Fr.
58/E5 Limón, CR
42/F5 Limpopo (riv.), Afr.
30/C2 Linchuan, China
54/B3 Lincoln, Il,US
53/H2 Lincoln (cap.), Ne,US
47/K4 Line (isls.), Kiri.
36/B3 Lingga (isl.), Indo.
22/E4 Linköping, Swe.
21/G1 Linz, Aus.
20/D3 Lions (gulf), Fr.
29/J3 Lioyang, China
21/G4 Lipari (isls.), It.
23/E3 Lipetsk, Rus.
62/E8 Lipez (mts.), Bol.
20/A4 Lisbon (cap.), Port.
18/C3 Lisburn, NI,UK
19/K3 Lithuania
59/E4 Little Cayman (isl.), Cay.
52/E4 Little Colorado (riv.), US
53/J4 Little Rock (cap.), Ar,US
30/A3 Liuzhou, China
18/D3 Liverpool, Eng,UK
50/E3 Livingstone (range), Ab,Can
42/B2 Livingstone (falls), D.R. Congo
42/E4 Livingstone, Zam.
21/F3 Livorno (Leghorn), It.
21/G2 Ljubljana (cap.), Slov.
56/C3 Llano Estacado (plain), US
62/D3 Llanos (plain), SAm.
20/D3 Lleida (Lérida), Sp.
64/C1 Llullaillaco (vol.), Chile
42/B3 Lobito, Ang.
54/E3 Lockport, NY,US
52/B3 Lodi, Ca,US
19/J4 Łódź, Pol.
22/D2 Lofoten (isls.), Nor.
49/D3 Logan (mt.), ,Can
52/E2 Logan, Ut,US
54/C3 Logansport, In,US
20/C3 Logroño, Sp.
20/C2 Loire (riv.), Fr.
41/N8 Loita (hills), Kenya
40/C6 Loma (mts.), SLeo.
64/E3 Lomas de Zamora, Arg.
63/H3 Lombarda (mts.), Braz.
37/E5 Lombok (isl.), Indo.
40/F6 Lomé (cap.), Togo
18/C2 Lomond (lake), Sc,UK
52/B4 Lompoc, Ca,US
54/D3 London, On,Can
18/E4 London (cap.), Eng,UK
18/C2 Londonderry, NI,UK
64/F1 Londrina, Braz.
59/F3 Long (isl.), Bahm.
25/T2 Long (str.), Rus.
55/F3 Long (isl.), NY,US
52/C4 Long Beach, Ca,US
54/F3 Long Branch, NJ,US
55/G2 Longfellow (mts.), Me,US
53/F2 Longmont, Co,US
55/K2 Long Range (mts.), Nf,Can
56/E3 Longview, Tx,US
50/C4 Longview, Wa,US
35/J5 Long Xuyen, Viet.
30/C2 Longyan, China
25/R4 Lopatka (cape), Rus.
30/E3 Lop Nur (Lop Nor) (dry lake), China
54/D3 Lorain, Oh,US
46/E8 Lord Howe (isl.), Austl.
20/C2 Lorient, Fr.
20/E1 Lorraine (reg.), Fr.
53/F4 Los Alamos, NM,US
52/C4 Los Angeles, Ca,US
59/N8 Los Mochis, Mex.
62/E1 Los Roques (isls.), Ven.
62/E1 Los Teques, Ven.
35/H4 Louangphrabang, Laos
30/B2 Loudi, China
56/E4 Louisiana (state), US
54/C4 Louisville, Ky,US
20/C3 Lourdes, Fr.
53/F2 Loveland, Co,US
55/G3 Lowell, Ma,US
24/K3 Lower Tunguska (riv.), Rus.
42/E4 Lower Zambezi Nat'l Park, Zam.
47/V12 Loyalty (isls.), NCal.
42/E1 Lualaba (riv.), D.R. Congo
42/B2 Luanda (cap.), Ang.
42/F3 Luangwa (riv.), Moz., Zam.
42/F3 Luangwa Nat'l Park, Zam.
42/E3 Luanshya, Zam.
56/C3 Lubbock, Tx,US
18/G3 Lübeck, Ger.
19/K4 Lublin, Pol.
42/E3 Lubumbashi, D.R. Congo
20/F2 Lucerne (Luzern), Swi.
34/D2 Lucknow, India
29/J4 Lüda (Dalian), China
33/L2 Ludhiana, India
56/E4 Lufkin, Tx,US
21/F2 Lugano, Swi.
42/G3 Lugenda (riv.), Moz.
20/B3 Lugo, Sp.
23/E4 Luhans'k, Ukr.
22/G2 Luleå, Swe.
57/J3 Lumberton, NC,US
18/G3 Lüneburg, Ger.
29/G5 Luoyang, China
42/E2 L'Upemba Nat'l Park, D.R. Congo
42/G3 Lúrio (riv.), Moz.
42/E4 Lusaka (cap.), Zam.
18/D4 Luton, Eng,UK
23/C3 Luts'k, Ukr.
18/F4 Luxembourg
18/F4 Luxembourg (cap.), Lux.
32/B3 Luxor, Egypt
30/D4 Luzon (isl.), Phil.
23/B4 Lviv, Ukr.
18/D4 Lyme (bay), Eng,UK
57/J2 Lynchburg, Va,US
55/G3 Lynn, Ma,US
20/E2 Lyon, Fr.
23/E4 Lysychans'k, Ukr.

M

22/H1 Maanselkä (mts.), Fin.
18/F4 Maas (riv.), Neth.
18/F4 Maastricht, Neth.
64/B6 Maca (mtn.), Chile
63/H3 Macapa, Braz.
30/B3 Macau, Port.
45/C3 Macdonnell (ranges), Austl.
21/J3 Macedonia, Former Yugoslav Republic of
63/L5 Maceió, Braz.
62/B4 Machala, Ecu.
62/D6 Machu Picchu (ruins), Peru
49/E3 Mackenzie (riv.), NW,Can
54/B3 Macomb, Il,US
20/E2 Mâcon, Fr.
57/H3 Macon, Ga,US
45/D4 Macquarie (riv.), Austl.
32/C2 Ma'daba, Jor.
42/K10 Madagascar
62/F5 Madeira (riv.), Braz.
40/B1 Madeira (isls.), Port.
54/B3 Madison (cap.), Wi,US
36/D5 Madiun, Indo.
62/E6 Madre de Dios (riv.), Bol.
58/A4 Madre del Sur, Sierra (mts.), Mex.
59/N8 Madre Occidental, Sierra (range), Mex.
58/A2 Madre Oriental, Sierra (range), Mex.
20/C3 Madrid (cap.), Sp.
36/D5 Madura (isl.), Indo.
34/C6 Madurai, India
29/M4 Maebashi, Japan
25/R4 Magadan, Rus.
55/J2 Magdalen (isls.), Qu,Can
62/D3 Magdalena (riv.), Col.
18/G3 Magdeburg, Ger.
36/C5 Magelang, Indo.
64/B7 Magellan (str.), SAm.
24/F4 Magnitogorsk, Rus.
19/M3 Mahilyow, Bela.
40/H5 Maiduguri, Nga.
41/L8 Maiko Nat'l Park, D.R. Congo
18/G4 Main (riv.), Ger.
55/G3 Maine (gulf), US
55/G2 Maine (state), US
18/G4 Mainz, Ger.
20/E4 Majorca (isl.), Sp.
46/G4 Majuro (atoll), Mrsh.
34/E2 Makālu (peak), China, Nepal
37/E4 Makassar (str.), Indo.
23/G5 Makhachkala, Rus.
23/E4 Makiyivka, Ukr.
33/H3 Makran (reg.), Iran, Pak.
33/G3 Makran Coast (reg.), Asia
34/B5 Malabar (coast), India
40/G7 Malabo (cap.), EqG.
36/A3 Malacca (str.), Asia
20/B4 Málaga, Sp.
36/D5 Malang, Indo.
42/C2 Malange, Ang.
23/E6 Malatya, Turk.
42/F3 Malawi
36/B2 Malay (pen.), Asia
36/B3 Malaya (reg.), Malay.
32/E2 Malāyer, Iran
36/C2 Malaysia
27/G9 Maldives
27/G9 Male (cap.), Mald.
34/B3 Malegaon, India
40/E4 Mali
22/E5 Malmö, Swe.
62/B3 Malpelo (isl.), Col.
21/G5 Malta
37/J4 Mamberamo (riv.), Indo.
54/C4 Mammoth Cave Nat'l Pk., Ky,US
62/F4 Manacapura, Grande de (lake), Braz.
37/F3 Manado, Indo.
58/D5 Managua (cap.), Nic.
32/F3 Manama (cap.), Bahr.
34/D2 Manaslu (mtn.), Nepal
54/E4 Manassas, Va,US
62/F4 Manaus, Braz.
18/D4 Manchester, Eng,UK
55/G3 Manchester, NH,US
29/J3 Manchuria (reg.), China
35/G3 Mandalay, Myanmar
51/H4 Mandan, ND,US
41/P5 Mandeb, Bab el (str.), Afr., Asia
21/H3 Manfredonia (gulf), It.
63/J6 Mangabeiras (uplands), Braz.
34/B5 Mangalore, India
53/H3 Manhattan, Ks,US
50/D5 Manila (cap.), Phil.
23/C6 Manisa, Turk.
18/C3 Man, Isle of (isl.), UK
51/J2 Manitoba (prov.), Can.
54/D2 Manitoulin (isl.), On,Can
54/C2 Manitowoc, Wi,US
62/C2 Manizales, Col.
51/K5 Mankato, Mn,US
34/C6 Mannar (gulf), India, SrL.
18/G4 Mannheim, Ger.
54/D3 Mansfield, Oh,US
62/B4 Manta, Ecu.
63/K8 Mantiqueira (mts.), Braz.
21/F2 Mantova, It.
62/D6 Manú (riv.), Peru
45/H6 Manukau, NZ
62/D6 Manú Nat'l Park, Peru
59/P10 Manzanillo, Mex.
37/J4 Maoke (mts.), Indo.
30/B3 Maoming, China
42/F6 Maputo (cap.), Moz.
63/J3 Maracá (isl.), Braz.
62/D1 Maracaibo, Ven.
62/D2 Maracaibo (lake), Ven.
63/H7 Maracaju (mts.), Braz.
62/E1 Maracay, Ven.
32/E1 Marāgheh, Iran
63/J4 Marajó (bay), Braz.
63/H4 Marajó (isl.), Braz.
62/C4 Marañón (riv.), Peru
20/B4 Marbella, Sp.
64/D3 Mar Chiquita (lake), Arg.
33/K2 Mardān, Pak.
64/E4 Mar del Plata, Arg.
63/F1 Margarita (isl.), Ven.
41/L7 Margherita (peak), D.R. Congo
58/E3 Marianao, Cuba
21/G2 Maribor, Slov.
43/T Marie Byrd Land (reg.), Ant.
57/G3 Marietta, Ga,US
63/H8 Marília, Braz.
63/H8 Maringá, Braz.
54/C3 Marion, In,US
54/D3 Marion, Oh,US
23/E4 Mariupol', Ukr.
54/E3 Markham, On,Can
23/C5 Marmara (sea), Turk.
20/E1 Marne (riv.), Fr.
63/H3 Maroni (riv.), Braz.
47/M5 Marquesas (isls.), FrPol.
54/C2 Marquette, Mi,US
41/K5 Marrah, Jabal (mts.), Sudan
62/E3 Marrahuaca (mtn.), Ven.
40/D1 Marrakech, Mor.
20/E3 Marseille, Fr.
56/E3 Marshall, Tx,US
46/G3 Marshall Islands
53/J2 Marshalltown, Ia,US
36/D4 Martapura, Indo.
55/G3 Martha's Vineyard (isl.), Ma,US
19/J4 Martin, Slvk.
59/J4 Martinique, Fr.
59/J4 Martinique Passage (chan.), West Indies
24/G6 Mary, Trkm.
54/E4 Maryland (state), US
55/L2 Marystown, Nf,Can
40/H3 Marzūq, Sahrā (des.), Libya
42/G1 Masai Steppe (grsld.), Tanz.
29/K4 Masan, SKor.
30/D5 Masbate (isl.), Phil.
42/E6 Maseru (cap.), Les.
32/G1 Mashhad, Iran
33/H3 Māshkel, Hāmūn-i (lake), Pak.
33/G4 Masira (gulf), Oman
32/E2 Masjed-e Soleymān, Iran
53/J2 Mason City, Ia,US
55/F3 Massachusetts (state), US
20/D2 Massif Central (plat.), Fr.
54/D3 Massillon, Oh,US
42/B2 Matadi, D.R. Congo
56/D4 Matagorda (isl.), Tx,US
58/B2 Matamoros, Mex.
55/H1 Matane, Qu,Can
58/E3 Matanzas, Cuba
37/E5 Mataram, Indo.
46/H6 Mata Utu (cap.), Wall.
63/G6 Mato Grosso (plat.), Braz.
29/L5 Matsuyama, Japan
20/E2 Matterhorn (mt.), Eur.
54/B4 Mattoon, Il,US
62/F2 Maturín, Ven.
47/K2 Maui (isl.), Hi,US
40/C4 Mauritania
15/M7 Mauritius
55/F4 May (cape), NJ,US
59/G3 Mayaguana (isl.), Bah.
59/H4 Mayagüez, PR
23/F5 Maykop, Rus.
39/G6 Mayotte, Fr.
33/J1 Mazar-i-Sharif, Afg.
59/N9 Mazatlán, Mex.
19/K3 Mazury (reg.), Pol.
19/M3 Mazyr, Bela.
42/F6 Mbabane (cap.), Swaz.
41/J7 Mbandaka, D.R. Congo
42/F2 Mbeya, Tanz.
42/F2 Mbeya (range), Tanz.
42/D2 Mbuji-Mayi, D.R. Congo
53/J4 McAlester, Ok,US
56/D5 McAllen, Tx,US
15/N8 McDonald (isls.), Austl.
54/E3 McKeesport, Pa,US
49/B3 McKinley (mt.), Ak,US
49/G2 M'Clintock (chan.), Can.
52/D3 Mead (lake), US
63/J5 Mearim (riv.), Braz.
32/C4 Mecca, SAr.
18/G3 Mecklenburger Bucht (bay), Ger.
19/K2 Mecsek (mts.), Hun.
36/A3 Medan, Indo.
62/C2 Medellín, Col.
50/C5 Medford, Or,US
52/F2 Medicine Bow (range), Wy,US
50/F3 Medicine Hat, Ab,Can
32/C4 Medina, SAr.
15/K4 Mediterranean (sea)
34/C2 Meerut, India
40/D1 Meknès, Mor.
35/J5 Mekong (riv.), Asia
35/J6 Mekong, Mouths of the (riv.), Viet.
36/B3 Melaka (Malacca), Malay.
46/E5 Melanesia (reg.), Pacific
45/D4 Melbourne, Austl.
57/H4 Melbourne, Fl,US
20/C5 Melilla, Sp.
23/E4 Melitopol', Ukr.
45/C2 Melville (isl.), Austl.
49/F2 Melville (isl.), Can.
49/J3 Melville (pen.), Can.
18/G5 Memmingen, Ger.
57/F3 Memphis, Tn,US
64/C3 Mendoza, Arg.
54/B3 Menominee Falls, Wi,US
36/A4 Mentawai (isls.), Indo.
54/D3 Mentor, Oh,US
20/E2 Mercantour Nat'l Park, Fr.
52/B3 Merced, Ca,US
64/C3 Mercedario (mtn.), Arg.
35/G5 Mergui (arch.), Myanmar
58/D3 Mérida, Mex.
20/B4 Mérida, Sp.
62/D2 Mérida, Ven.
62/E2 Mérida (mts.), Ven.
57/F3 Meridian, Ms,US
64/E3 Merlo, Arg.
41/M4 Meroe (ruins), Sudan
23/D6 Mersin, Turk.
52/E4 Mesa, Az,US
52/E3 Mesa Verde Nat'l Pk., Co,US
64/E3 Mesopotamia (reg.), Arg.
32/D2 Mesopotamia (reg.), Iraq
56/D3 Mesquite, Tx,US
21/G4 Messina, It.
21/J4 Messini (gulf), Gre.
21/G2 Mestre, It.
62/D2 Meta (riv.), Ven.
57/F4 Metairie, La,US
20/E1 Metz, Fr.
20/E1 Meuse (riv.), Eur.
59/L7 Mexicali, Mex.
63/J3 Mexicana (isl.), Braz.
58/A3 Mexico
58/C3 Mexico (gulf), NAm.
58/B4 Mexico (cap.), Mex.
33/H1 Meymaneh, Afg.
57/H5 Miami, Fl,US
57/H5 Miami Beach, Fl,US
28/E5 Mianyang, China
24/F4 Miass, Rus.
54/C2 Michigan (lake), US
54/C2 Michigan (state), US
54/C3 Michigan City, In,US
54/C2 Michipicoten (isl.), On,Can
23/F3 Michurinsk, Rus.
46/E3 Micronesia (reg.), Pacific
46/D4 Micronesia, Fed. States of
55/F3 Middlebury, Vt,US
18/D3 Middlesbrough, Eng,UK
54/E2 Midland, On,Can
54/C3 Midland, Mi,US
56/C4 Midland, Tx,US
46/H2 Midway Islands, PacUS
53/H4 Midwest City, Ok,US
21/K4 Mikonos (isl.), Gre.
62/C4 Milagro, Ecu.
21/F2 Milan, It.
51/K4 Mille Lacs (lake), Mn,US
54/C3 Milwaukee, Wi,US
37/F3 Minahasa (pen.), Indo.
18/C2 Minch, The (sound), Sc,UK
30/D6 Mindanao (isl.), Phil.
30/D5 Mindoro (isl.), Phil.
23/G5 Mingäçevir, Azer.
33/K2 Mingāora, Pak.
51/K4 Minneapolis, Mn,US
51/K4 Minnesota (state), US
20/B3 Miño (riv.), Sp.
20/E3 Minorca (Menorca) (isl.), Sp.
51/H3 Minot, ND,US
19/L3 Minsk (cap.), Bela.
36/D3 Miri, Malay.
64/F3 Mirim (lake), Braz.
33/L1 Mīrpur, Pak.
21/J4 Mirtóön (sea), Gre.
54/C3 Mishawaka, In,US
64/F2 Misiones (mts.), Arg.
21/J1 Miskolc, Hun.
37/H4 Misool (isl.), Indo.
40/J1 Miṣrātah, Libya
56/D5 Mission, Tx,US
52/C4 Mission Viejo, Ca,US
57/F4 Mississippi (riv.), US
57/F3 Mississippi (state), US
50/E4 Missoula, Mt,US
53/J3 Missouri (riv.), US
53/J3 Missouri (state), US
62/D7 Misti, El (mt.), Peru
41/L8 Mitimbu (mts.), D.R. Congo
58/B4 Mitla (ruin), Mex.
29/M4 Mito, Japan
64/C7 Mitre (pen.), Arg.
42/E3 Mitumba (mts.), D.R. Congo
29/L5 Miyazaki, Japan
57/F4 Mobile, Al,US
21/F2 Modena, It.
52/B3 Modesto, Ca,US
41/Q7 Mogadishu (cap.), Som.
31/A3 Moinkum (des.), Kaz.
52/C4 Mojave (des.), Ca,US
62/E6 Mojos (plain), Bol.
29/K5 Mokp'o, SKor.
19/M5 Moldova
21/K2 Moldoveanu (peak), Eur.
54/B3 Moline, Il,US
47/K2 Molokai (isl.), Hi,US
37/G4 Molucca (sea), Indo.
37/G3 Moluccas (isls.), Indo.
42/G1 Mombasa, Kenya
62/E6 Momoré (riv.), Bol.
49/H4 Mona (passage), NAm.
20/E3 Monaco
50/D3 Monashee (mts.), BC,Can
55/H2 Moncton, NB,Can
28/D2 Mongolia
56/E3 Monroe, La,US
54/D3 Monroe, Mi,US
40/C6 Monrovia (cap.), Libr.
18/E4 Mons, Belg.
50/F4 Montana (state), US
62/D6 Montaña, La (reg.), Peru
21/F3 Montecristo (isl.), It.
59/F4 Montego Bay, Jam.
21/H3 Montenegro (rep.), Yugo.
63/L7 Monte Pascoal Nat'l Park, Braz.
52/B3 Monterey, Ca,US
62/C2 Montería, Col.
58/A2 Monterrey, Mex.
63/K7 Montes Claros, Braz.
64/E3 Montevideo (cap.), Uru.
57/G3 Montgomery (cap.), Al,US
54/F2 Mont-Laurier, Qu,Can
55/G2 Montmagny, Qu,Can
55/F2 Montpelier (cap.), Vt,US
20/D3 Montpellier, Fr.
54/F2 Montréal, Qu,Can
55/N6 Mont-Royal, Qu,Can
59/J4 Montserrat, UK
20/D3 Montserrat (mt.), Sp.
35/F3 Monywa, Myanmar
21/F2 Monza, It.
53/H4 Moore, Ok,US
47/K6 Moorea (isl.), FrPol.
51/J4 Moorhead, Mn,US
55/G2 Moosehead (lake), Me,US
50/G3 Moose Jaw, Sk,Can
34/C1 Moradabad, India
19/J4 Morava (riv.), Eur.
21/J3 Morava (riv.), Yugo.
19/J4 Moravia (reg.), Czh.
18/D2 Moray (firth), Sc,UK
58/A4 Morelia, Mex.
20/B4 Morena, Sierra (range), Sp.
52/C4 Moreno Valley, Ca,US
57/F4 Morgan City, La,US
54/E4 Morgantown, WV,US
29/N4 Morioka, Japan
30/D6 Moro (gulf), Phil.
40/C1 Morocco
64/E3 Morón, Arg.
39/G6 Moroni (cap.), Com.
37/G3 Morotai (isl.), Indo.
57/H2 Morristown, Tn,US
63/J6 Morro Alto (peak), Braz.
63/H6 Mortes (riv.), Braz.
23/E2 Moscow (cap.), Rus.
50/D4 Moscow, Id,US
18/F4 Mosel (riv.), Ger.
20/E1 Moselle (riv.), Fr.
50/D4 Moses Lake, Wa,US
58/E5 Mosquito Coast (reg.), Nic.
58/E6 Mosquitos (gulf), Pan.
63/L5 Mossoró, Braz.
57/F4 Moss Point, Ms,US
19/H4 Most, Czh.
40/E1 Mostaganem, Alg.
21/H3 Mostar, Bosn.
32/D1 Mosul, Iraq
58/D5 Motagua (riv.), Guat.
18/D3 Motherwell, Sc,UK
35/G4 Moulmein, Myanmar
55/L2 Mount Pearl, Nf,Can
50/C4 Mount Rainier Nat'l Pk., Wa,US
54/B4 Mount Vernon, Il,US
54/D3 Mount Vernon, Oh,US
50/C3 Mount Vernon, Wa,US
42/G4 Mozambique
39/G6 Mozambique (chan.), Afr.
42/F3 Muchinga (mts.), Zam.
29/K3 Mudanjiang, China
42/E3 Mufulira, Zam.
42/E2 Muhila (mts.), D.R. Congo
19/K4 Mukacheve, Ukr.
19/H4 Mulde (riv.), Ger.
20/C4 Mulhacén (mt.), Sp.
20/E2 Mulhouse, Fr.
32/K2 Multan, Pak.
34/B4 Mumbai (Bombay), India
54/C3 Muncie, In,US
18/G4 Munich (München), Ger.
64/B7 Muñoz Gamero (pen.), Chile
18/F4 Münster, Ger.
36/C4 Muntok, Indo.

70

Mupa - Quetta

42/C4 Mupa Nat'l Park, Ang.
64/B6 Murallón (mtn.), Chile
20/C4 Murcia, Sp.
21/J2 Mureş (riv.), Rom.
57/G3 Murfreesboro, Tn,US
33/G3 Mūrī ān, Hāmūn-e Jaz (lake), Iran
17/H2 Murmansk, Rus.
21/G2 Mur (Mura) (riv.), Eur.
23/F2 Murom, Rus.
45/D4 Murray (riv.), Austl.
45/D4 Murrumbidgee (riv.), Austl.
33/G3 Musandam (pen.), Oman
33/G4 Muscat (cap.), Oman
45/C3 Musgrave (ranges), Austl.
54/C3 Muskegon, Mi,US
53/J4 Muskogee, Ok,US
42/F4 Mutare, Zim.
34/E2 Muzaffarpur, India
42/F1 Mwanza, Tanz.
42/E2 Mweru (lake), Afr.
35/G3 Myanmar (Burma)
23/D4 Mykolayiv, Ukr.
57/J3 Myrtle Beach, SC,US
34/C5 Mysore, India
35/J5 My Tho, Viet.

N

23/H2 Naberezhnye Chelny, Rus.
32/C2 Nabulus, WBnk.
56/E4 Nacogdoches, Tx,US
35/F2 Nagaland (state), India
29/M4 Nagano, Japan
29/M4 Nagaoka, Japan
29/K5 Nagasaki, Japan
34/C6 Nagercoil, India
23/G6 Nagorno-Karabakh (reg.), Azer.
29/M4 Nagoya, Japan
34/C3 Nagpur, India
30/E2 Naha, Japan
64/B5 Nahuel Huapi Nat'l Park, Arg.
41/M8 Nairobi (cap.), Kenya
32/F2 Najafābād, Iran
32/D3 Najd (reg.), SAr.
35/H6 Nakhon Si Thammarat, Thai.
23/F5 Nalchik, Rus.
31/E5 Nam (lake), China
32/F2 Namak (lake), Iran
31/B3 Namangan, Uzb.
35/J3 Nam Dinh, Viet.
42/B5 Namib (des.), Namb.
42/C5 Namibia
35/F2 Namjagbarwa (peak), China
50/D5 Nampa, Id,US
29/K4 Namp'o, NKor.
18/F4 Namur, Belg.
50/C3 Nanaimo, BC,Can
30/C2 Nanchang, China
28/F5 Nanchong, China
20/E1 Nancy, Fr.
33/K1 Nanga Parbat (mt.), Pak.
29/H5 Nanjing (Nanking), China
30/A3 Nanning, China
30/C2 Nanping, China
20/C2 Nantes, Fr.
29/J5 Nantong, China
55/G3 Nantucket (isl.), Ma,US
28/G5 Nanyang, China
52/B3 Napa, Ca,US
21/G3 Naples, It.
57/H5 Naples, Fl,US
29/M5 Nara, Japan
34/F3 Nārāyanganj, Bang.
34/C3 Narmada (riv.), India
24/G3 Narodnaya (mtn.), Rus.
55/G3 Nashua, NH,US
57/G2 Nashville (cap.), Tn,US
34/B4 Nasik, India
59/F2 Nassau (cap.), Bahm.
41/M3 Nasser (lake), Egypt
63/L5 Natal, Braz.
57/F4 Natchez, Ms,US
56/E4 Natchitoches, La,US
52/C4 National City, Ca,US
36/C3 Natuna (isls.), Indo.
58/B4 Naucalpan, Mex.
46/F5 Nauru
25/T3 Navarin (cape), Rus.
64/C7 Navarino (isl.), Chile
33/J3 Nawābshāh, Pak.
24/G5 Nawoiy, Uzb.
23/F6 Naxçıvan, Azer.
21/K4 Náxos (isl.), Gre.
28/B2 Nayramadlïn Orgil (mtn.), Mong.
32/C2 Nazareth, Isr.
40/J5 N'Djamena (cap.), Chad
42/E3 Ndola, Zam.
18/C3 Neagh (lake), NI,UK
24/F6 Nebitdag, Trkm.
62/E3 Neblina (peak), Braz.
53/G2 Nebraska (state), US
18/G4 Neckar (riv.), Ger.
54/B2 Neenah, Wi,US
23/H2 Neftekamsk, Rus.
32/B2 Negev (reg.), Isr.
64/D5 Negro (riv.), Arg.
62/F4 Negro (riv.), Braz.
64/E3 Negro (riv.), Uru.
30/D6 Negros (isl.), Phil.
28/G3 Nei Monggol (plat.), China
62/C3 Neiva, Col.
50/D3 Nelson, BC,Can
49/H4 Nelson (riv.), Mb,Can
19/K3 Nemunus (riv.), Eur.
34/D2 Nepal
18/C2 Ness (lake), Sc,UK
18/F3 Netherlands
59/H5 Netherlands Antilles (isls.), Neth.
19/H3 Neubrandenburg, Ger.
20/E2 Neuchatel, Swi.
64/C4 Neuquén (riv.), Arg.
52/C3 Nevada (state), US
52/C3 Nevada, Sierra (mts.), US
59/J4 Nevis (isl.), StK.
54/C4 New Albany, In,US
54/F3 Newark, NJ,US
54/D3 Newark, Oh,US
55/G3 New Bedford, Ma,US
57/J3 New Bern, NC,US
56/D4 New Braunfels, Tx,US
46/D5 New Britain (isl.), PNG
55/F3 New Britain, Ct,US
55/H2 New Brunswick (prov.), Can.
46/F6 New Caledonia, Fr.
45/E4 Newcastle, Austl.
55/H2 Newcastle, NB,Can
54/C4 New Castle, In,US
54/D3 New Castle, Pa,US
18/D3 Newcastle upon Tyne, Eng,UK
34/C2 New Delhi (cap.), India
55/K1 Newfoundland (prov.), Can.
55/L1 Newfoundland (isl.), Nf,Can
46/E5 New Georgia (isl.), Sol.
55/J2 New Glasgow, NS,Can
46/C5 New Guinea (isl.), Pacific
55/G3 New Hampshire (state), US
46/D5 New Hanover (isl.), PNG
55/F3 New Haven, Ct,US
46/F6 New Hebrides (isls.), Van.
56/F4 New Iberia, La,US
46/E5 New Ireland (isl.), PNG
54/F3 New Jersey (state), US
55/F3 New London, Ct,US
54/E2 Newmarket, On,Can
52/F4 New Mexico (state), US
57/F4 New Orleans, La,US
18/D4 Newport, Wal,UK
54/C4 Newport, Ky,US
55/G3 Newport, RI,US
54/E4 Newport News, Va,US
59/F3 New Providence (isl.), Bahm.
18/C3 Newry, NI,UK
25/P2 New Siberian (isls.), Rus.
45/D4 New South Wales (state), Austl.
53/H3 Newton, Ks,US
55/G3 Newton, Ma,US
51/K4 New Ulm, Mn,US
50/C3 New Westminster, BC,Can
54/F3 New York (state), US
54/F3 New York, NY,US
45/H6 New Zealand
33/G1 Neyshābūr, Iran
36/D3 Ngabang, Indo.
35/J5 Nha Trang, Viet.
54/E3 Niagara Falls, On,Can
54/E3 Niagara Falls, NY,US
40/F5 Niamey (cap.), Niger
36/A3 Nias (isl.), Indo.
58/D5 Nicaragua
58/E5 Nicaragua (lake), Nic.
20/E5 Nice, Fr.
35/F6 Nicobar (isls.), India
32/B1 Nicosia (cap.), Cyp.
58/D6 Nicoya (pen.), CR
63/G2 Nieuw-Nickerie, Sur.
40/G4 Niger
40/G6 Niger (riv.), Afr.
40/G6 Nigeria
40/G7 Niger, Mouths of the (delta), Nga.
29/M4 Niigata, Japan
47/J2 Niihau (isl.), Hi,US
18/F4 Nijmegen, Neth.
23/D4 Nikopol', Ukr.
41/M2 Nile (riv.), Afr.
54/D3 Niles, Oh,US
20/E3 Nimes, Fr.
32/D1 Nineveh (ruins), Iraq
30/D2 Ningbo (Ningpo), China
40/C5 Niokolo-Koba Nat'l Park, Sen.
54/B1 Nipigon (lake), On,Can
54/E2 Nipissing (lake), On,Can
21/J3 Niš, Yugo.
63/K8 Niteroi, Braz.
47/J7 Niue, NZ
23/H2 Nizhnekama (res.), Rus.
24/H3 Nizhnevartovsk, Rus.
23/F2 Nizhniy Novgorod, Rus.
24/G4 Nizhniy Tagil, Rus.
19/J4 Nízke Tatry Nat'l Park, Slvk.
40/G7 N'Kongsamba, Camr.
52/E5 Nogales, Az,US
23/E2 Noginsk, Rus.
49/A3 Nome, Ak,US
24/J2 Nordenskjöld (arch.), Rus.
22/H1 Nordkapp (cape), Nor.
53/H2 Norfolk, Ne,US
54/E4 Norfolk, Va,US
46/F7 Norfolk I. (terr.), Austl.
24/J3 Noril'sk, Rus.
54/B3 Normal, Il,US
53/H4 Norman, Ok,US
20/C1 Normandy (reg.), Fr.
49/E3 Norman Wells, Can.
22/F4 Norrköping, Swe.
64/E4 Norte (pt.), Arg.
63/J3 Norte (cape), Braz.
62/G6 Norte (mts.), Braz.
18/E2 North (sea), Eur.
45/H6 North (isl.), NZ
49/* North America
18/D3 Northampton, Eng,UK
55/F3 Northampton, Ma,US
50/F2 North Battleford, Sk,Can
54/F2 North Bay, On,Can
57/H3 North Carolina (state), US
50/C3 North Cascades Nat'l Pk., Wa,US
57/J3 North Charleston, SC,US
51/H4 North Dakota (state), US
18/C3 Northern Ireland, UK
46/D3 Northern Marianas (isls.), PacUS
21/J4 Northern Sporades (isls.), Gre.
45/C2 Northern Territory, Austl.
51/K4 Northfield, Mn,US
18/F3 North Frisian (isls.), Eur.
29/K3 North Korea
52/D3 North Las Vegas, Nv,US
53/J4 North Little Rock, Ar,US
49/G2 North Magnetic Pole, Can.
53/G2 North Platte (riv.), US
53/G2 North Platte, Ne,US
57/G3 Northport, Al,US
50/F2 North Saskatchewan (riv.), Can.
24/K2 North Siberia Lowland (plain), Rus.
45/H6 North Taranaki (bight), NZ
55/J2 Northumberland (str.), Can.
45/A3 North West (cape), Austl.
18/D3 North York Moors Nat'l Park, Eng,UK
49/A3 Norton (sound), Ak,US
54/C3 Norton Shores, Mi,US
22/C3 Norway
17/D2 Norwegian (sea), Eur.
18/E3 Norwich, Eng,UK
55/G2 Notre Dame (mts.), Qu,Can
18/D3 Nottingham, Eng,UK
40/B4 Nouakchott (cap.), Mrta.
47/V13 Nouméa (cap.), NCal.
63/K8 Nova Friburgo, Braz.
63/K8 Nova Iguaçu, Braz.
55/J2 Nova Scotia (prov.), Can.
20/F2 Novara, It.
25/R2 Novaya Sibir' (isl.), Rus.
24/E2 Novaya Zemlya (isls.), Rus.
19/J5 Nové Zámky, Slvk.
23/D2 Novgorod, Rus.
21/H2 Novi Sad, Yugo.
23/F4 Novocherkassk, Rus.
64/F2 Novo Hamburgo, Braz.
23/G3 Novokuybyshevsk, Rus.
24/J4 Novokuznetsk, Rus.
23/E3 Novomoskovsk, Rus.
23/E5 Novorossiysk, Rus.
24/J4 Novosibirsk, Rus.
33/K2 Nowshera, Pak.
41/M5 Nūbah, Jibāl An (des.), Sudan
40/M3 Nubian (des.), Sudan
56/D4 Nueces (riv.), Tx,US
58/A2 Nueva Laredo, Mex.
47/H7 Nuku'alofa (cap.), Tonga
24/F5 Nukus, Uzb.
45/B4 Nullarbor (plain), Austl.
49/A3 Nunivak (isl.), Ak,US
19/G4 Nürnberg, Ger.
49/M3 Nuuk (cap.), Grld.
41/K5 Nyala, Sudan
42/F3 Nyasa (lake), Afr.
21/J2 Nyíregyháza, Hun.
19/L3 Nyoman (riv.), Bela.

O

51/H4 Oahe (lake), US
47/K2 Oahu (isl.), Hi,US
52/B3 Oakland, Ca,US
57/G2 Oak Ridge, Tn,US
58/B4 Oaxaca, Mex.
24/H3 Ob' (gulf), Rus.
24/G3 Ob' (riv.), Rus.
37/G4 Obi (isls.), Indo.
29/N3 Obihiro, Japan
23/E2 Obninsk, Rus.
57/H4 Ocala, Fl,US
62/C3 Occidental, Cordillera (mts.), SAm.
46/* Oceania
52/C4 Oceanside, Ca,US
59/F4 Ocho Rios, Jam.
25/L2 October Revolution (isl.), Rus.
22/D5 Odense, Den.
19/H3 Oder (Odra) (riv.), Eur.
23/D4 Odesa, Ukr.
56/C4 Odessa, Tx,US
18/F4 Offenburg, Ger.
41/P6 Ogaden (reg.), Eth.
40/F6 Ogbomosho, Nga.
52/E2 Ogden, Ut,US
40/G8 Ogooué (riv.), Gabon
54/B4 Ohio (riv.), US
54/B4 Ohio (state), US
21/J3 Ohrid (lake), Eur.
63/H3 Oiapoque (riv.), Braz., FrG.
20/D1 Oise (riv.), Fr.
29/L5 Oita, Japan
64/C2 Ojos del Salado (mt.), SAm.
23/F2 Oka (riv.), Rus.
33/K2 Okāra, Pak.
29/L5 Okayama, Japan
29/M5 Okazaki, Japan
57/H5 Okeechobee (lake), Fl,US
25/Q4 Okhotsk (sea), Rus.
30/E2 Okinawa (isl.), Japan
53/H4 Oklahoma (state), US
53/H4 Oklahoma City (cap.), Ok,US
53/J4 Okmulgee, Ok,US
22/F4 Öland (isl.), Swe.
53/J3 Olathe, Ks,US
21/F3 Olbia, It.
18/G3 Oldenburg, Ger.
54/E3 Olean, NY,US
23/D4 Oleksandriya, Ukr.
25/N2 Olenek (riv.), Rus.
20/D2 Oleron (isl.), Fr.
63/M5 Olinda, Braz.
62/E8 Ollagüe (vol.), Bol.
19/J4 Olomouc, Czh.
25/S3 Oloy (range), Rus.
19/K3 Olsztyn, Pol.
25/S3 Olyatorskiy (bay), Rus.
50/C4 Olympia (cap.), Wa,US
50/C4 Olympic (mts.), Wa,US
50/B4 Olympic Nat'l Pk., Wa,US
21/J3 Olympus (mt.), Gre.
53/J2 Omaha, Ne,US
33/G4 Oman
33/G4 Oman (gulf), Asia
37/F5 Ombai (str.), Indo.
41/M4 Omdurman, Sudan
24/H4 Omsk, Rus.
29/L5 Omuta, Japan
17/H2 Onega (lake), Rus.
40/G6 Onitsha, Nga.
54/C1 Ontario (prov.), Can.
54/E3 Ontario (lake), NAm.
18/E4 Oostende, Belg.
57/G3 Opelika, Al,US
56/E4 Opelousas, La,US
19/J4 Opole, Pol.
21/J2 Oradea, Rom.
40/E1 Oran, Alg.
42/C6 Orange (riv.), Afr.
45/D4 Orange, Austl.
63/H3 Orange (cape), Braz.
63/G3 Orange (mts.), Sur.
56/E4 Orange, Tx,US
54/D3 Orangeville, On,Can
59/G5 Oranjestad (cap.), Aru.
28/F4 Ordos (des.), China
23/E5 Ordu, Turk.
22/E4 Orebro, Swe.
50/C4 Oregon (state), US
50/C4 Oregon City, Or,US
23/E3 Orel, Rus.
52/E2 Orem, Ut,US
24/F4 Orenburg, Rus.
20/B3 Orense, Sp.
62/C5 Oriental, Cordillera (mts.), SAm.
54/E2 Orillia, On,Can
62/F2 Orinoco (riv.), SAm.
62/F2 Orinoco (delta), Ven.
34/D3 Orissa (state), India
18/D2 Orkney (isls.), Sc,UK
57/H4 Orlando, Fl,US
20/D2 Orléans, Fr.
55/H2 Oromocto, NB,Can
55/G2 Orono, Me,US
19/M3 Orsha, Bela.
24/F4 Orsk, Rus.
32/E1 Orūmīyah (Urmia), Iran
62/E7 Oruro, Bol.
29/M5 Osaka, Japan
63/J8 Osasco, Braz.
31/B3 Osh, Kyr.
54/E3 Oshawa, On,Can
54/B2 Oshkosh, Wi,US
40/F6 Oshogbo, Nga.
21/H2 Osijek, Cro.
31/D1 Öskemen, Kaz.
22/D3 Oslo (cap.), Nor.
23/E6 Osmaniye, Turk.
18/G3 Osnabrück, Ger.
64/B5 Osorno, Chile
19/J4 Ostrava, Czh.
54/E3 Oswego, NY,US
21/H3 Otranto (str.), Eur.
29/M4 Otsu, Japan
54/F2 Ottawa (cap.), Can.
54/E2 Ottawa (riv.), Can.
53/J2 Ottumwa, Ia,US
21/F2 Ötztal Alps (range), Eur.
56/E3 Ouachita (mts.), Ar,Ok,US
41/J5 Ouaddaï (reg.), Chad
40/E5 Ouagadougou (cap.), Burk.
40/C3 Ouarane (reg.), Mrta.
40/E1 Oujda, Mor.
20/E1 Our (riv.), Eur.
18/B2 Outer Hebrides (isls.), Sc,UK
53/J3 Overland Park, Ks,US
20/B3 Oviedo, Sp.
54/C4 Owensboro, Ky,US
54/D2 Owen Sound, On,Can
18/D3 Oxford, Eng,UK
40/F6 Oyo, Nga.
53/J3 Ozarks (mts.), US
53/J3 Ozarks, Lake of the (lake), Mo,US
25/S4 Ozernoy (cape), Rus.

P

62/F6 Pacaás Novos Nat'l Park, Braz.
62/F6 Pacaás Novas (mts.), Braz.
62/F3 Pacaraima (mts.), Braz.
62/C6 Pachacamac (ruins), Peru
58/B3 Pachuca, Mex.
14/B4 Pacific (ocean)
50/B3 Pacific (ranges), BC,Can
36/B4 Padang, Indo.
36/A3 Padangsidempuan, Indo.
18/G3 Paderborn, Ger.
21/F2 Padova (Padua), It.
54/B4 Paducah, Ky,US
47/H6 Pago Pago (cap.), ASam.
36/B3 Pahang (riv.), Malay.
52/E4 Painted (des.), Az,US
36/B3 Pakanbaru, Indo.
33/H3 Pakistan
35/J4 Pakxe, Laos
21/G3 Palagruža (isls.), Cro.
36/D4 Palangkaraya, Indo.
46/C4 Palau
30/C6 Palawan (chan.), Phil.
30/C6 Palawan (isl.), Phil.
36/B4 Palembang, Indo.
21/G4 Palermo, It.
46/E4 Palikir (cap.), Micr.
63/J6 Palma (riv.), Braz.
20/D4 Palma de Mallorca, Sp.
40/D7 Palmas (cape), Libr.
57/H4 Palm Bay, Fl,US
52/C4 Palmdale, Ca,US
62/C3 Palmira, Col.
52/C4 Palm Springs, Ca,US
47/J4 Palmyra (atoll), PacUS
52/B3 Palo Alto, Ca,US
36/C3 Pamangkat, Indo.
31/B4 Pamir (plat.), Asia
57/J3 Pamlico (sound), NC,US
56/C3 Pampa, Tx,US
64/D4 Pampa Humida (reg.), Arg.
64/D4 Pampas (reg.), Arg.
64/C4 Pampa Sec (reg.), Arg.
20/C3 Pamplona, Sp.
34/B4 Pānāji, India
58/E6 Panama
59/E6 Panama (can.), Pan.
59/F6 Panamá (cap.), Pan.
59/F6 Panama (gulf), Pan.
59/F5 Panama (isth.), Pan.
57/G4 Panama City, Fl,US
30/D5 Panay (isl.), Phil.
21/J2 Pančevo, Yugo.
19/L3 Panevėžys, Lith.
36/C4 Pangkalpinang, Indo.
63/G7 Pantanal (reg.), Braz.
21/G4 Pantelleria (isl.), It.
21/H2 Pápa, Hun.
58/D5 Papagayo (gulf), CR
47/X15 Papeete (cap.), FrPol.
46/D5 Papua New Guinea
30/B4 Paracel (isls.)
53/K3 Paragould, Ar,US
63/L6 Paraguaçu (riv.), Braz.
63/G7 Paraguai (riv.), Braz.
62/D1 Paraguaná (pen.), Ven.
61/D5 Paraguay
64/E1 Paraguay (riv.), SAm.
63/K8 Paraíba do Sul (riv.), Braz.
63/G2 Paramaribo (cap.), Sur.
62/C2 Paramillo Nat'l Park, Col.
25/R4 Paramushir (isl.), Rus.
64/D3 Paraná, Arg.
61/D5 Paraná (riv.), SAm.
63/J7 Paranaíba (riv.), Braz.
64/G1 Paranapiaca (mts.), Braz.
63/H8 Paranapanema (riv.), Braz.
63/H8 Pardo (riv.), Braz.
36/D5 Pare, Indo.
62/F6 Parecis (mts.), Braz.
37/E4 Parepare, Indo.
62/F1 Paría (gulf)
62/F1 Paría (pen.), Ven.
62/F3 Parima (mts.), Braz.
62/E7 Parinacota (mtn.), Bol.
20/D1 Paris (cap.), Fr.
56/E3 Paris, Tx,US
54/D4 Parkersburg, WV,US
21/F2 Parma, It.
54/D3 Parma, Oh,US
63/K4 Parnaíba, Braz.
63/K4 Parnaíba (riv.), Braz.
21/J3 Parnassós (Parnassus) (mt.), Gre.
19/L2 Pärnu, Est.
21/K3 Páros (isl.), Gre.
49/F2 Parry (chan.), Can.
54/D2 Parry Sound, On,Can
53/J3 Parsons, Ks,US
52/C4 Pasadena, Ca,US
56/E4 Pasadena, Tx,US
57/F4 Pascagoula, Ms,US
50/D4 Pasco, Wa,US
30/D5 Pasig, Phil.
19/H4 Passau, Ger.
64/F2 Passo Fundo, Arg.
62/C3 Pasto, Col.
64/B6 Patagonia (reg.), Arg.
54/F3 Paterson, NJ,US
33/L2 Pathānkot, India
62/C3 Patía (riv.), Col.
33/L2 Patiala, India
34/E2 Patna, India
63/L5 Patos, Braz.
64/F3 Patos (lake), Braz.
21/J3 Pátrai, Gre.
63/L5 Paulo Afonso, Braz.
24/H4 Pavlodar, Kaz.
55/G3 Pawtucket, RI,US
24/G3 Pay-Khoy (mts.), Rus.
49/F4 Peace (riv.), Can.
21/J3 Peć, Yugo.
17/K2 Pechora (riv.), Rus.
56/C4 Pecos, Tx,US
57/G5 Pecos (riv.), Tx,US
21/H2 Pécs, Hun.
35/G4 Pegu, Myanmar
23/C2 Peipus (lake), Eur.
36/C5 Pekalongan, Indo.
54/B3 Pekin, Il,US
28/H4 Peking (Beijing) (cap.), China
21/G5 Pelagie (isl.), It.
54/D3 Pelée (pt.), On,Can
59/J5 Pelée (mt.), Mart.
50/E2 Pelican (mts.), Ab,Can
21/J4 Peloponnisos (reg.), Gre.
64/F3 Pelotas, Braz.
64/F2 Pelotas (riv.), Braz.
36/A3 Pematangsiantar, Indo.
42/G2 Pemba (isl.), Tanz.
54/E2 Pembroke, On,Can
64/A6 Penas (gulf), Chile
40/F5 Pendjari Nat'l Park, Ben., Burk.
50/D4 Pendleton, Or,US
50/D4 Pend Oreille (lake), Id,US
20/A3 Peneda Geres Nat'l Park, Port.
54/E2 Penetanguishene, On,Can
30/C3 Penghu (isls.), Tai.
20/C4 Penibetico, Sistema (range), Sp.
63/J5 Penitente (mts.), Braz.
18/D3 Pennine Chain (range), Eng,UK
54/E3 Pennsylvania (state), US
57/G4 Pensacola, Fl,US
50/D3 Penticton, BC,Can
23/G3 Penza, Rus.
54/B3 Peoria, Il,US
55/H1 Percé, Qu,Can
62/C3 Pereira, Col.
20/D2 Périgueux, Fr.
62/D2 Perija (mts.), Col., Ven.
32/D6 Perim (isl.), Yem.
64/B6 Perito Moreno Nat'l Park, Arg.
23/J2 Perm', Rus.
20/D3 Perpignan, Fr.
32/E3 Persian (gulf), Asia
45/A4 Perth, Austl.
54/E2 Perth, On,Can
18/D2 Perth, Sc,UK
62/C5 Peru
21/G3 Perugia, It.
30/C3 Pescadores (Penghu) (isls.), Tai.
21/G3 Pescara, It.
33/K2 Peshawar, Pak.
62/E1 Petare, Ven.
54/E2 Peterborough, On,Can
18/D3 Peterborough, Eng,UK
54/E4 Petersburg, Va,US
55/H2 Petitcodiac, NB,Can
32/C2 Petra (ruins), Jor.
25/M2 Petra (isls.), Rus.
52/E4 Petrified Forest Nat'l Pk., Az,US
24/G4 Petropavl, Kaz.
25/R4 Petropavlovsk-Kamchatskiy, Rus.
63/K8 Petrópolis, Braz.
17/H2 Petrozavodsk, Rus.
35/H5 Phanom Dongrak (mts.), Camb., Thai.
56/D5 Pharr, Tx,US
57/G3 Phenix City, Al,US
54/F4 Philadelphia, Pa,US
30/D4 Philippine (sea), Phil.
30/D5 Philippines
35/H5 Phnom Penh (cap.), Camb.
47/H5 Phoenix (isls.), Kiri.
52/D4 Phoenix (cap.), Az,US
21/F2 Piacenza, It.
62/F3 Pica da Neblina Nat'l Park, Braz.
20/D1 Picardy (reg.), Fr.
57/H3 Piedmont (plat.), US
51/H4 Pierre (cap.), SD,US
42/F6 Pietermaritzburg, SAfr.
53/F3 Pike's (peak), Co,US
64/D1 Pilcomayo (riv.), SAm.
64/E2 Pilcomayo Nat'l Park, Arg.
19/H4 Pilsen (Plzeň), Czh.
58/E3 Pinar del Río, Cuba
30/D4 Pinatubo (mtn.), Phil.
63/J4 Pindaré (riv.), Braz.
21/J3 Pindus (mts.), Gre.
53/J4 Pine Bluff, Ar,US
28/G5 Pingdingshan, China
30/D3 Pingtung, Tai.
35/J3 Pingxiang, China
29/H4 Pingyang, China
58/E3 Pinos (Juventud) (isl.), Cuba
19/L3 Pinsk, Bela.
21/F3 Piombino, It.
54/C3 Piqua, Oh,US
63/J8 Piracicaba, Braz.
21/J4 Piraiévs, Gre.
21/F3 Pisa, It.
64/C2 Pissis (mtn.), Arg.
47/N7 Pitcairn (isl.), UK
21/K2 Pitești, Rom.
53/J3 Pittsburg, Ks,US
54/D3 Pittsburgh, Pa,US
55/F3 Pittsfield, Ma,US
62/B5 Piura, Peru
23/C4 Pivdenyy Buh (riv.), Ukr.
56/C3 Plainview, Tx,US
56/D3 Plano, Tx,US
57/H5 Plantation, Fl,US
64/E3 Plata, Río de la (est.), SAm.
53/H2 Platte (riv.), Ne,US
54/F2 Plattsburgh, NY,US
35/J5 Pleiku, Viet.
45/H6 Plenty (bay), NZ
21/K3 Pleven, Bulg.
19/J3 Plock, Pol.
21/K2 Ploiești, Rom.
21/K3 Plovdiv, Bulg.
59/J4 Plymouth (cap.), Monts.
18/C4 Plymouth, Eng,UK
19/H4 Plzeň (Pilsen), Czh.
21/F2 Po (riv.), It.
50/E5 Pocatello, Id,US
23/E2 Podol'sk, Rus.
29/K4 P'ohang, SKor.
46/E4 Pohnpei (isl.), Micr.
42/B1 Pointe-Noire, Congo
54/D3 Pointe Pelee Nat'l Pk., On,Can
19/J3 Poland
19/M3 Polatsk, Bela.
33/J1 Pol-e-Khomri, Afg.
23/D4 Poltava, Ukr.
47/J3 Polynesia (reg.), Pacific
19/H3 Pomerania (reg.), Eur.
19/H3 Pomeranian (bay), Eur.
57/H5 Pompano Beach, Fl,US
21/G3 Pompei (ruins), It.
53/H3 Ponca City, Ok,US
59/H4 Ponce, PR
34/C5 Pondicherry, India
64/F2 Ponta Grossa, Braz.
57/F4 Pontchartrain (lake), La,US
54/D3 Pontiac, Mi,US
36/C4 Pontianak, Indo.
21/G3 Ponziane (isls.), It.
62/E7 Poopó (lake), Bol.
62/C3 Popayán, Col.
53/K3 Poplar Bluff, Mo,US
49/C3 Porcupine (riv.), NAm.
22/H1 Porsangen (fjord), Nor.
54/C3 Portage, Mi,US
51/J3 Portage la Prairie, Mb,Can
50/B3 Port Alberni, BC,Can
50/B3 Port Angeles, Wa,US
56/E4 Port Arthur, Tx,US
59/G4 Port-au-Prince (cap.), Haiti
35/F5 Port Blair, India
57/H5 Port Charlotte, Fl,US
42/E7 Port Elizabeth, SAfr.
40/G7 Port Harcourt, Nga.
55/J2 Port Hawkesbury, NS,Can
54/D3 Port Huron, Mi,US
55/G3 Portland, Me,US
50/B4 Portland, Or,US
15/M6 Port Louis (cap.), Mrts.
20/A4 Portmaio, Port.
46/D5 Port Moresby (cap.), PNG
64/F3 Porto Alegre, Braz.
59/J5 Port-of-Spain (cap.), Trin.
40/F6 Porto-Novo (cap.), Ben.
20/A3 Porto (Oporto), Port.
62/F5 Porto Velho, Braz.
62/B4 Portoviejo, Ecu.
32/B2 Port Said, Egypt
18/D4 Portsmouth, Eng,UK
55/G3 Portsmouth, NH,US
54/D4 Portsmouth, Oh,US
54/E4 Portsmouth, Va,US
41/N4 Port Sudan, Sudan
20/A4 Portugal
46/F6 Port-Vila (cap.), Van.
64/E2 Posadas, Arg.
54/E4 Potomac (riv.), US
62/E7 Potosí, Bol.
19/H3 Potsdam, Ger.
54/F3 Pottstown, Pa,US
54/F3 Poughkeepsie, NY,US
52/E3 Powell (lake), US
50/B3 Powell River, BC,Can
30/C2 Poyang (lake), China
58/B3 Poza Rica, Mex.
19/J3 Poznań, Pol.
19/H4 Prague (Praha) (cap.), Czh.
21/F2 Prato, It.
37/E5 Praya, Indo.
52/D4 Prescott, Az,US
63/H8 Presidente Prudente, Braz.
19/J4 Prešov, Slvk.
21/J3 Prespa (lake), Eur.
55/G2 Presque Isle, Me,US
18/D3 Preston, Eng,UK
42/E6 Pretoria (cap.), SAfr.
57/F5 Prichard, Al,US
21/H2 Prijedor, Bosn.
23/G4 Prikaspian (plain), Kaz., Rus.
50/G2 Prince Albert, Sk,Can
15/L8 Prince Edward (isls.), SAfr.
55/J2 Prince Edward Island (prov.), Can.
50/C2 Prince George, BC,Can
49/G2 Prince of Wales (isl.), Can.
49/E2 Prince Patrick (isl.), NW,Can
49/E4 Prince Rupert, Can.
45/D2 Princess Charlotte (bay), Austl.
19/M4 Pripyat' (riv.), Eur.
21/J3 Priština, Yugo.
21/J3 Prizren, Yugo.
36/D5 Probolinggo, Indo.
27/H4 Prokop'yevsk, Rus.
35/C4 Prome, Myanmar
20/E2 Provence (reg.), Fr.
55/G3 Providence (cap.), RI,US
62/F6 Providência (mts.), Braz.
58/E5 Providencia (isl.), Col.
52/E2 Provo, Ut,US
49/C2 Prudhoe (bay), Ak,US
21/K2 Prut (riv.), Eur.
23/C2 Pskov, Rus.
58/B4 Puebla de Zaragoza, Mex.
53/F3 Pueblo, Co,US
62/F1 Puerto La Cruz, Ven.
64/B5 Puerto Montt, Chile
59/H4 Puerto Rico, US
59/N9 Puerto Vallarta, Mex.
50/C4 Puget (sound), Wa,US
47/J6 Pukapuka (atoll), Cook Is.
50/D4 Pullman, Wa,US
62/B4 Puna (isl.), Ecu.
34/B4 Pune (Poona), India
33/K2 Punjab (plain), Pak.
64/B7 Punta Arenas, Chile
58/E5 Punta Gorda (bay), Nic.
62/C3 Puracé (vol.), Col.
62/C3 Puracé Nat'l Park, Col.
62/F4 Purus (riv.), SAm.
36/C5 Purwokerto, Indo.
29/K4 Pusan, SKor.
19/M2 Pushkin, Rus.
24/K3 Putorana (mts.), Rus.
62/D4 Putumayo (riv.), Col., Peru
50/C4 Puyallup, Wa,US
24/J2 Pyasina (riv.), Rus.
23/F5 Pyatigorsk, Rus.
29/K4 P'yŏngyang (cap.), NKor.
20/C3 Pyrenees (mts.), Eur.

Q

49/L2 Qaanaaq, Grld.
32/F1 Qā'emshahr, Iran
40/G1 Qafsah, Tun.
33/J2 Qandahār, Afg.
31/B2 Qaraghandy, Kaz.
32/F3 Qatar
41/L1 Qattâra (depr.), Egypt
32/E1 Qazvin, Iran
49/M3 Qeqertarsuaq, Grld.
23/G6 Qezel Owzan (riv.), Iran
28/D4 Qilian (mts.), China
41/M2 Qinā, Egypt
29/J4 Qingdao (Tsingtao), China
28/D4 Qinghai (lake), China
29/H3 Qinhuangdao, China
29/J2 Qiqihar, China
29/L2 Qitaihe, China
24/G5 Qizilqum (des.), Uzb.
32/F2 Qom (Qum), Iran
24/G4 Qostanay, Kaz.
30/B2 Quanzhou, China
50/G3 Qu'Appelle (riv.), Sk,Can
55/G1 Québec (prov.), Can.
55/G2 Québec (cap.), Qu,Can
49/D4 Queen Charlotte (isls.), BC,Can
49/E2 Queen Elizabeth (isls.), Can.
43/A Queen Maud Land (reg.), Ant.
45/D3 Queensland (state), Austl.
63/H4 Queimada (isl.), Braz.
58/A3 Querétaro, Mex.
50/C2 Quesnel, BC,Can
33/J2 Quetta, Pak.

71

Queza – Tanza

58/C5 Quezaltenango, Guat.
30/D5 Quezon City, Phil.
29/H4 Qufu, China
42/B2 Quiçama Nat'l Park, Ang.
64/B5 Quilán (cape), Chile
20/B1 Quimper, Fr.
54/B4 Quincy, Il,US
55/G3 Quincy, Ma,US
35/J5 Qui Nhon, Viet.
62/C4 Quito (cap.), Ecu.
30/C2 Quzhou, China
24/G5 Qyzylordā, Kaz.

R

40/D1 Rabat (cap.), Mor.
46/E5 Rabaul, PNG
41/K3 Rabyanāh, Sahra' (des.), Libya
49/M5 Race (cape), Nf,Can
54/C3 Racine, Wi,US
19/K4 Radom, Pol.
21/H4 Ragusa, It.
33/K3 Rahīmyār Khān, Pak.
50/C4 Rainier (mt.), Wa,US
51/K3 Rainy (lake), NAm.
34/D3 Raipur, India
34/D4 Rajahmundry, India
36/D3 Rajang (riv.), Malay.
34/B3 Rajkot, India
34/E3 Rājshāhi, Bang.
33/K1 Rakaposhi (mtn.), Pak.
57/J3 Raleigh (cap.), NC,US
63/K6 Ramalho (mts.), Braz.
18/E4 Ramsgate, Eng,UK
34/E3 Ranchi, India
54/B3 Rantoul, Il,US
47/L7 Rapa (isl.), FrPol.
51/H4 Rapid City, SD,US
54/E4 Rappahannock (riv.), Va,US
47/J7 Rarotonga (isl.), Cook Is.
64/D5 Rasa (pt.), Arg.
41/N5 Ras Dashen Terara (mt.), Eth.
32/E1 Rasht, Iran
32/F3 Ra's Tannūrah (cape), SAr.
45/H6 Raupehu (mtn.), NZ
34/D3 Raurkela, India
21/G2 Ravenna, It.
21/F2 Ravensburg, Ger.
33/K2 Ravi (riv.), Asia
33/K2 Rawalpindi, Pak.
50/G5 Rawlins, Wy,US
55/K2 Ray (cape), Nf,Can
21/K3 Razgrad, Bul.
18/D4 Reading, Eng,UK
54/F3 Reading, Pa,US
62/E7 Real (mts.), Bol.
63/M5 Recife, Braz.
32/C4 Red (sea)
27/K7 Red (riv.), Asia
53/J5 Red (riv.), US
50/E2 Red Deer, Ab,Can
50/F3 Red Deer (riv.), Ab,Can
52/B2 Redding, Ca,US
51/J4 Red River of the North (riv.), US
41/N3 Red Sea (hills), Sudan
52/A2 Redwood Nat'l Pk., Ca,US
18/C3 Ree (lake), Ire.
18/G4 Regensburg, Ger.
21/G4 Reggio di Calabria, It.
21/F2 Reggio nell'Emilia, It.
51/G3 Regina (cap.), Sk,Can
20/E1 Reims, Fr.
64/A7 Reina Adelaida (arch.), Chile
49/G4 Reindeer (lake), Can.
54/E2 Renfrew, On,Can
20/C1 Rennes, Fr.
52/C3 Reno, Nv,US
28/H4 Renqiu, China
53/H2 Republican (riv.), US
64/E2 Resistencia, Arg.
21/J2 Reşiţa, Rom.
21/J2 Retrezap Nat'l Park, Rom.
15/M7 Réunion, Fr.
18/G4 Reutlingen, Ger.
50/D3 Revelstoke, BC,Can
49/F8 Revillagigedo (isls.), Mex.
50/F5 Rexburg, Id,US
22/N7 Reykjavík (cap.), Ice.
58/B2 Reynosa, Mex.
18/F3 Rhine (riv.), Eur.
55/G3 Rhode Island (state), US
23/C6 Rhodes (isl.), Gre.
23/C6 Rhodes (Ródhos), Gre.
18/D4 Rhondda, Wal,UK
20/E2 Rhône (riv.), Eur.
18/C2 Rhum (isl.), Sc,UK
36/B3 Riau (arch.), Indo.
63/J8 Ribeirão Preto, Braz.
19/M5 Rîbniţa, Mol.
50/D4 Richland, Wa,US
54/C4 Richmond, In,US
54/C4 Richmond, Ky,US
54/E4 Richmond (cap.), Va,US
51/H3 Riding Mtn. Nat'l Pk., Mb,Can
40/E1 Rif, Er (mts.), Mor.
19/L2 Riga (cap.), Lat.
19/K2 Riga (gulf), Lat.
33/H2 Rīgestan (des.), Afg.
21/G2 Rijeka, Cro.
21/K2 Rimimicu Vîlcea, Rom.
21/G2 Rimini, It.
55/G1 Rimouski, Qu,Can
62/C5 Río Abiseo Nat'l Park, Peru
62/E5 Rio Branco, Braz.
63/J8 Rio Claro, Braz.
64/D3 Río Cuarto, Arg.
63/K8 Rio de Janeiro, Braz.
56/C4 Rio Grande (riv.), NAm.
62/F4 Rio Jaú Nat'l Park, Braz.
64/E3 Rio Negro (res.), Uru.
62/D2 Ritacuba (mtn.), Col.
45/D4 Riverina (reg.), Austl.
52/C4 Riverside, Ca,US
57/H5 Riviera Beach, Fl,US
55/G2 Rivière-du-Loup, Qu,Can
23/C3 Rivne, Ukr.
32/E4 Riyadh (cap.), SAr.
23/F5 Rize, Turk.
29/H4 Rizhao, China
59/J4 Road Town (cap.), BVI
54/E4 Roanoke, Va,US
57/J2 Roanoke Rapids, NC,US
55/F1 Roberval, Qu,Can
45/A3 Robinson (ranges), Austl.
51/K4 Rochester, Mn,US
55/G3 Rochester, NH,US
54/E3 Rochester, NY,US
54/B3 Rockford, Il,US
45/E2 Rockhampton, Austl.
57/H3 Rock Hill, SC,US
54/B3 Rock Island, Il,US
50/F5 Rock Springs, Wy,US
49/E4 Rocky (mts.), NAm.
57/J3 Rocky Mount, NC,US
50/E2 Rocky Mountain House, Ab,Can
53/F2 Rocky Mountain Nat'l Pk., Co,US
53/J3 Rogers, Ar,US
21/J2 Romania
21/G3 Rome (cap.), It.
57/G3 Rome, Ga,US
54/F3 Rome, NY,US
63/H6 Roncador (mts.), Braz.
43/W Ronne Ice Shelf, Ant.
63/H6 Ronuro (riv.), Braz.
43/N Roosevelt (isl.), Ant.
62/F6 Roosevelt (riv.), Braz.
62/F2 Roraima (mtn.), Guy.
64/D3 Rosario, Arg.
59/J4 Roseau (cap.), Dom.
50/C5 Roseburg, Or,US
18/F5 Rosenheim, Ger.
43/P Ross (sea), Ant.
43/P Ross Ice Shelf, Ant.
18/H3 Rostock, Ger.
23/E4 Rostov, Rus.
53/F4 Roswell, NM,US
18/D3 Rotherham, Eng,UK
18/F4 Rotterdam, Neth.
46/G6 Rotuma (isl.), Fiji
20/D1 Rouen, Fr.
54/E1 Rouyn-Noranda, Qu,Can
52/D2 Roy, Ut,US
42/F2 Ruaha Nat'l Park, Tanz.
32/E5 Rub' al Khali (des.), Asia
24/G4 Rūdnyy, Kaz.
42/G2 Rufiji (riv.), Tanz.
19/H3 Rügen (isl.), Ger.
42/F2 Rukwa (lake), Tanz.
59/G3 Rum (cay), Bahm.
54/E1 Rupert (riv.), Qu,Can
21/K3 Ruse, Bulg.
24/H3 Russia
23/G5 Rust'avi, Geo.
56/E3 Ruston, La,US
55/F3 Rutland, Vt,US
42/G3 Ruvuma (riv.), Tanz.
42/E1 Rwanda
23/E3 Ryazan', Rus.
23/E2 Rybinsk, Rus.
23/E2 Rybinsk (res.), Rus.
23/G4 Ryn-Peski (des.), Kaz.
46/B2 Ryukyu (isls.), Japan
19/K4 Rzeszów, Pol.

S

50/C3 Saanich, BC,Can
18/F4 Saarbrücken, Ger.
19/K2 Saaremaa (isl.), Est.
21/H2 Šabac, Yugo.
20/D3 Sabadell, Sp.
37/E2 Sabah (reg.), Malay.
56/E4 Sabine (riv.), US
55/H3 Sable (cape), NS,Can
55/J3 Sable (isl.), NS,Can
33/G1 Sabzevar, Iran
55/H2 Sackville, NB,Can
52/B3 Sacramento (cap.), Ca,US
52/B2 Sacramento (riv.), Ca,US
53/F4 Sacramento (mts.), NM,US
40/H1 Safāqis (Sfax), Tun.
40/D1 Safi, Mor.
33/H2 Safid (mts.), Afg.
29/L5 Saga, Japan
54/D3 Saginaw, Mi,US
55/G1 Saguenay (riv.), Qu,Can
40/G3 Sahara (des.), Afr.
33/L3 Saharanpur, India
33/K2 Sāhīwāl, Pak.
35/J5 Saigon (Ho Chi Minh City), Viet.
50/E2 St. Albert, Ab,Can
57/H4 St. Augustine, Fl,US
54/E3 St. Catharines, On,Can
53/K3 St. Charles, Mo,US
51/K4 St. Cloud, Mn,US
51/K4 St. Croix (riv.), US
59/H4 St. Croix (isl.), USVI
54/F2 Ste-Agathe-des-Monts, Qu,Can
55/G2 Ste-Foy, Qu,Can
20/E2 St-Étienne, Fr.
55/K1 St. George (cape), Nf,Can
18/C4 St. George's (chan.), Eur.
59/J5 St. George's (cap.), Gren.
42/C7 St. Helena (bay), SAfr.
14/J6 St. Helena & Dependencies, UK
50/C4 St. Helens (mt.), Wa,US
18/D4 St. Helier (cap.), Jersey, Chl.,UK
55/F2 St-Hyacinthe, Qu,Can
55/F1 St-Jean (lake), Qu,Can
55/F2 St-Jérôme, Qu,Can
55/H2 St. John, NB,Can
55/H2 St. John (riv.), NAm.
59/J4 St. Johns (cap.), Anti.
55/L2 St. John's (cap.), Nf,Can
53/J3 St. Joseph, Mo,US
59/J4 St. Kitts (isl.), StK.
59/J4 St. Kitts & Nevis
63/H2 Saint-Laurent-du-Maroni, FrG.
55/J1 St. Lawrence (gulf), Can.
55/G1 St. Lawrence (riv.), NAm.
49/A3 St. Lawrence (isl.), Ak,US
53/K3 St. Louis, Mo,US
59/J5 St. Lucia
20/C1 Saint-Malo, Fr.
20/C1 Saint-Malo (gulf), Fr.
59/J4 Saint Martin (isl.), Fr.
55/F2 St-Maurice (riv.), Qu,Can
20/C2 St-Nazaire, Fr.
51/K4 St. Paul (cap.), Mn,US
18/D4 St. Peter Port (cap.), Guernsey, Chl.,UK
19/M2 St. Petersburg, Rus.
57/H5 St. Petersburg, Fl,US
55/K2 St. Pierre & Miquelon, Fr.
57/H4 St. Simons (isl.), Ga,US
55/H2 St. Stephen, NB,Can
54/D3 St. Thomas, On,Can
59/H4 St. Thomas (isl.), USVI
59/J5 St. Vincent & the Grenadines
46/D3 Saipan (isl.), NMar.
29/M5 Sakai, Japan
51/H4 Sakakawea (lake), ND,US
23/D5 Sakarya (riv.), Turk.
25/Q4 Sakhalin (gulf), Rus.
25/Q4 Sakhalin (isl.), Rus.
30/D3 Sakishima (isls.), Japan
64/D2 Salado (riv.), Arg.
20/B3 Salamanca, Sp.
14/D7 Sala y Gómez (isl.), Chile
40/D1 Salé, Mor.
24/G3 Salekhard, Rus.
34/C5 Salem, India
55/G3 Salem, NH,US
50/C4 Salem (cap.), Or,US
54/D4 Salem, Va,US
21/G3 Salerno, It.
53/H3 Salina, Ks,US
52/B3 Salinas, Ca,US
18/D4 Salisbury, Eng,UK
54/F4 Salisbury, Md,US
50/E4 Salmon (riv.), Id,US
50/E4 Salmon River (mts.), Id,US
41/K8 Salonga Nat'l Park, D.R. Congo
64/C1 Salta, Arg.
58/A2 Saltillo, Mex.
52/E2 Salt Lake City (cap.), Ut,US
64/E3 Salto Grande (res.), Arg., Uru.
52/C4 Salton Sea (lake), Ca,US
57/H3 Saluda (riv.), SC,US
63/H2 Salut (isls.), FrG.
63/L6 Salvador, Braz.
27/J8 Salween (riv.), Asia
21/G2 Salzburg, Aus.
18/G3 Salzgitter, Ger.
30/E5 Samar (isl.), Phil.
23/H3 Samara, Rus.
37/E4 Samarinda, Indo.
24/G6 Samarqand, Uzb.
36/C3 Sambas, Indo.
47/H6 Samoa
21/K4 Sámos (isl.), Gre.
21/K3 Samothráki (isl.), Gre.
23/E5 Samsun, Turk.
32/D5 Sanaa (San'a) (cap.), Yem.
58/E5 San Andrés (isl.), Col.
56/C4 San Angelo, Tx,US
56/D4 San Antonio, Tx,US
52/C4 San Bernardino, Ca,US
64/B3 San Bernardo, Chile
52/C4 San Clemente (isl.), Ca,US
46/F6 San Cristobal (isl.), Sol.
62/D2 San Cristóbal, Ven.
52/C4 San Diego, Ca,US
54/D3 Sandusky, Oh,US
52/E2 Sandy, Ut,US
57/G3 Sandy Springs, Ga,US
57/H4 Sanford, Fl,US
55/G3 Sanford, Me,US
57/J3 Sanford, NC,US
52/B3 San Francisco, Ca,US
62/C4 Sangay Nat'l Park, Ecu.
34/B4 Sāngli, India
53/F3 Sangre de Cristo (mts.), US
52/B3 San Joaquin (val.), Ca,US
64/C6 San Jorge (gulf), Arg.
58/E6 San José (cap.), CR
52/B3 San Jose, Ca,US
62/J8 San José dos Campos, Braz.
64/C3 San Juan, Arg.
59/H4 San Juan (cap.), PR
52/E3 San Juan (riv.), US
21/F2 Sankt Gallen, Swi.
62/B4 San Lorenzo (cape), Ecu.
59/N9 San Lucas (cape), Mex.
52/B4 San Luis Obispo, Ca,US
58/A3 San Luis Potosí, Mex.
56/D4 San Marcos, Tx,US
21/G3 San Marino
52/B3 San Mateo, Ca,US
64/D5 San Matías (gulf), Arg.
62/F6 San Miguel (riv.), Bol.
58/D5 San Miguel, ESal.
64/C2 San Miguel de Tucumán, Arg.
52/C4 San Nicolas (isl.), Ca,US
58/A2 San Nicolás de los Garzas, Mex.
25/P2 Sannikova (str.), Rus.
64/C1 San Pedro (vol.), Chile
58/D4 San Pedro Sula, Hon.
62/C3 Sanquianga Nat'l Park, Col.
20/E3 San Remo, It.
59/G3 San Salvador (isl.), Bahm.
58/D5 San Salvador (cap.), ESal.
64/C1 San Salvador de Jujuy, Arg.
20/C3 San Sebastián, Sp.
58/D5 Santa Ana, ESal.
52/C4 Santa Ana, Ca,US
52/C4 Santa Barbara, Ca,US
52/C4 Santa Catalina (isl.), Ca,US
64/G2 Santa Catarina (isl.), Braz.
59/E3 Santa Clara, Cuba
62/F7 Santa Cruz, Bol.
40/B2 Santa Cruz (isls.), Sol.
52/B3 Santa Cruz, Ca,US
40/B2 Santa Cruz de Tenerife, Sp.
64/D3 Santa Fe, Arg.
53/F4 Santa Fe (cap.), NM,US
64/B7 Santa Inés (isl.), Chile
64/F2 Santa Maria, Braz.
52/B4 Santa Maria, Ca,US
62/D1 Santa Marta, Col.
20/C3 Santander, Sp.
20/F3 Sant'Antioco (isl.), It.
63/H4 Santarém, Braz.
52/B3 Santa Rosa, Ca,US
57/J3 Santee (riv.), SC,US
64/B3 Santiago (cap.), Chile
59/G4 Santiago, DRep.
56/C4 Santiago (mts.), Tx,US
20/A3 Santiago de Compostela, Sp.
59/F4 Santiago de Cuba, Cuba
64/D2 Santiago del Estero, Arg.
64/G1 Santo Andre, Braz.
59/H4 Santo Domingo (cap.), DRep.
62/B3 Santo Domingo de los Colorados, Ecu.
64/G1 Santos, Braz.
64/B6 San Valentín (mtn.), Chile
63/J8 São Carlos, Braz.
64/G2 São Francisco (isl.), Braz.
63/L5 São Francisco (riv.), Braz.
63/K4 São João (isls.), Braz.
62/F5 São João (mts.), Braz.
63/K8 São João del Rei, Braz.
63/J8 São José do Rio Preto, Braz.
63/J8 São José dos Campos, Braz.
63/G7 São Lourenço (riv.), Braz.
63/K4 São Luís, Braz.
63/K4 São Marcos (bay), Braz.
20/E2 Saône (riv.), Fr.
64/G1 São Paulo, Braz.
63/M5 São Roque (cape), Braz.
63/K8 São Tomé (cape), Braz.
40/G7 São Tomé (cap.), SaoT.
40/F7 São Tomé and Príncipe
20/A4 São Vincent (cape), Port.
29/N3 Sapporo, Japan
20/C3 Saragossa, Sp.
21/H3 Sarajevo (cap.), Bosn.
23/G3 Saransk, Rus.
23/H2 Sarapul, Rus.
57/H5 Sarasota, Fl,US
54/F3 Saratoga Springs, NY,US
23/G3 Saratov, Rus.
36/D3 Sarawak (reg.), Malay.
21/F3 Sardinia (isl.), It.
33/K2 Sargodha, Pak.
32/F1 Sāri, Iran
54/D3 Sarnia, On,Can
29/K5 Sasebo, Japan
50/G2 Saskatchewan (prov.), Can.
51/G2 Saskatchewan (riv.), Can.
50/G3 Saskatoon, Sk,Can
20/F3 Sassari, It.
34/C3 Satpura (range), India
21/J2 Satu Mare, Rom.
32/D4 Saudi Arabia
54/C2 Sault Ste. Marie, On,Can
54/C2 Sault Ste. Marie, Mi,US
21/H2 Sava (riv.), Eur.
47/H9 Savai'i (isl.), Sam.
57/H3 Savannah (riv.), US
57/H3 Savannah, Ga,US
35/H4 Savannakhet, Laos
42/F5 Save (riv.), Moz.
20/F2 Savona, It.
37/F5 Savu (sea), Indo.
52/F3 Sawateh (range), Co,US
41/M2 Sawhāj, Egypt
52/D1 Sawtooth (mts.), Id,US
18/D3 Scarborough, Eng,UK
21/F2 Schaffhausen, Swi.
54/F3 Schenectady, NY,US
18/G4 Schwäbische Alb (range), Ger.
18/G4 Schweinfurt, Ger.
18/G3 Schwerin, Ger.
18/C4 Scilly (isls.), Eng,UK
54/D4 Scioto (riv.), Oh,US
43/W Scotia (sea), Ant.
18/C2 Scotland, UK
52/G2 Scottsbluff, Ne,US
57/G3 Scottsboro, Al,US
52/E4 Scottsdale, Az,US
54/F3 Scranton, Pa,US
21/H3 Scutari (lake), Eur.
50/C4 Seattle, Wa,US
62/B5 Sechura (bay), Peru
62/B5 Sechura (des.), Peru
53/J3 Sedalia, Mo,US
20/B3 Segovia, Sp.
20/D1 Seine (riv.), Fr.
40/E7 Sekondi, Gha.
50/D3 Selkirk (mts.), BC,Can
51/J3 Selkirk, Mb,Can
57/G3 Selma, Al,US
62/E5 Selvas (for.), Braz.
36/D5 Semarang, Indo.
31/D1 Semey, Kaz.
40/B5 Senegal
40/B4 Senegal (riv.), Afr.
29/K4 Seoul (cap.), SKor.
55/H1 Sept-Îles, Qu,Can
52/C3 Sequoia Nat'l Pk., Ca,US
36/C3 Serasan (str.), Malay.
42/F1 Serengeti (plain), Tanz.
42/F1 Serengeti Nat'l Park, Kenya, Tanz.
63/H5 Seringa (mts.), Braz.
24/G4 Serov, Rus.
23/E3 Serpukhov, Rus.
63/K5 Serra da Capivara Nat'l Park, Braz.
62/E3 Serrania de la Neblina Nat'l Park, Ven.
40/G1 Sétif, Alg.
20/A4 Setúbal, Port.
20/A4 Setúbal (bay), Port.
23/G5 Sevan (lake), Arm.
23/E5 Sevastopol', Ukr.
21/J2 Severnaya Zemlya (isls.), Rus.
17/H2 Severodvinsk, Rus.
52/D3 Sevier (riv.), Ut,US
20/B4 Seville, Sp.
49/C3 Seward, Ak,US
15/M6 Seychelles
23/E6 Seyhan (riv.), Turk.
18/F3 's Gravenhage (The Hague) (cap.), Neth.
34/C2 Shahjahanpur, India
35/G3 Shan (plat.), Myanmar
29/J4 Shandong (pen.), China
29/J5 Shanghai, China
30/C2 Shangrao, China
18/B3 Shannon (riv.), Ire.
25/P4 Shantar (isls.), Rus.
30/B3 Shaoguan, China
30/D2 Shaoxing, China
30/B2 Shaoyang, China
54/D3 Sharon, Pa,US
52/B2 Shasta (lake), Ca,US
52/B2 Shasta (mt.), Ca,US
32/E2 Shatt-al-'Arab (riv.), Asia
40/G1 Shaṭṭ al Jarīd (depr.), Tun.
55/F2 Shawinigan, Qu,Can
53/H4 Shawnee, Ok,US
54/C3 Sheboygan, Wi,US
18/D3 Sheffield, Eng,UK
33/K2 Shekhūpura, Pak.
25/S2 Shelagskiy (cape), Rus.
57/H3 Shelby, NC,US
25/R3 Shelekhov (gulf), Rus.
54/E4 Shenandoah Nat'l Pk., Va,US
29/J3 Shenyang (Mukden), China
55/G2 Sherbrooke, Qu,Can
50/G4 Sheridan, Wy,US
56/D3 Sherman, Tx,US
18/F3 's Hertogenbosch, Neth.
50/E2 Sherwood Park, Ab,Can
18/D1 Shetland (isls.), Sc,UK
51/J4 Sheyenne (riv.), ND,US
31/E3 Shihezi, China
28/G4 Shijiazhuang, China
29/L5 Shikoku (isl.), Japan
35/F2 Shillong, India
29/M5 Shimizu, Japan
29/L5 Shimonoseki, Japan
32/F3 Shiraz, Iran
30/B2 Shishou, China
28/G5 Shiyan, China
28/F4 Shizuishan, China
29/M5 Shizuoka, Japan
21/H3 Shkodër, Alb.
34/C4 Sholapur, India
56/E3 Shreveport, La,US
29/L2 Shuangyashan, China
32/B2 Shubrā al Khaymah, Egypt
21/K3 Shumen, Bul.
31/A3 Shymkent, Kaz.
33/H2 Siāh (mts.), Afg.
33/K2 Sialkot, Pak.
19/K3 Šiauliai, Lith.
24/K3 Siberia (reg.), Rus.
21/K2 Sibiu, Rom.
30/D5 Sibuyan (sea), Phil.
21/G4 Sicily (isl.), It.
40/E1 Sidi Bel-Abbès, Alg.
40/K1 Sidra (gulf), Libya
18/G4 Siegen, Ger.
62/D3 Sierra de la Macarena Nat'l Park, Col.
40/C6 Sierra Leone
52/C3 Sierra Nevada (mts.), US
62/D2 Sierra Nevada Nat'l Park, Ven.
52/E5 Sierra Vista, Az,US
29/M2 Sikhote-Alin' (mts.), Rus.
34/E2 Sikkim (state), India
19/H4 Silesia (reg.), Pol.
34/E2 Silīguri, India
54/D3 Simcoe, On,Can
54/E2 Simcoe (lake), On,Can
41/N5 Simēn (mts.), Eth.
23/D5 Simferopol', Ukr.
45/C3 Simpson (des.), Austl.
32/B3 Sinai (pen.), Egypt
36/B3 Singapore
36/B3 Singapore (cap.), Sing.
36/C3 Singkawang, Indo.
23/E5 Sinop, Turk.
59/J4 Sint Maarten (isl.), NAnt.
29/J3 Sinŭiju, NKor.
42/D4 Sioma Ngwezi Nat'l Park, Zam.
53/H2 Sioux City, Ia,US
51/J5 Sioux Falls, SD,US
29/J3 Siping, China
21/G4 Siracusa (Syracuse), It.
21/K2 Siret (riv.), Rom.
35/F3 Sitākunda, Bang.
49/D4 Sitka, Ak,US
23/E6 Sivas, Turk.
41/L2 Siwah (oasis), Egypt
34/D2 Siwalik (range), India, Nepal
22/D4 Skagerrak (str.), Eur.
41/G1 Skikda, Alg.
21/K4 Skiros (isl.), Gre.
21/J3 Skopje (cap.), FYROM
18/C2 Skye (isl.), Sc,UK
49/F4 Slave (riv.), Can.
21/H2 Slavonski Brod, Cro.
57/F4 Slidell, La,US
18/B3 Sligo, Ire.
21/K3 Sliven, Bul.
19/J4 Slovakia
21/G2 Slovenia
19/J3 Sl'upsk, Pol.
21/J2 Smederevo, Yugo.
50/B2 Smithers, BC,Can
54/E2 Smiths Falls, On,Can
53/G3 Smoky Hill (riv.), Ks,US
23/D3 Smolensk, Rus.
57/G3 Smyrna, Ga,US
50/D5 Snake (riv.), US
18/C3 Snowdon (mt.), Wal,UK
63/K6 Sobradinho (res.), Braz.
23/E5 Sochi, Rus.
37/K6 Society (isls.), FrPol.
27/E8 Socotra (isl.), Yem.
21/J3 Sofia (cap.), Bulg.
23/F5 Sokhumi, Geo.
62/C1 Soledad, Col.
62/E4 Solimões (Amazon) (riv.), Braz.
46/E5 Solomon (sea)
46/E6 Solomon Islands
18/C3 Solway (firth), UK
41/Q6 Somalia
49/H2 Somerset (isl.), NW,Can
20/D1 Somme (riv.), Fr.
29/K2 Songhua (riv.), China
35/H6 Songkhla, Thai.
55/F2 Sorel, Qu,Can
63/K8 Sorocaba, Braz.
37/H4 Sorong, Indo.
19/J4 Sosnowiec, Pol.
55/J2 Souris, PE,Can
51/H3 Souris (riv.), NAm.
45/H7 South (isl.), NZ
42/D6 South Africa
61/* South America
49/J3 Southampton (isl.), NW,Can
18/D4 Southampton, Eng,UK
45/C3 South Australia (state), Austl.
54/C3 South Bend, In,US
55/F2 South Burlington, Vt,US
57/H3 South Carolina (state), US
27/L8 South China (sea), Asia
51/H4 South Dakota (state), US
45/G7 Southern Alps (mts.), NZ
45/B2 Southesk Tablelands (plat.), Austl.
43/X South Georgia (isl.), Ant.
29/K4 South Korea
52/C3 South Lake Tahoe, Ca,US
43/W South Orkney (isls.), Ant.
24/E5 South Ossetia (reg.), Geo.
53/G2 South Platte (riv.), US
43/A South Pole
43/Y South Sandwich (isl.), Ant.
50/F3 South Saskatchewan (riv.), Can.
34/E3 South Suburban, India
42/E6 Soweto, SAfr.
20/B3 Spain
59/F4 Spanish Town, Jam.
52/C3 Sparks, Nv,US
57/H3 Spartanburg, SC,US
21/J4 Sparta (Spárti), Gre.
45/C4 Spencer (gulf), Austl.
24/B2 Spitsbergen (isl.), Nor.
21/H3 Split, Cro.
50/D4 Spokane, Wa,US
30/B5 Spratly (isls.)
19/H4 Spree (riv.), Ger.
53/J3 Springdale, Ar,US
54/B4 Springfield (cap.), Il,US
54/E3 Springfield, Ma,US
53/J3 Springfield, Mo,US
54/D4 Springfield, Oh,US
50/C4 Springfield, Or,US
54/F3 Springfield, Vt,US
55/H2 Springhill, NS,Can
50/C3 Squamish, BC,Can
33/K3 Sri Gangānagar, India
34/D6 Sri Lanka
33/K2 Srinagar, India
23/E4 Stakhanov, Ukr.
54/F3 Stamford, Ct,US
64/E7 Stanley (cap.), Falk.
41/L8 Stanley (falls), D.R. Congo
25/N4 Stanovoy (range), Rus.
21/K3 Stara Zagora, Bulg.
57/F3 Starkville, Ms,US
23/E3 Staryy Oskol, Rus.
54/E3 State College, Pa,US
57/H3 Statesboro, Ga,US
57/H3 Statesville, NC,US
54/E4 Staunton, Va,US
22/C4 Stavanger, Nor.
23/F5 Stavropol', Rus.
53/G2 Sterling, Co,US
24/F4 Sterlitamak, Rus.
54/D3 Steubenville, Oh,US
54/B2 Stevens Point, Wi,US
45/G7 Stewart (isl.), NZ
53/H3 Stillwater, Ok,US
18/D2 Stirling, Sc,UK
22/F4 Stockholm (cap.), Swe.
18/D3 Stockport, Eng,UK
52/B3 Stockton, Ca,US
56/C4 Stockton (plat.), Tx,US
18/D3 Stoke-on-Trent, Eng,UK
25/P2 Stolbovoy (isl.), Rus.
55/Q9 Stoney Creek, On,Can
19/H3 Stralsund, Ger.
20/E1 Strasbourg, Fr.
54/D3 Stratford, On,Can
21/G4 Stromboli (isl.), It.
21/J3 Sturma (riv.), Bul.
45/D3 Sturt (des.), Austl.
18/G4 Stuttgart, Ger.
53/K4 Stuttgart, Ar,US
21/H2 Subotica, Yugo.
62/E7 Sucre (cap.), Bol.
62/G5 Sucunduri (riv.), Braz.
63/H7 Sucuriú (riv.), Braz.
41/L5 Sudan
40/H5 Sudan (reg.), Afr.
54/D2 Sudbury, On,Can
19/H4 Sudeten (mts.), Eur.
32/B3 Suez, Egypt
32/B2 Suez (canal), Egypt
32/B3 Suez (gulf), Egypt
54/E4 Suffolk, Va,US
28/F1 Sühbaatar, Mong.
36/C5 Sukabumi, Indo.
33/J3 Sukkur, Pak.
37/G4 Sula (isls.), Indo.
33/J3 Sulaimān (range), Pak.
37/E4 Sulawesi (Celebes) (isl.), Indo.
53/J5 Sulphur, La,US
37/E2 Sulu (sea), Asia
37/F3 Sulu (arch.), Phil.
36/B4 Sumatra (isl.), Indo.
37/E5 Sumba (isl.), Indo.
37/E5 Sumba (str.), Indo.
37/E5 Sumbawa (isl.), Indo.
55/J2 Summerside, PE,Can
23/K5 Sumqayıt, Azer.
57/H3 Sumter, SC,US
23/D3 Sumy, Ukr.
36/D4 Sunda (isls.), Indo.
36/B5 Sunda (str.), Indo.
18/D3 Sunderland, Eng,UK
25/P3 Suntar-Khayata (mts.), Rus.
54/C2 Superior (lake), NAm.
54/A2 Superior, Wi,US
23/G3 Sura (riv.), Rus.
36/D5 Surabaya, Indo.
36/D5 Surakarta, Indo.
34/B3 Surat, India
24/H3 Surgut, Rus.
63/G3 Suriname
50/C3 Surrey, BC,Can
40/H1 Sūsah, Tun.
54/E4 Susquehanna (riv.), US
46/G6 Suva (cap.), Fiji
57/H4 Suwannee (riv.), US
29/J5 Suzhou, China
24/B2 Svalbard (isls.), Nor.
49/G2 Sverdrup (isls.), NW,Can
25/P2 Svyatyy Nos (cape), Rus.
58/E4 Swan (Santanilla) (isls.), Hon.
18/C4 Swansea, Wal,UK
42/F6 Swaziland
22/E3 Sweden
56/C3 Sweetwater, Tx,US
50/F5 Sweetwater (riv.), Wy,US
50/G3 Swift Current, Sk,Can
18/D4 Swindon, Eng,UK
20/E2 Switzerland
45/E4 Sydney, Austl.
55/J2 Sydney, NS,Can
54/E3 Syracuse, NY,US
24/G5 Syrdar'ya (riv.), Kaz.
32/C1 Syria
32/C2 Syrian (des.), Asia
24/G3 Syzran', Rus.
19/H3 Szczecin, Pol.
21/J2 Szeged, Hun.
21/H2 Székesfehérvár, Hun.
21/H2 Szombathely, Hun.

T

63/K6 Tabatinga (mts.), Braz.
50/E3 Taber, Ab,Can
42/F2 Tabora, Tanz.
23/G6 Tabriz, Iran
47/K4 Tabuaeran (isl.), Kiri.
32/C3 Tabūk, SAr.
50/C4 Tacoma, Wa,US
62/D7 Tacora (vol.), Chile
40/H2 Tadrart (mts.), Afr.
29/K4 T'aebaek (mts.), NKor., SKor.
29/K4 Taegu, SKor.
29/K4 Taejŏn, SKor.
40/G3 Tafassasset, Ténéré du (reg.), Niger
23/E4 Taganrog, Rus.
63/J7 Taguatinga, Braz.
20/B4 Tagus (riv.), Eur.
47/L6 Tahiti (isl.), FrPol.
52/C3 Tahoe (lake), US
29/H4 Tai'an, China
30/D3 T'aichung, Tai.
30/D3 T'ainan, Tai.
21/J4 Tainaron, Ákra (cape), Gre.
30/D2 T'aipei (cap.), Tai.
36/B3 Taiping, Malay.
30/D3 Taiwan (Rep. of China)
30/C3 Taiwan (str.), China, Tai.
28/G4 Taiyuan, China
32/D6 Ta'izz, Yem.
24/H6 Tajikistan
32/F1 Tajrīsh, Iran
58/C4 Tajumulco (vol.), Guat.
29/L5 Takamatsu, Japan
29/M4 Takaoka, Japan
45/H6 Takapuna, NZ
31/D4 Takla Makan (des.), China
40/E6 Takoradi, Gha.
37/G3 Taland (isls.), Indo.
64/B4 Talca, Chile
64/B4 Talcahuano, Chile
57/G3 Talladega, Al,US
57/G4 Tallahassee (cap.), Fl,US
19/L2 Tallinn (cap.), Est.
33/J1 Tālogān, Afg.
40/E6 Tamale, Gha.
23/F3 Tambov, Rus.
57/H5 Tampa, Fl,US
22/G3 Tampere, Fin.
58/B3 Tampico, Mex.
41/N5 Tana (lake), Eth.
45/C2 Tanami (des.), Austl.
64/E4 Tandil, Arg.
35/G4 Tanem (range), Thai.
40/E3 Tanezrouft (des.), Afr.
42/G2 Tanga, Tanz.
42/F2 Tanganyika (lake), Afr.
31/E5 Tanggula (mts.), China
40/D1 Tangier, Mor.
29/H4 Tangshan, China
37/H5 Tanimbar (isls.), Indo.
36/C5 Tanjungkarang, Indo.
32/B2 Tanta, Egypt
42/F2 Tanzania

Taos – Zwoll